Revisiting Suicide

This book provides a socio-psychological enquiry of the phenomenon of suicide in the Indian context. It addresses the rising trend of suicides across the world and through case studies explores its primary reasons, the after-effects on survivors and families and measures to prevent them.

The volume focuses on deciphering the social and psychological meanings associated with suicide. Through an examination of psycho-social autopsies of numerous cases, it highlights the patterns and trends which emerge around mental well-being, suicide and bereavement. It examines the primary roadblocks for robust suicide prevention measures and provides great insights into behavioral and personality categories and their relationship with suicide.

Offering theoretical and empirical perspectives on the issue of suicide and self-harm, this book will be of interest to students, researchers, and faculty of behavioral sciences, psychology, social anthropology, demography, criminology, social work and sociology. It will also be an essential read for psychologists and counselors, policy makers, NGOs, CSOs, legal experts and media personnel working in the area of suicide prevention and research.

Kanchan Bharati is an Assistant Professor at the Centre for Culture and Development, Vadodara. For a year she worked as Academic Associate at the Indian Institute of Management, Bengaluru. She completed her higher education in the field of Sociology and Social Gerontology. She has authored and co-authored papers on aging and other socially relevant issues in important journals, edited books and co-edited *Marriage and Divorce in India: Shifting Concepts and Changing Practices* (2019) with Lancy Lobo.

Lancy Lobo holds a Master's degree in Anthropology and a Doctoral degree in Sociology from the Delhi School of Economics, University of Delhi, India. He has authored, co-authored and edited 25 books, and scores of mimeographs and articles based on research over 40 years. He has been a Professor and the Director of Centre for Social Studies, based in Surat, an institute under the Indian Council of Social Science Research, Delhi. He was an International Visiting Fellow at the Woodstock Centre, Georgetown University, Washington, D.C., in the year 1999–2000. He is the Founder Director of Centre for Culture and Development, Vadodara, which is completing 20 years. Some of his latest publications include the following: with Jayesh Shah (eds.), *The Legacy of Nehru: Appraisal and Analysis* (2018); with A.M. Shah and Lancy Lobo (eds.), *Essays on Suicide and Self-Immolation* (2018); with Kanchan Bharati (eds.), *Marriage and Divorce in India: Changing Concepts and Practices* (2019); and with Jayesh Shah, *How People Vote? Civic Literacy and Political Participation* (2019).

Jayesh Shah is working as a Research Consultant at the Centre for Culture and Development, Vadodara. He also holds post-graduate diplomas in Industrial Relations, Labor Laws, Organization Behavior, Clinical Psychology and Computer Science. He has served as Chief Executive Officer in a leading international company for more than ten years. Earlier he worked as freelance Management Consultant for more than ten years in Gujarat. He has conducted extensive research on labor, employment and industry in his career. Some of his publications include the following, with Lancy Lobo; *How People Vote? Civic Literacy and Political Participation* (2019); *Gujaratna Shalakiya Sikshanno Xray* (Gujarati) (2019); (eds.), *The Legacy of Nehru: Appraisal and Analysis* (2018); and (eds.), *Democracy in India: Current Debates and Emerging Challenges* (2017).

Revisiting Suicide

From a Socio-Psychological Lens

Kanchan Bharati,
Lancy Lobo and
Jayesh Shah

Routledge
Taylor & Francis Group
LONDON AND NEW YORK

First published 2021
by Routledge
2 Park Square, Milton Park, Abingdon, Oxon OX14 4RN

and by Routledge
52 Vanderbilt Avenue, New York, NY 10017

Routledge is an imprint of the Taylor & Francis Group, an informa business

British Library Cataloguing-in-Publication Data
A catalogue record for this book is available from the British Library

Library of Congress Cataloging-in-Publication Data
A catalog record has been requested for this book

ISBN: 978-0-367-48073-8 (hbk)
ISBN: 978-1-003-05434-4 (ebk)

Typeset in Sabon
by codeMantra

Contents

List of figures vii
List of tables ix
Preface xi
List of abbreviations xiii

1 Suicide: actors and factors 1

2 Psychological and sociological autopsy: making the paradigm explicit 37

3 Demystifying suicide: insights from primary research 62

4 Pathways to suicide: inferences and theoretical interpretations 130

5 The way forward: implications for prevention policy and interventions 147

Annexure 1: checklist-cum-interview schedule 175
Annexure 2: socio-demographic profile and inherent aspects of suicide act: case narratives 179
References 187
Index 211

Figures

1.1 Socio-psychological perspective to suicide 31
2.1 Data analysis of the empirical case studies, Vadodara 52
2.2 Reasons for the difficulty in accessing empirical insights on suicides 60
3.1 Dynamics behind suicide act 63
3.2 General cognitive pattern behind suicide of case-narratives 125
4.1 Assumptions of interpersonal theory of suicide 131
4.2 Completed-suicide: press/pain/perturbation 134
4.3 Emile Durkheim's social integration and social regulation 136
4.4 Biosocial development model of borderline personality 138
4.5 Beck's hopelessness model 140
4.6 Relationship between the suicide rate and unemployment rate 143
4.7 Relationship between the suicide rate and GDP per capita growth rate 144
4.8 Relationship between the suicide rate and industrial growth rate 144
4.9 Relationship between the suicide rate and urbanization 145

Tables

1.1	Number of suicides and suicide rate in Vadodara	29
1.2	Characteristics of registered suicide-death cases in Vadodara	32
4.1	Five clusters of psychological needs	135
4.2	Suicide rate during economic and political turmoil years	142
A.1	Gender distribution by marital status and age, case narratives (in numbers)	179
A.2	Educational distribution by gender, marital status and age, case narratives (in numbers)	179
A.3	Occupational distribution by gender and age, case narratives (in numbers)	180
A.4	Causal distribution of suicide by gender, marital status and age, case narratives (in numbers)	181
A.5	Distribution of adopted suicide methods by suicide status, gender and marital status, case narratives (in numbers)	182
A.6a	Distribution of various inherent aspects of suicidal act, case narratives (in numbers)	183
A.6b	Distribution of various inherent aspects of suicidal act, case narratives (in numbers)	184
A.7	Responses over suicidal act of the family/self of suicide-attempters and the family of suicide-completers (in numbers)	185

Preface

The Centre for Culture and Development (CCD) at Vadodara brought out a book, *Essays on Suicide and Self-Immolation*, edited by A.M. Shah and Lancy Lobo, with Foreword by Professor Ashis Nandy (Delhi: Primus Publications, 2018). This is a collection of papers reprinted from the almost forgotten *Journal of Anthropological Society of Bombay*, published in 1886–1936. Its Part I includes essays analyzing statistics of suicide in Bombay, and Part II has historical essays on suicide and self-immolation in India. Emile Durkheim's classic sociological work on suicide came out much later than these journal essays.

Encouraged by response to this work in social history and following our concern for understanding the increasing numbers of suicide in modern India, CCD planned to carry out an empirical study in contemporary society. In 2018, CCD completed a study on the patterns and trends of suicide, with their socio-economic and psychological dimensions, in India. The empirical work was focused on Gujarat State in general and Vadodara city in particular. The present volume is a result of this empirical study.

CCD also held in 2018 a national seminar on 'suicide and self-harm' where social scientists and psychiatrists shared their research on the problem of suicide. The proceedings of this seminar are in the process of being edited for publication.

We are grateful to Mr. D.R. Patel (DG-Crime 1, CID Crime, Gujarat, Gandhinagar) and Mr. Sanjiv Srivastava (Add. DGP – Gujarat, Gandhinagar) for providing us secondary data on suicidal deaths in various districts of Gujarat. We are thankful to Mr. Uday Rawal (PI) and Mr. D.B. Vala (PSI) of the Crime Analysis Unit, CID-Crime, Gandhinagar, for assembling the data district wise. Mr. E. Radhakrishnan and Mr. M. Shashidhar (CP, Vadodara City) and Mr. Saurabh Toulambia (SP, Vadodara Rural) were helpful in securing data on suicide cases under various police stations of Vadodara district. Dr. Rajeev Deveshwar (MS-Orthopedic) (Medical Superintendent and Medico-Legal Officer of Shree Sayaji General Hospital, Vadodara) helped us in accessing the medical records of suicide cases. These were helpful in finalizing our case studies. We thank them all.

We have consulted the leading psychiatrist Dr. Yogesh Patel (MD) of Vadodara for his expert views on the issue of suicide. Under the guidance of Dr. Jamila Firdaus (Clinical Psychologist), Mansi Jadeja, Mallika Pathak and Sahil Gehlot conducted the case studies for this study with great interest. We are grateful to them.

Professor Biswaroop Das had been closely guiding this project from time to time. We have benefitted from peer group reviews and comments from him on the draft report of this study. Later on Professor Rajlakshmi Sriram has given valuable comments and suggestions on the manuscript. We gratefully acknowledge their contributions.

We thank Amba, Priya, Soma and Champak of secretarial staff at CCD for having done data entry and word processing, and Gopi Shah for editing the language of the report.

CCD acknowledges the financial assistance provided by Indian Council of Social Science Research (New Delhi) for this study.

Our work with Shoma Choudhury and her team at Routledge has been one of our best experiences with publishers.

Vadodara
October 1, 2020

Abbreviations

AAS	American Association of Suicidology
APA	American Psychological Association
BP	Blood Pressure
CAT	Common Aptitude Test
CBT	Cognitive Behavior Therapy
CP	Commissioner of Police
CT	Computed Tomography
DBT	Dialectical Behavior Therapy
DGP	Director General of Police
DGC	Director General, Crime
DMHP	District Mental Health Programme
ECDS	Empirical Criteria for the Determination of Suicide
FIRR	First Information Register Report
GOI	Government of India
GST	General Strain Theory
HICs	High-Income Countries
HL	Health Literacy
HPA	The Hypothalamic-Pituitary-Adrenal
IIM-A	Indian Institute of Management-Ahmedabad
ILA	Indian Lunacy Act
IMHA	The Mental Health Care Act - India
IMV	Integrated Motivational Volitional
INSERM	*Institut national de la santé et de la recherche médicale* (National Institute for Health and Medical Research)
IO	Investigative Officer
IPT	Interpersonal Therapy
ITI	Industrial Training Institute
LGBTQ	Lesbian Gay Bisexual Transgender and Queer
LIG	Low-income group
MBA	Master's in Business Administration
MCI	Medical Council of India
MDMH	Missouri Department of Mental Health
mhGAP	Mental Health Gap Action Program

MHCB	Mental Health Care Bill
MHC	Mental Health Care
MLC	Mental Health Literacy
MLO	Medico-legal Officer
NCRB	National Crime Records Bureau
NGOs	Nongovernmental Organizations
NIMHANS	National Institute of Medical Health and Neurosciences
DIMHANS	Dharwad Institute of Medical Health and Neurosciences
NMHP	National Mental Health Programme
NPA	National Psychiatric Association
OCDS	Operational Criteria for the Determination of Suicide
PA	Psychological Autopsy
PHR	Police/Hospital Record
PHC	Primary Health Care
PHCC	Primary Healthcare Centres
PMI	Persons with Mental Illness or Disorders
PSA	Psycho-Sociological Autopsy, or Psycho-Social Autopsy
RPDA	Rights of Persons with Disability Act
RTI	Right to Information
SA	Sociological Autopsy
SAMH	Scottish Association for Mental Health
SAMHSA	Substance Abuse and Mental Health Services Administration
SCRB	State Crime Records Bureau
SDRs	Suicide Death Rates
SP	Superintendent of Police
SSRIs	Selective Serotonin Reuptake Inhibitors
SUPRE	Suicide Prevention
TB	Tuberculosis
UK	United Kingdom
UN-CRPD	UN-Convention on the Rights of Persons with Disabilities
WHO	World Health Organization

1 Suicide

Actors and factors

The rising trend of suicides and deaths is a major cause of concern for the society and policy makers. Preventing and reducing suicidal behavior are now important targets of the World Health Organization (WHO), which estimates that, worldwide, about 1 million people die by suicide every year.[1] This represents a global annual suicide rate of 16 per lakh people. In addition, the suicide-attempt rate is about 10–15 times more than the suicide rate. Asia alone contributes as many as 60% of the world's suicides. Despite this, suicide has received relatively less attention in Asia including India than it has in Europe and the USA (Hendin 2008).

Twenty-first century is seen as 'a century full of stress and tensions'. The virtue of patience has been disappearing from the families and more particularly among the youth and the teenagers. The demand is for instantaneous fulfillment of needs and desires. This combined with high aspirations for educational achievement; successful career and upward mobility in the social ladder have become the mandates that need to be 'met at any cost'. This phenomenon plays out differently across various social contexts, making young people and their families 'anxious and be on the edge' all the time. There is no systemic input for life skills training, or positive coping through parenting and schooling.

As a result there is an increase in anxiety, stress and depression. Such a situation is a fertile soil for emergence of suicidal tendencies because depression and suicide are closely interlinked. People with depression are often stigmatized and excluded by family and society. They also tend to under-perform in education and work, thereby remain increasingly deprived of economic and social opportunities, with a decreased quality of life. Depression also escalates the cycle of poverty and poor health, the impact which is huge but unmeasured. India is home to an estimated 57 million people[2] (18% of the global estimate) who are affected by depression. With India witnessing significant changes (including globalization, urbanization, migration and modernization) that is coupled with rapid socio-demographic transition, depression is likely to increase in the coming years.

Much has been written about suicide and the nature of the act by philosophers and theologians through the ages. However, it has especially fascinated social scientists for two reasons: first, because of its universality and, second, because of its very nature and definition, suicide constitutes a form of deviant behavior. Both of these reasons make suicide an important and major object of social inquiry. In the eighteenth-century West, the social meaning and perception of suicide was largely shaped by religion, and it was regarded as a moral problem, but since the beginning of the twentieth century it has come to be regarded as a social problem requiring explanation (Lukes 1973).

In India, research on suicide and suicidal behavior has received less attention despite a good proportion of population being under the threat of suicidal death. Only about 25% of the deaths in India are registered, and only about 10% are medically certified (Hendin 2008). Studies of large-scale verbal autopsy of all deaths in rural regions reveal that the suicide rate in the rural areas is three to four times higher than that reported by the government (Gajalakshmi and Peto 2007), so the official suicide rate reported in the country is probably lower than the actual rate (Sahoo et al. 2010). Hence, crucial challenge in studying suicide in Asia including India is the availability and quality of suicide data. In countries where data are available, there are problems of underestimation due to inaccurate ascertainment and delay in reporting suicidal deaths (Chen et al. 2012).

There are many research studies on suicide for different states of India but there is no specific study based on social demography and mental health of the citizen of the country. This book offers theoretical and empirical perspectives to the issue of suicide. It concentrates on the social, economic and psychological determinants within the family correlating with the social, cultural and economic attributes of those families where suicidal deaths and attempts had occurred. It thus explores the nature of the problem and networks of underlying reasons for suicide. It also attempts to understand the survivor's dilemmas – those who survived suicide-attempt, their families and response of bereaved families. It brings out the transformational change that happened on individuals and the families as an outcome of suicide-attempt/death.

The study has tried to assess the prime reasons for suicide and the life of the family after such act. By looking suicide as a social problem, this study contemplates some important queries:

1 In what way the social-psychological conditions and issues (such as disrupted social relations, social isolation, family discords, illness and psychopathology) are found to be associated with suicide-attempts/deaths?
2 Are there any patterns of suicide emerging and between different groups of people who are considered to be influenced by social conditions (e.g., people's relationships with one another; their position in society; their

access to resources; and their inadequate social integration/regulations, status integration, cultural norms, values and beliefs)?

3 Does specific age group, marital status, gender group and income-group have any specific relevance with suicidal tendencies?

Suicide is a complex phenomenon largely associated with social and psychological distress of the person as well as of the family. Pattern of suicidal deaths is a reflection of the prevailing social set-up and mental health status of humans who live therein and hence demands attention not only to examine the magnitude but also decipher the patterns.

Understanding suicide: theoretical perspectives

Throughout human history numerous theories have been advanced in an effort to explain why people seek to take their own lives. In general, these theories can be classified into four groups such as biological (including biochemical, neurotransmitters), psychological, psychiatric and sociological. Suicide finds mention even in ancient literature, religious or non-religious literature. But it was Emile Durkheim (1951 [orig. 1897]), a French sociologist, who made a sociological study of the suicide and presented its accounts in his book *Le Suicide*. He viewed suicide as a conscious act out of an individual's will, although a result of one's social conditions or circumstances. In other words, suicide is an individual act but the causes can ultimately be related to the social set-up, influenced by various interacting factors of social, psychological, economic, biological/psychiatric, cultural and environmental domains. Following the footsteps of Durkheim, sociologists have studied the phenomenon of suicide as a behavior determined by number of individual and social factors.

Suicide is not one thing, even though it is one word (Interian et al. 2018). As a discipline, suicidology cuts across various academic disciplines and perspectives, making the real world of suicide as complex and interdisciplinary. It is important to recognize that different perspectives or approaches are complementary and consideration of their mutual relevance is significant for effective understanding and for preventive measures.

Sociological dimension of suicide

Sociological theories focus on the significance of the social environment; social relationships; and other social, economic and cultural factors in the etiology of suicide.

Durkheim presented the sociological dimension of suicide through his work on understanding suicidal rates among Catholics and Protestants.[3] It inferred the explanation of suicide through the lens of social integration and regulation. To him though suicide is an individual act, its causes are rooted in an individual's social setting. Essentially, he regarded man to be a social being whose sense of self-belonging depended highly on his/her interaction with his/her community/society. In his view, suicide is the result of social disorganization, the lack of social integration and/or social solidarity *vis-à-vis* individual which shows certain suicidal patterns. Based on individuals' relationship with society he pointed out four types of suicides:

1 Altruistic suicide, i.e., a suicide due to a highly intimate interaction, integration and interconnection shared between an individual and a group/community/society
2 Egoistic suicide, i.e., a suicide of a self-centered person who lacks altruistic feelings and is usually cut off from the mainstream society due to little social integration
3 Anomic suicide, i.e., a suicide by individuals due to exceedingly limited social regulation and integration
4 Fatalistic suicide, i.e., suicide because of heightened overregulation in society and the inability to cope with it

Durkheim established that the more a person feels socially integrated and connected, or has a sense of belonging socially, the likeliness of him/her dying by suicide is less. Similarly the more unstable an individual's social integration, the individual is more likely to end life. He opined that suicide incidences or rates could diminish when there is a balance of regulation and integration. It is essential that individual's desires and expectations must be regulated and monitored by the social ties in order to keep them under check (Mukherjee and Kumar 2017). Durkheim's approach had received its share of criticism major being his failure in operationalizing the definition of social facts, issues with the use of official statistical data involving inaccuracy, overemphasizing externality and less importance to individuals thoughts. Nonetheless, his work is still relevant as it gave significant insights to the problem of suicide and patterns through wider aspects of human-society relationship. People who attempt suicide are much more likely to say they feel lonely and isolated from others and claim disconnections from society, confirming what Durkheim hypothesized over 100 years ago (Zhang 2019).

Another social explanation that stands out is the social interaction and social interpretive approach of actions and behavior, seeing the social meaning, pioneered by Max Weber, Jacob, Douglas and writers on phenomenological philosophy. This approach studies suicide by unearthing the complexity of shared and individual meanings of the actions and reasons involved in the process of the act through careful description and analysis of features of the social, cultural and interpersonal milieu or context in which an individual engages in suicidal behavior (Maskill et al. 2005).

Jacobs (1967) used interpretive approach to understand the suicides of adult and adolescents in Los Angeles through analyzing suicide notes.

Studying 112 suicide notes written by the young and old people who had either attempted or died by suicide, he came out with the explanation that suicide notes offer an important source of information in gaining some insights into the motives, thoughts and emotions of individuals that brought them to adopt such form of behavior. Since note-writers put rational arguments for wanting to end life by suicide, one can categorize predominant reasons and patterns behind suicide. His analysis of suicide notes predominantly showed that suicidal person perceived their problems as unbearable and insoluble, death as an answer to end all their problems and the situations during the suicidal act was considered beyond the personal control.

While looking at the social meanings of suicide Douglas (1967) believed that suicidal actions have very specific meanings to the suicidal individual. Such actions show something fundamental both about the person and about the situation of person highlighting 'cause' of the suicidal action. For him the meaningfulness lays in the motives, intentions or needs of person contemplating suicide. Diaries, notes written by suicidal person and observers' reports were the valuable source of information in digging out meanings of their suicide. Based on these sources he highlighted common patterns of suicidal actions:

1 Sympathy suicide, i.e., suicide as a mean of achieving sympathy and fellow feeling, or as a cry for help
2 Revenge suicide, i.e., suicide as a mean of getting revenge. An expression of aggression towards others or to attach guilt and blame to those who wronged a person
3 Escape suicide, i.e., suicide as a mean to escape from the unbearable situations or misery of life
4 Repentance suicide, i.e., suicide as a self-punishment to show repentance for the wrongdoing

The interpretive or social meaning perspective would see suicide among the old or infirm members of certain societies due to limited food supplies and resources. In communities such as the Eskimos and the *Chuckchee*, old people who displayed signs of weakness, fatigue and inability to hunt or work on their own chose suicide over becoming a burden to their tribes. This sacrificial act helps in retaining and contributing supplies and resources to fitter members of the community. Similarly, suicide practiced in wars by prisoners of war, victims and/or combatants is mainly to avoid being captured and humiliated into slavery, or to escape from the disgraceful feeling of being defeated (Douglas 1967; Marshall and Meier 2011: 319).

Unlike Durkheim, Baechler's (1979) social interpretive approach claimed that suicide could only be explained by the influence of personal factors rather than external factors, and like him, he distinguished four different types of suicides underlying social meaning behind such action:

1 Escapist suicide, i.e., a suicide because of being unable to cope or escape an unbearable situation
2 Aggressive suicide, i.e., a suicide that aims to hurt or harm somebody else as an act of vengeance to make someone feel guilty about his or her actions
3 Oblative suicide, i.e., a suicide practiced due to the submission to sacrificial feelings, giving up of one's life to save and/or help others
4 Ludic suicide, i.e., suicidal attempt performed with intentional risk factors, leading to death

Based on Durkheim's concept of anomie,[4] strain theory also proposes social dimension of suicide. It states that social structures within society pressure individuals to become delinquent and engage in delinquency. It is a theory of social deviance developed by Merton (1938) where he mentioned that strain leads the individuals to commit crimes when they find themselves under social pressure to achieve socially accepted goals that they are lacking in. His theory was largely developed due to the social and economic circumstances occurring in the U.S.' society during the early 1900s when achieving success (monetary) was highly valued. Since some groups are relatively disadvantaged in getting success due to the gap between aspirations and means to achieve goals, they end up taking other routes, which may include crime, mental illness or substance abuse. As a concept of anomie it differs from Durkheim's conception where suicide act is due to the absence of norms to regulate human needs and actions. Merton believed it to be a strain or stress resulting from the presence of norms.

Preposition of strain theory has been further developed by Agnew (1992), terming it as General Strain Theory (GST). It is neither structural nor interpersonal but rather individual and emotional with a special attention to an individual's immediate social environment. The core idea of it is that people who experience strain or stress become distressed or upset which may lead them to commit a crime or self-harm in order to cope with it. The strains either subjective (like relative deprivation) or objective (dictatorial behavior of parents, physical attack, financial problems, victim of deviant activities, etc.) can end up with anger, and introjections of anger can propel the person towards suicide and suicidal tendency. Deviant behaviors due to micro psycho-social factors are kind of adjustment strategies to strain resources and are responses to the anger (Broidy and Agnew 1997).

Psychological dimension of suicide

Psychological perspective on suicide divulges more on behavior per se than the social structure. It focuses more on the intra-psychic processes of the individual, as well as on the cognitive, emotional and personality variables, which influence suicidal behavior which could be classified into non-psychoanalytic and psychoanalytic.

An earliest psychological explanation can be traced to Clark (1922), Gordon (1922), Crichton-Miller (1931) and Williams (1936). Clark holds that basic to all suicides is an inversion or an incest motive. The result is an imbalance in the will to live, an increase of intra-psychic tension, an affective fixation of infantile attachment and finally a suicidal act. Gordan believed that man being a social animal possesses an intrinsic element in his personality, i.e., a capacity to adapt to the progressive evolution of the social environment. He contends that suicide represents a failure in the adaptive process – a denial and shirking of the duty of the individual as an integral part of the universal whole.

Crichton-Miller, like Gordan, also attributes suicide act to the individuals' inability to adapt himself and holds that it constitutes a final regression from reality. He proposes motivations for suicides into three groups:

1. Physical pain and frustration of instinctual needs
2. Social sufferings and fears including remorse for wrongdoings and an impulse towards penance and an exaggerated self-love which prohibits the acceptance of any form of social humiliation
3. Doubts and dreads pertaining to the hereafter and manifest in the suicides of Messianic character in which there occurs a supreme sacrifice of the total personality for some redemptive purpose

Williams stated two dominant reasons for suicide-disappointment and frustration. Since all persons experience such feelings, he postulates in the rigid personality the presence of a strong narcissistic component, which cannot accept defeats or combat reverses and is unable to adapt easily to reality. The result of which is suicide.

Freud (1923) outlined important psychoanalytic theory of suicide. He provides a detailed psychological interpretation of self-destruction, where he claims that suicide is essentially a basic concept of the human mind and every individual is vulnerable to suicide, to a certain extent. Freud considered suicide to be an intra-psychic phenomenon primarily, originating within the unconscious mind. The inherent 'death instinct' with an individual is responsible for violent behaviors, externalized as anger or internalized as suicidal behaviors (Mukherjee and Kumar 2017). The pressures compelling an individual to end life by suicide could increase, depending on one's life events, situations, stress and anxiety levels. Freud reiterated that life and death instincts are in constant conflict within the individual, hence depicting suicide as the potent outcome of an intra-psychic struggle between the forces of life and death (Berman and Jobes 1991; Stillion and McDowell 1996). Zilboorg (1937) criticized Freud's take on suicide and expanded the psychoanalytic approach by stating that suicide is a result of potential negative triggers, such as revenge, fear, spite and escapist fantasies leading to the act of suicide. He, further, proposed that most suicidal acts are impulsive in nature and that external factors definitely play a role simultaneously with the internal mechanisms proposed by Freud (Williams and Pollock 2000).

Another important genre of psychological dimensions was provided by the cognitive psychologists under cognitive theories that propose individuals becoming suicidal as a result of disruption in the components of cognitive triad, i.e., beliefs about self, others and future. They emphasized suicide as an outcome of interaction between vulnerability factors and life stressors.

Focusing on individual's intra-psychic factors and suicide vulnerability, suicidologist Shneidman's work deserves special attention. As far as the aspect of pain goes in relation to suicide, Shneidman (1985, 1996) coined the term 'psychache' referring to the severe psychological pain as a result of unmet psychological needs. He narrated that all those who die by suicide experience 'psychache' before their death. However, he also points that not all those who experience 'psychache' will die by suicide, in fact, the additional factor of lethality is necessary for the suicide to occur. He also claims that suicide is the ultimate escape from this 'psychache'.

Beck's (1967) cognitive theory based on research conducted with clinically depressed patients proposes that an individual's lineage of thoughts, ideologies and interpretations of life events is correlated to the manner in which s/he responds to events, both emotionally and behaviorally (Brown et al. 2006). Clinically depressed people habitually displayed a certain pattern of thinking, which involved them having a rather negative view of themselves, their future and the world, resulting in a self-perpetuating cycle of negativity and an increased sense of hopelessness for their future. Individuals restrained to such a lineage of thoughts, ideologies, beliefs and values are limited by their inability to perceive and cope with their problems differently; hence, they view suicide as the only means to liberate thermally from existence. Thus, evolved the 'Hopelessness theory of Suicide', which claimed that hopelessness behaves like a catalyst, thereby participating in the manifestation of suicidal behavior. Hopelessness is a key variable in individuals inclined towards suicidal tendencies and the act per se; they inevitably view their experiences as negative in nature, and strongly believe that their attempts to achieve goals will end in no more than failure, thereby displaying that hopelessness, depression and suicidal behavior are interconnected (Beck et al. 1975).

The interpersonal theory of suicide proposed by Joiner (2005) states that an individual will not die by suicide unless s/he has both the desire to die by suicide and the ability to do so. It asserts that when people hold two specific psychological states, i.e., low belongingness or social alienation and perceived burdensomeness in mind for long enough, they develop the desire for death. Ability to a suicide-attempt comes with the element of acquired ability for lethal self-injury, i.e., the acquired ability to overcome one's natural fear of death. It is hypothesized that the capability for suicide is acquired largely through repeated exposure to painful or fearsome experiences resulting in habituation and a higher tolerance for pain and a sense of fearlessness in the face of death. A clear implication of this is that past suicidal behavior will habituate individuals to the pain and fear of self-injury, making future suicidality, on average, more likely.

More recent and comprehensive psychological perspective was of O'Connor's (2011) Integrated Motivational-Volitional (IMV) model of suicidal behavior that describes three stages of suicidality. The first is pre-motivational stage, marked by background factors and triggering events; the second is motivational stage, marked by suicidal thoughts and formation of intent; and the third is volitional stage marked by behavioral action and engaging in serious suicidal behaviors. Motivational and volitional moderators that can influence the progression of suicidal behavior moderate the progress from the first stage to third stage.

Biological dimension of suicide

The primary biological focus of suicide studies has been oriented towards the affirmative association to biological changes in functioning of the brain. It brings out the interrelated aspects of personality traits or temperament, role of genetics and neurological and neurobiological differences to the suicidal behavior.

The hypothalamic-pituitary-adrenal (HPA) axis (a system tying together the hypothalamus and the pituitary gland in the brain with the adrenal glands near the kidneys) controls our body's responses to actual, anticipated or perceived harm. In addition, the HPA axis regulates our ability to adapt to stressors over time. Exactly how the HPA axis influences suicidal behavior is not yet clear. Some researchers suggest the contributions of two genes that control the regulation of the neurotransmitters (chemical messengers in the brain and nervous system): norepinephrine and serotonin (substances that influence mood regulation) (Reiss and Mark n.d.; Yohn et al. 2017). One of the most consistent findings in biological studies in both suicide-attempters and individuals who died from suicide showed low serotonin levels (or poor ability to receive serotonin) and higher levels of noradrenaline in the brain stem, resulting in mood disorders (Traskman-Bendz et al. 1992; Traskman-Bendz and Mann 2000). Suicidal people also seem to have lower levels of norepinephrine (also called epinephrine or adrenaline) in the part of the brain called the locus ceruleus. Norepinephrine is a chemical messenger that affects the central nervous system and the bloodstream. When one confronts with danger, epinephrine is released into the bloodstream, increasing the heart rate and blood pressure, readying one for action (Reiss and Mark undated).

Personality is the relatively stable set of characteristics called traits. It is composed of learned characteristics, and genetically based individual differences in attention, arousal and reactivity to new or novel situations called temperament. Adults and adolescents with suicidal behavior tend to display characteristic temperaments of depressive/withdrawn, impulsive/aggressive/negativistic or high in neuroticism. Individuals with such temperaments show high levels of negative, depressive or angry moods with difficulty in controlling their emotions. They are also likely to develop depression and anxiety disorders and often die by suicide as a result. Moreover, people with such traits are often diagnosed with antisocial personality disorders or risky behaviors (ibid.).

In recent years, a growing body of biological research on suicide also supports the notion that genetic factors are highly related to a person's risk for ending life by suicide. The evidence of such research is based on the two things: first, suicide often runs in families, and adoption studies suggest that genes are likely to account for familial clustering of suicidal behavior (Turecki 2005). Brent and Mann (2005) reviewed a host of family genetic studies (adopted children, twins and family studies) to investigate its impact on an individual's ideation towards suicide. They concluded that suicide and suicidal behavior belong to the same clinical phenotype and maybe attributed to the genetic transmission of impulsive aggression. Sexual and physical abuse, early parental loss, imitation, family instability and transmission of psychopathology are some of the identified potential environmental variables of suicidal behavior link. Supporting a genetic link to suicide among twins it is stated that if monozygotic twin (i.e., genetically identical) takes her own life, the other has an 11.3 fold increased risk of suicide as well. Also there is a higher concordance rate for suicide among identical twins than the dizygotic (i.e., genetically non-identical) twins (11.3% vs. 1.8%) (Reiss and Mark undated).

Economic dimension of suicide

This dimension presents an economic interpretation to suicide while considering the effects of societal influences and individual factors on suicidal behavior. Durkheim's sociological perspective to suicide has established the economic association with suicide by providing the evidence of correlations between the two in terms that equality in income and wealth (affluence or poverty) and income inequality threatening social integration resulting in anomie (Bantjes et al. 2016; Durkheim 1951).

Hamermesh and Soss (1974) were the first to develop an economic theory of suicide. They directly model and empirically explore suicide in economics, using time series and cross-sectional variation in the USA to argue that suicide rates increase with aggregate measures of unemployment. Suicide risk is significantly related to unemployment and decreases in permanent income.

The impact of unemployment on suicide has been extensively investigated in the wake of global economic crises, especially in high-income countries (HICs). For instance, an Australian study reported higher rates of suicide following the 2006–2008 economic crisis (Milner et al. 2014). Following the 1997–1998 Asian economic crisis, a study of 54 HICs showed that increased rates of unemployment following the crisis were associated with increase in suicide rates, although the strength of the association varied by gender and region (Chang et al. 2013). Suicide rates in Korea, Japan and Hong Kong rose at a significantly greater rate in the poorest sections of society left behind during the economic recovery (Hong et al. 2011). It was hypothesized that it takes much longer for the benefits of economic recovery to trickle down to the most economically vulnerable individuals, thus leaving them susceptible to suicide despite recovery (Chan et al. 2014). Yong-Hwan (2009) supports that higher income is associated with higher suicide rates. Evidence shows effect of unemployment on suicide rates is larger for countries with higher income, as compared to those with lower-income levels.

Economic outcomes throughout India remain closely tied to agriculture. Climate variability critically affects agricultural incomes, and with over 30% of the population lying below the poverty line, climate shocks can have dire consequences for households relying on agriculture. Negative income shocks induced by agricultural income variability may increase the stress or exacerbate existing risk factors such as family challenges or mental and physical health for some individuals. Such a scenario raises the probability that individual will contemplate, attempt or die by suicide (Chemin et al. 2013; Rehkopf and Buka 2006; Stack 2000b). Further, the small and marginal farmers in India have greater debt burden and crop failure due to climate disturbances or due to crop failure, pest attack, etc., which constantly pose a threat of repaying debt and the resultant crisis situation. Hence, some farmers resort to suicide when they are unable to pay the debt, or when their mortgaged land is auctioned (Gill 2005).

Pandey and Kaur (2009) through their time series analysis (period of 1967–2006) suggested that industrial growth encourages the incidence of suicide. This is probably because industrial growth requires skilled labor and those who are unskilled may lose their jobs which may increase the chance of suicide. It also showed that the incidence and rate of suicide increases with increase in inflation rate, which has been confirmed by the occurrence of farmers' suicides in India.

The different dimensions to suicide differ with the focus either on social structure, individual behavior or genes. They, however, overlap conceptually in several ways, thus proposing a 'socio-psycho-bio approach', which sounds more holistic. Suicide becomes the inevitable end-result when there is a combination of socio-economic, psychological and biological risk factors. Such a perspective brings out broader understanding of suicide by examining the social meanings of suicide and suicidal behavior in their social and individual contexts. For instance, applied in the milieu of family, it would claim that family plays a critical role in an individual's suicidal behavior by creating social pressures and stress in order to follow social obligations. Psychological approach would recognize the presence of psychiatric disorders as a result of family creating a pathological home environment (exposure to abuse, socio-economic constraints), while biological dimension could recognize role of parents (in some cases) in passing abnormal behavior (aggressive, impulsive) due to genetic disorders (Maris et al. 2000).

Suicide risk groups and vulnerability

Suicide is a personal act, which often harnesses a breakdown of common conscience and depicts the flaw in the social fabric of society where individuals find themselves placed. Hence, understanding of suicide calls for a comprehension of various factors and structure of the society. When a person's behavior, action or situation questions their adherence to the expected norms, it places them in a dilemma. Suicide is, thus, a personal disorganization resulting in an individual's deviation from the social norms, values or rules (Spaulding and Simpson 1951). How to prevent or diminish such deviancy lays in the fact of first understanding the risk factors and contexts. It would allow one to reflect upon the situations and scenarios that shape the mindset of individuals to end their lives.

Suicide is rarely, if ever, the outcome of a single antecedent event. Rather, a constellation of risk and protective factors, external and internal to the individual, interacts with each other to produce the complex outcome of suicide (Moscicki 1997). From an epidemiologic perspective, distal risk factors mean underlying vulnerability or the predisposing factors for suicidal behavior. They can occur at both the individual and environmental levels, and represent an edge above which individual vulnerability to proximal risk factors increases. Exposure to distal risk factors is necessary for attempted- and completed-suicide; however, they alone are not sufficient (Rothman 1986). Proximal risk factors are more immediately antecedent to the suicidal event itself, and can act as precipitants. However, the interaction of powerful distal risk factors with proximal circumstances can have a cumulative effect of environmental and individual burden that produces the necessary and sufficient conditions for suicide. The co-occurrence of distal and proximal risk processes in individual, family and environmental domains is likely to be associated with the greatest risk for suicide (Lewinsohn et al. 1996; Shaffer et al. 1996; Wagner 1997).

Suicide risk groups

Age and gender

Suicide occurs throughout the lifespan but generation of youth or young people is among those most affected and at a greater risk. Globally, suicide is now the second leading cause of death for those between the ages of 15 and 29 years. According to estimates of suicide mortality across world regions, young adults in low- and middle-income countries have much higher suicide rates than their counterparts in high-income countries. In some regions, a peak in suicide rates in young adults subsides in middle age while in others suicide rates increase steadily with age. In high-income countries, suicide is most common among middle-aged and elderly men (WHO 2018a, 2014).

Studies have demonstrated that the onset of suicidal behavior increases considerably at the start of adolescence (age 12), peaks at 16 years and stays elevated into early adulthood (Nock and Mendes 2008). Thus, adolescence and adulthood present the greatest risk for the first onset of suicidal behavior. It is not surprising then that most suicides are occurring among school and college students with studies showing the range from 32% to 70% suicide ideations in college students (Gutierrez et al. 2000). Country-specific studies point out that the trend of suicides among adolescent and young continues to be a great societal concern in the USA (NIMH 2004), in African region (Ludman et al. 1996; NIMSS 2004; WHO 2014) and in South Korea.[5] The youth and young adult suicide rate in India has been relatively constant at around 15 per lakh since 1967. In the late 1970s there occurred a dip, which later on remained stable at a lower level around 15 per lakh until 1995 and recent trends infer that there is a little change in the rates since then (Mayer 2016).

According to the Registrar General, India (2014), among the ten leading causes of death in young people aged 15–24, non-medical causes are dominant. Suicide-deaths stand first with 18%, three times more than the tuberculosis. Motor vehicle accidents and unintentional injuries are the second and third leading cause of death, respectively. For rural women both young and middle age (15–44), suicide is described as the top killer.

Adolescent suicidal behavior is a common problem in low- and middle-developed or high-income countries. However, in African countries, the higher prevalence of suicidal behaviors might be partly explained by the predominance of HIV/AIDS, political instability, food and/or financial scarcity (Cluver et al. 2015). Likewise, in high-income countries and in several low- and middle-income countries suicidal behaviors among adolescents could be correlated to psychological factors such as depression, low self-esteem, hopelessness and weak social relationships (King et al. 2001; Pagee and West 2011).

Pillai et al. (2009) observed that among young people, suicidal behavior was found to be associated with certain features like gender, premarital sex, sexual abuse, domestic violence, patients diagnosed with mental disorders, school or college dropouts and so on. According to them, violence and psychological distress were associated with suicidal behavior. They opine that factors associated with gender disadvantage increase ones vulnerability towards suicide, which is particularly noted in rural women.

For older age groups Rao (1972) found the association between depression and suicidal behavior with the fact that the risk of completed-suicide among the aged attempters being two times higher compared to the younger generation. Shukla et al. (1990) however found the low prevalence of suicide among the elderly in India because the aged are well-integrated and respected individuals of the family and children take responsibility for their care. In addition, life expectancy in the elderly is lower in India than elsewhere, contributing to the comparatively lower suicide rate. Presently, the explanation for elderly suicides, however, needs further research and understanding considering the changing social status of the elderly in India.

Gender is also a factor in suicidal behavior. Suicide patterns suggest that in the Western world, males die more than females by suicide (Phillips et al. 1999; Stack 2000). There is a higher rate of ideation and suicide-attempts among women (Borges et al. 2010; Lester 2000; Nock et al. 2013); however, rates of suicide-deaths are generally higher in men which is estimated at 15 per 1,00,000 men *vs.* eight per 1,00,000 women, worldwide (Canetto and Sakinofsky 1998; WHO 2014). Global male-to-female suicide ratio is of 1.8:1. Suicide gender ratio is less in Asia when compared to Western countries (Varnik 2012). In India, the ratio is near equal (1.4:1) while in China the ratio is reversed with the female rate being higher than the male rate (0.9:1). In Taiwan, Hong Kong and Singapore it is at 1.2:1 (Chen et al. 2012; Mayer and Tahereh 2002; Vijayakumar 2007; Yip and Liu 2006). In richer countries, three times as many men die of suicide than women do, but in low-and middle-income countries, the male-to-female ratio is much lower at 1.5 men to each woman (WHO 2014).

A large proportion of the suicide-deaths in India in 2016 was in the age groups 15–39 years in both women (71.2%) and men (57.7%). Suicide was the leading contributor to deaths in these age groups among women, and the second leading contributor among men in India. Statewise distribution shows that suicide-deaths ranked first among all causes of death in women aged 15–29 years in 26 of the 31 states, and in women aged 15–39 years in 24 states. For men, suicide was the leading cause of death in 9 states among those aged 15–29 years and in 10 states in those aged 15–39 years (Dandona et al. 2018).

The battle to reduce suicide has also been more successful among women than men. Across nations, suicide rates for men are three to seven times higher. The same pattern prevails in India across most age groups, though the gender gap is less sharp (Kaushal 2019). Youth suicide rates vary greatly between states of India for males and females. For young males, in 28 states/union territories and for females in 12 states/union territories, the suicide rates were at or above the crisis level. Based on data from around 2000, if individual Indian states were nations, then the 15 highest youth female suicide rates in the world would all have been Indian (Mayer 2016).

As a part of The Million Death Study,[6] the study by Gomes et al. (2017) showed that young adults end life by suicides far more than the Government of India reports. In addition, most of the suicides were among young adults rather than older farmers, who had been thought to have the highest numbers of suicide. Suicide rates in young adults were particularly high in south India, and many of the suicides were by ingesting organophosphate pesticide (Patel et al. 2012). Yet there has been no public recognition of the seriousness of youth suicide in the country (Mayer 2016).

Within the aged group one finds the increased prevalence of suicide among older men to that of women. This may be because older women are more willing and flexible in adapting to changing life situations than men as a result of a lifetime of socialization. Therefore, they may be less likely to respond to severely stressful life events in later stages, such as the death of a spouse, feeling of loneliness with lethal self-destructive behavior (Canetto 1992).

Tousignant et al. (1998) conducted a survey among a diverse group of people (such as university professors, inspectors, crime reporters and nurses) in the city of Bangalore to investigate the perceptions of male and female suicides. The narratives of suicide derived from the survey suggest a series of accusations against women over the suicides. Women were blamed for their own and for their husband's suicide. If women die by suicide, they were said to be ashamed of having transgressed a rule; if men end their lives, it was thought to have been the victim of some form of abuse at the hands of women. However, they also found that in some situations women were viewed more often as victims of life adversities than the men.

Students

Every hour one student takes his/her life in India, according to NCRB (2015) data. The number of student suicides stood at 9,905 in 2017 and 10,159 in 2018, which in 2019 raised to 10,335. In nine years, i.e., from 2011 to 2019, 79, 652 students had killed themselves. These were reported data, but there may be more cases of unreported attempted suicides. Their suicides could be related to the pressure of performance, aspirations and failures. The educational system, teachers and parents can be regarded equally responsible for the phenomenon of increasing suicides among the students. We have an education system that judges the capacity and performance of a student based on marks in exams. Such system along with parent's expectations puts all kinds of pressure on the students to excel at any cost and score as high as possible (Peenikaparambil 2018). In pressure and fear of failing hopes of parents, school or their teachers, students feel better to die by suicide. In some cases, children take their lives before they appear for examination or before their results are out due to anticipation of getting low marks. In Sweden, parents place a strong emphasis on performance and success on children. Hence, suicide in Swedish society is followed by the failure to perform and/or the result of low self-esteem. In order to reduce suicides among students it is important to prepare them to face failures and difficult situations in life. They are to be taught that failures do not define their life. By facing failures and going through struggles one can rather bring out the best in one's life. Increasing mental strength should be core focus as it will not make him/her to end life when faced with adverse situations (ibid.).

Chatterjee and Basu (2010) probed the intrinsic and extrinsic factors that induces suicidal ideation among female college students. Almost 12% of the total studied females showed high suicidal ideation of suicidal thought within past one month. Academic, interpersonal and environment-related factors were reasons behind suicidal ideations. Events like public embarrassment, harassment, rape, being rejected in love were highly rated while academic failures and career issues were moderately important. Reasons for ending life by suicide due to death of loved one and financial crisis were less significant. The issues of sexual harassment and love affairs as significant factor for suicidal ideation could be because of the matter of immense shame and trauma as such incidents are unacceptable to self and society. Since such instances are highly stressful, they form extreme risk to suicidal thought.

A study on the prevalence of suicidal behavior and its epidemiological correlates among adolescent school and college students of 14–19 years in Delhi uncovered their suicidal thoughts. Attempted-suicide was more prevalent in females than in males. Some females reported to have seriously thought about suicide, whereas some went ahead and truly attempted it. Few females and males even reported of multiple attempts at ending their lives within a span of one year. Range of socio-demographic factors like higher-age groups, single living parent, working mothers and role models engaging in negative health risk behaviors (smoking, drinking, etc.) all showed the association with the suicide-risk behavior of students. For instance, neglect of parental role and support risks students' (of single parent or working mothers) proneness to suicide as there would be limited communication and availability of parents support to ensure that they overcome various stress including unsafe health behaviors and any thoughts of self-harming (Sharma et al. 2008).

Vulnerability to suicidal behavior is multifaceted, and personality trait is one of them. Devi and Prakash (2015) highlighted relationship between personality traits and suicidal ideation among college students of 18–26 years in Imphal (Manipur). It showed that individuals with elevated neuroticism are more susceptible to psychological distress and suicidal behaviors.

Since they have poor adaptation and coping capability, because of coping ineffectively with stress, they resort to suicidal behaviors in adverse situations. Individual personality trait of introverted and socially withdrawn is also equally vulnerable to suicide ideation. The personality features of individuals who have a low opinion of their abilities and low self-esteem or feel hopeless, and those who are unreliable, lack motivation and often act without considering the consequences are also at the risk of suicidal ideation which later becomes serious suicidal behavior.

Among students, one can assume that examinations, parental control and expectations for good academic performance, classroom bullying and peer pressure put a considerable strain on young students. Hence, lower academic performance, anxiety, depression and other mental health problems may be shown as associated with academia-related stress, which could lead to many of them, turning towards self-destruction (Kaila 2005; Lakshmi and Arora 2006).

Suicide because of a failure in love affairs has become quite prevalent nowadays. The widespread use of mobile phones and impact of media offers enough ground for boys and girls students to get intimately involved with each other. Eventually, the growth of such relations may take harmful form to the individuals involved, a betrayal of these relations also suffices as reason enough for suicide. The attitude of families who consciously choose to undermine and not accept their children' love affairs may further add a reason for young students to end life by suicide.

Farmers

Among occupational risk groups, the plight of farmers has captured the greatest attention with their suicides being linked to income. Behere and Behere (2008) noted certain causes among the farmers of Vidharba region, like chronic indebtedness and inability to pay debts accumulated over the years, rising costs of agricultural inputs and falling prices of agricultural produce, family disputes, depression, alcoholism and possibly delay of monetary compensation to the family following a suicide. Similarly, according to a report of seven districts in the state of Punjab, the debt-related suicides have increased at an alarming rate (above 90%) during 2010–2016 (Vasudeva 2017). Considering that there are 20 lakh cultivators and 15 lakh agricultural laborers in Punjab, an average of 18 farmers and 18 agricultural laborers die by suicide per lakh workers per annum (Singh 2018). Another study in relation to the large number of farmers deaths by suicide in the same state revealed that the farmers who died by suicide were under huge debts, and the income acquired from agriculture was not adequate to repay the borrowed money. In the absence of any help, farmers chose to end their lives (Chavan et al. 2008).

On the nature and causes of farmers' suicides in Karnataka, Nagathan et al. (2011) study explains that spread of suicide was largely concentrated between the age group of 36 and 50 years (middle age). Farmers' dependency upon agriculture especially on dry farming with negligible supplementary enterprises further risks their vulnerability to suicide. Debt burden was found to be the major cause forcing farmers to take extreme step of ending life by suicide. Loss in agricultural activities and poor repaying capacity of borrowed money were other important reasons. According to the authors, Indian farmer is caught in the debt trap because commercial farming force farmer to invest heavily by taking risk in anticipation of higher returns. But the intervening factors such as drought, failure of water sources, crop failure and non-remunerative prices increase the debt over years. Social obligations like marriage and education of children further raise their debt. Debt trap thus keeps working in a vicious way. Socio-psychological features revealed that many farmers suffered from stress, which could be due to heavy pressure and humiliation from private moneylenders, crop failure, debt burden, etc.

Shiva and Jalees (n.d.) also views rapid increase in indebtedness as the root of farmers taking their lives. For them the rising costs of production and falling prices of farm commodities (products of policies of trade liberalization and corporate globalization) affected the debt scenario for farmers. They argue that rising farmer suicides is allied to economic processes linked to globalization such as rise in indebtedness and increased frequency of crop failure. This happens due to higher ecological vulnerability, arising from climate change, drought and higher economic risks due to introduction of untested, unadapted seeds. Since corporate seeds replaced farm-saved seeds that need fertilizers, pesticides and cannot be saved, peasants are forced to buy seed for every planting season. This increases poverty and indebtedness which when become unpayable due to crop failure and lead farmers to die by suicide. Seed monopolies controlled by a handful of agribusiness corporations resulted in negative effects for farmers in Andhra Pradesh (Warangal District) and Bihar with hybrid Bt cotton and hybrid corn, respectively.

According to Mayer (2016), though many farmers end life by suicide due to financial debt, their numbers to total suicidal deaths in the country are lower. Rate of suicide-deaths by farmers is lower than that of housewives, the retired and civil servants. Official statistics record nearly four housewives death from suicide for every one of farmer.

Suicide risk factors

Marital status

It is believed strongly that marriage is not a protective factor against suicide-attempts. In India, 68.8% and 66.7% of all those who took own lives were married in 2018 and 2019, respectively (NCRB 2018; 2019). Various individual research studies also indicated that most married individuals were likely to die by suicide as opposed to the unmarried people (Latha et al. 1996; Srivastava et al. 2004). Other studies however pointed out the tendency for suicide ideations and attempts among other marital groups (Narang et al. 2000; Sharma 1998). Suicide rates for divorced and widowed women and men are higher than rates for married persons (Monk 1987; Smith et al. 1988). In the case of divorce or separation, it is not clear whether the disruption of the marriage itself leads to suicide, or whether persons who are more likely to be suicidal also are more likely to be in an unstable marriage. A disrupted family environment that includes violence in the form of physical and sexual abuse or family history of suicide and/or mental or addictive disorders may also contribute to suicide risk (Briere and Zaidi 1989; De Wilde et al. 1991; Egeland and Sussex 1985).

Even The Million Death study, revealed that unlike most Western countries where likelihood of married women ending lives by suicide is less than once married women, in India it is the opposite. Married women are more at risk and more likely to die by suicide than the divorced, widowed or separated women. This could be due to psychological and physical torture that women suffer in marital home at the hands of husband or in-laws. However, there are differences in the suicide rates among young married women within India. South Indian states, well known for better gender relations and empowerment than north Indian states, have much higher youth female mortality. Maybe there is a greater socio-cultural tolerance of suicide as a way out of mental stress in south India (Kaushal 2019).

Marital problems and social pressure have extensive implications on females leading to suicide. For instance, the exceedingly high rate of suicide among Chinese women could be attributed to the negative social situation of women in the country (Zhang et al. 2002). Their status in society depends on their marital and maternal responsibilities. In pre-revolutionary China, they were legitimately sold off much unlike commodities: to overcome poverty, to pay off gambling debts, either eventually to become a wife or concubine or to work in a brothel as a Geisha or a prostitute (Hershatter 1991; Ocko 1991). In contemporary times, the social situation continues to remain poor despite individual rights being officially announced yet not enforced by the system. Moreover, most females were pressurized to conceive and bear a male child in order to ensure that the elderly were taken care of and one's family lineage continued through a male child. In addition to this, the one-child policy in China resulted in the maximization in parent's preferences towards the birth of a male child: eventually, leading to the mistreatment, divorce and suicide of many young mothers, thus creating suicidal tendencies among them. Further, failing to recognize psychiatric illnesses of depression such as withdrawn and uncommunicative behavior has led to the exponential increase in suicide rates in the country. A young female generally experiences an acute amount of interpersonal or financial crisis leading to depression and eventually, to the act of suicide through the consumption of lethal pesticides or poisons (Chen et al. 2012; Pearson

1995). Cultural-socio-economic disadvantages of the Chinese rural females and their cultural attitude towards suicide are particularly noteworthy, as far as suicide is concerned (Law and Liu 2008).

In Asian families of the United Kingdom (UK), arranged marriage, dowry and other cultural pressures were reported in women who reacted under extraordinary pressure and struggled to conform to the norms of the society. Moreover, individuals who face dilemmas due to what they and others perceive to be their roles increases stressful life events and vulnerabilities. Trapped in between such conflicts women were left with the option to choose self-harming practices or attempt to end life by suicide as an outlet and/or expression of being in distress (Bhugra 2002). Such scenarios partially reaffirm the claim that being married is not necessarily a protective factor for females; suicide-attempts are closely viewed as an impact of family relationships. In Asia, young married women face multiple atrocities and find themselves situated in the lowest ranks, which acts as a higher risk factor for suicides (Gururaj et al. 2004).

Though determinant of risk to suicide, one should understand that the quality of the marital relationship, emotional warmth, extended family support and the ability to handle stress related to marriage and child-rearing are more important than marital status, per se, in leading a person to suicide act. But, to study these qualifiers is rather difficult (Radhakrishnan and Andrade 2012).

Education and occupation status

Analysis of NCRB data on the educational status of those died by suicide across regions over five decades (census years) indicates that most were educated anywhere upto primary to higher-secondary. The trend over years showed growth under these educational categories (Lobo and Bharati 2018). This observation is similar to a time series study by Pandey and Kaur (2009), which conveyed the exponential rise of suicides of individuals from the primary, matriculate and/or higher-secondary education while suicides by the highly educated, diploma holders and above were relatively smaller in number. Such scenario implies a declining tendency of suicide among illiterates compared to the formally educated people. A possible reason for it could be due to the academic, professional and social pressures among the educated persons.

Unemployment creates a series of stressful scenarios, which conjure multiple reactions comprising personal meanings such as loss of esteem and personal consequences which might include depression and hopelessness. Unemployment and suicide share a rather complimentary relationship reported to be stronger in men than that of in women (Kposowa 2001). Thus, unemployment and suicide may be the result of factors such as stress-induced mental health problems and the lack of protective supporting factors such as family and loved ones (Mishara 2008). In India, though there is a tendency to link suicides with income or economic distress, surprisingly the association between poverty and suicide mortality is not high. All India figures over five census years (2011, 2001, 1991, 1981 and 1971) show low percentages of suicide due to poverty (Lobo and Bharati 2018). Recently released data of NCRB (2019) showed suicides due to poverty at 0.8%. In 2018, it was 0.9%, which was the same even for 2016 and 2017. This suggests poverty as a single factor is less impactful for suicide, but in combination of other factors, it elevates the risk to suicide.

A study by Kar (2010), to understand the risk factors associated with suicide-attempts in Orissa, showed that persons with no formal or college education had around 40% attempts that were least rescuable, significantly more from the other educational groups. Further, in terms of occupational status, a sizeable proportion of attempters (other than students and housewives) were unemployed. However, significant number of employed respondents had planned attempts within one month before their suicide-attempts. Being unemployed is extremely stressful, but many skilled-workers, self-employed and professionals have attempted due to job uncertainties. Fear of no regular job, or impending financial loss lead to stress and attempt to suicide.

The process of urbanization also tends to give rise to multiple risk factors for suicide. For instance, young people migrating to cities often find it difficult to find job. Aged inhabitants in rural areas form a specific vulnerable group and is at a heightened risk of contemplating, attempting or ending lives by suicide (Hendin et al. 2008; Ji et al. 2001; Wu et al. 2012).

The need to focus on migrants as a specifically vulnerable group was brought out by the study of Chavan et al. (2008), who used psychological autopsies to reveal that almost 58% migrants from other parts of India were frequently male and young (20–28 years) and are at suicide risk.

Highlighting about suicides of public sector employees, Jain et al. (2012) states that workplace stress is the foremost reason for ending one's life. Based on reported suicide cases of certain public sectors like Railway, Research and Analysis Wing (RAW), Hindustan Aeronautics Limited (HAL) and Indian Armed Forces, authors identify that job stress has led many public sector employees to suffer from mental trauma, which they ended by suicide. Working conditions to the point of exhaustion, little room for flexibility and self-initiative are main reasons for their job stress. For employees the stress initially shows itself as irritability, mood changes and short temper, which later on lead to extreme measures like suicide. According to them, seniors in such companies should work to resolve the underlying causes of stress as a long-term idea. They should provide its employees a stress-free work environment besides recognizing the source of stress where it becomes a problem for staff, and should take action to reduce it.

Alcohol dependence

Self-injurious behavior and suicidal ideation link to alcohol dependence are well established. Globally, alcohol consumption has increased in recent decades, with all or most of that increase occurring in developing countries. Alcohol consumption has health and social consequences *via* intoxication (drunkenness), dependence (habitual, compulsive and long-term drinking) and biochemical effects. In addition to chronic diseases that may affect drinkers after many years of heavy use, alcohol contributes to traumatic outcomes that kill or disable at a relatively young age, resulting in the loss of many years of life to death or disability (Pompili et al. 2010).

Alcohol use and suicide are intimately linked, but they are both complex phenomena, springing from a multitude of factors. Menninger (1938) conceptualized addiction itself both as a form of chronic suicide and as a factor involved in focal suicide (deliberate self-harming accidents). Substance abusers are at greater risk for suicide, with alcoholics having an annual risk of suicide that is ten-fold that of the general population; co-morbid depression and antisocial personality disorder are significant contributing factors (Murphy and Wetzel 1999). Suicidal individuals show heavier drinking pattern, more alcohol-related medical problems, younger age of onset of alcohol misuse and longer duration of alcoholism (Cheng 1995; Conner and Duberstein 2004).

Borges and Rosovsky (1996) found that where more alcohol is consumed, greater is the risk of suicidal behavior. Alcohol intoxication increases suicide risk up to 90 times in comparison with abstinence. Individuals with alcoholism who attempted or completed suicide were characterized by major depressive episodes, stressful life events, high aggression/impulsivity, co-morbid substance, poor social support, negative affect, hopelessness and prior suicidal behavior (Sher 2006). Approximately one-half of alcohol-dependent women and one fourth of alcohol-dependent men have a lifetime history of depression (Kessler et al. 1997).

Psychiatric disorders

Studies in the recent past have shown the interconnected relationship of suicidal behavior with psychiatric illness or personality disorders. A patient diagnosed with a psychiatric disorder is 3–12 times more likely to die by suicide than the general populace (Crammer 1984; Roy 1989). Robins (1986) and Barraclough et al. (1974) analyzed several hundred cases of suicide and concluded that more than 90% of them had been suffering from mental illness during the time when they killed themselves. There is a high prevalence of mental illness (completed-suicide) in Western countries (Hawton and Heeringen 2001). In India although people with mental illness do die by suicide, the contribution of such suicides is small. Many suicides are impulsive and related to stress and conflict (Manoranjitham et al. 2010).

There are built up events associated with suicidal behavior. Underlying risk points the strongest association with the psychiatric disorders (Monk 1987; Moscicki 1995). More than 90% of completed-suicides are associated with mental or addictive disorders, the most common of which are depression, personality disorders and alcohol abuse (Rich et al. 1986; Runeson 1989). Co-morbid occurrence of more than one psychiatric disorder, and co-morbid mental and drug use disorders have been found frequently, suggesting that completed-suicide is associated with more severe forms of mental illness (Rich and Runeson 1992; Shafii et al. 1985). In addition, there is consistent evidence that biological risk factors may be associated with suicide and suicidal behavior with impulsivity (Kety 1986; Roy et al. 1991).

Psychiatric and physical illnesses, functional impairment, personality traits of neuroticism and social isolation are salient vulnerability factors among older as opposed to younger adults, which influence their suicidal behavior (Draper 1996). According to Rao and Madhavan (1983), the depressive illness is a major cause of suicidal ideation and the linkage between elders and their suicide-attempts. However, family and society neglect is largely due to perceiving and mistaking the illness as a part of the aging process. Due to changes in family structure and changing social role in the family, many elders feel neglected, lonely and isolated. Such feelings build up negative thoughts and turn up to become the cause of suicide. It is found that interpersonal relationships are regularly a factor in older adult suicides. If older adults find themselves not integral to the family or have trouble in establishing or maintaining relationships, they develop disturbed, insufferable interpersonal tragedies leading to a condition of self-harm (Das 2017).

As per National Mental Health Survey (NMHS) 2015–2016 in India, 1 in 20 (5.25%) people over 18 years of age have ever suffered (at least once in their lifetime) from depression amounting to a total of over 45 million persons with depression in 2015. Psychological autopsy studies reported a depression prevalence ranging from 22% to 38% among suicide decedents (Vijayakumar and Rajkumar 1999). The lifetime prevalence of depression in India was 5.25% among individuals aged 18+ years, and the current prevalence was 2.68%, highlighting the fact 1 out of 20 adult individuals has suffered from depression in the past with half of them suffering at present. Its current prevalence across the states ranged between 1.24% in Gujarat and 4.70% in Jharkhand. The reported prevalence was more in the 40–49 age groups (3.64%) and among females (2.97%). Prevalence among urban metro residents (5.17%) was two times higher than urban non-metro (1.90%) and rural residents (2.15%). Prevalence was more in those who were illiterate (3.63%); among the widowed, divorced or separated (5.23%); and among those in the lowest income quintile (3.42%) (*Ibid*). Every two of three individuals with depression reported disability in work life (67.30%), family life (70.20%) and social life (68.60%). Nearly

21% of affected individuals reported substantial difficulties in carrying out their daily activities. Difficulties of varying severity in carrying out their normal activity were present for an average of 20 days in the previous one-month period.

Social risks

Many social features of family life often cause stress to an individual's well-being, which could lead to anger with one of the consequences being suicide. For instance, perception of parent's neglect and rejection during childhood significantly predicts the lifetime suicide-attempts (Ehnvall et al. 2008). Problematic family circumstances, abusive experience, unemployment, social marginalization, isolation and psychiatric disorders are some factors that influence children's suicide (Kuhlberg et al. 2010; Platt 1992).

Vijayakumar (2003) observed family psychopathology, recent life events and alcoholism as significant psycho-social predictors of completed-suicides in India. Her study based in Chennai revealed that the history of psychopathology and suicidal behaviors in the family is known to be a risk factor for suicide, as it not only endows genetic vulnerability but also increases the discord at home and decreases the social support. Separation, widowhood or divorce are other factors which predispose a person to end life by suicide as these statuses result in economic changes as a shift in their roles, and its implications and/or effect on one's mental state. The study revealed that many of those who died by suicide had communicated their distress and suicidal intent, which largely went unheard.

In view of Bhatia et al. (1987), the joint family system and the extended interdependence of family members trigger individual suicides. While the closely knit family structure may ensure emotional stability in most circumstances, a crisis may cause a significant family disruption especially, if the family lacks social and emotional resources. In addition, the absence of stable interdependent relationships between an individual and one's family may result in a significant amount of emotional distress and, in such circumstances, may drive an individual to engage in suicidal behavior. Higher suicide rates among young adults could, therefore, be associated with the family domain such as greater socio-economic stresses, stress due to inability to meet role obligations. He also points that societal attitudes demeaning individuals who are dismissed as being unproductive and burdensome conjure feelings of despair and hopelessness, which could be a factor ultimately leading to increased levels of suicidal behavior especially among the elders.

Many suicides happen impulsively in moments of crisis with a breakdown in the ability to deal with life's stresses, such as financial problems, relationship break-up or chronic pain and illness. Experiencing conflict, disaster, violence, abuse, or loss and a sense of isolation are additionally associated with suicidal behavior (WHO 2018). Das et al. (2008), in their study on subjects with intentional self-harm attempts, reported that the majority of the subjects were married, educated beyond matriculation, were employed or retired, belonged to a nuclear family, were of a middle socio-economic status and came from an urban background.

Suicidal behavior is viewed and interpreted differently across cultures; Hendin's (1964) study of suicide in Scandinavian countries, such as in Denmark, noticed that guilt arousal was the major disciplinary technique employed by Danish mothers to control aggression, resulting in strong dependency needs in their sons. This marked dependency was the root of depression and suicidality after experiences of loss or separation. Further, fantasies of reunion with lost loved ones are commonly observed in those ending their life by suicide. Shame plays a significant role in Japan and is a reason good enough for suicide. This conceptual understanding gives meaning to the dramatic increase in peculiar kinds of suicide such as the forms of *Shinju*[7] and *inseki-jisatsu*, wherein the sense of belonging and feeling of oneness results in the need to take responsibility for some wrongdoing by recourse to suicide (Takahashi and Berger 1996).

Societies that are experiencing upheaval and unrest have higher rates of suicide. For instance, political violence can increase suicide rates – a long-standing civil war in Sri Lanka has been linked to a higher rate of suicide. Social change brought about by modernization, globalization, economic turmoil and/or new political systems (particularly when they result in the breakdown of traditional values and cultures) can also be accompanied by a rise in suicide rates. Since the fall of the Soviet Union, many Eastern European countries are dealing with increased rates of alcohol and drug abuse, and some of the highest suicide rates in the world today (Reiss and Mark: n.d.).

In terms of residence patterns, the suicide rate is generally reported to be higher in urban areas because of a variety of stresses related to living in and working in cities, including overcrowding and social isolation. In India, urban suicide rates increased from 11.3 in 2011 to 13.3 per lakh population in 2018 (NCRB 2018). Studies have been consistent in this regard, as suicide and attempted-suicide were found to be more common in inhabitants of urban areas (Khan et al. 2005). However, a systematic review of studies done by Rane and Nadkarni (2014) found that a higher suicide rate was seen in rural areas as opposed to urban areas both in India and in other countries with large agricultural populations (Patel et al. 2012). The likely explanations for the higher suicide rates in rural areas include rapid migration, economic hardship, lack of social support, isolation, relatively easy access to lethal means (e.g., pesticides) and the lack of high-quality resuscitation services (Hendin et al. 2008; NCRB 2008).

In recent times, there is also a frequent occurrence of suicide pacts and family suicides. Most of such suicides have been identified mainly due to economic bankruptcy or a result of social reasons. According to NCRB (2019), a total of 72 cases of mass family suicides were registered in the year comprising a total of 180 persons, with 126 being married and 54 unmarried. Maximum cases were from Tamilnadu (16) followed by Andhra Pradesh (14), Kerala (11), Punjab (9) and Rajasthan (7). Gururaj et al. (2004: 183ff), view such suicides as a protest against archaic societal norms and expectations.

The aftermath: suicide-attempters and suicide-completers

WHO (1968) defines suicidal act as the injury with varying degree of lethal intent. Such acts with no fatal outcome are labeled as suicide-attempts, attempted-suicide, para suicide or acts of intentional deliberate self-harm. Self-harm or suicide is difficult to understand because it goes against the natural human instinct of self-preservation. As a person cannot imagine ever being in a state of mind where s/he would hurt himself/herself, one cannot understand why anyone else would. This could make person to react in a negative, insensitive and judgmental way towards people involved in self-harm who are struggling with serious emotional turmoil.

Although completed- and attempted-suicides have common characteristics, there are also important differences. One important difference is that nearly 80% of the suicide-completers are men, while the majority of attempters are women. Another is that not all attempters injure themselves with the intent to die. Many do not have suicidal thoughts while self-injuring. In case there is strong intent to die, not all attempters injure themselves severely enough to cause death (Meehan et al. 1991). Some researchers have regarded attempted-suicide and completed-suicide as two quite different types of behavior. There is also some utility in considering deliberate self-harm where there is a small risk of death separately from attempted-suicide. However, there is a great deal of overlap between the risk factors for both these types of behavior, and a significant proportion of people who engage in low-risk deliberate self-harm or attempt suicide later go on to complete suicide. This suggests that deliberate self-harm, attempted-suicide and completed-suicide should be regarded as occurring on a continuum ranging from thoughts of suicide to completed-suicide (Kumar 2000; Lester 1989; Taylor 1988; Williams 1997). It is said that due emphasis should be given to the intention, lethality and rescuability in killing oneself to differentiate between attempters and completers (Kumar 2004). Nevertheless, all have its roots in the feeling of hopelessness, depression and worthlessness about self in relation to others – family or larger community.

Western and Indian studies had highlighted the younger age of attempters and higher age of completers (Hegde 1980; Roy 1995; Shukla et al. 1990). Probable causes for suicide and attempts in younger age could be due to the difficulties in securing stable jobs, financial problems and problems arising out of marriages, which take place increasingly during the early phase of life and might have enhanced their suicidal risk (Kumar 2004).

Contrary to Western reports, studies in India have highlighted that attempted suicides are significantly high among the married individuals in both genders. Shukla et al. (1990) have put forward several reasons. Marriage is a social obligation and is performed by the elders irrespective of the individuals' preparedness for it. Many marriages are being arranged, and marital partners are virtually strangers to each other and also the families. Hence, several adjustment problems could arise. Also as divorce is difficult and being socially looked down upon, suicide provides the only escape. He also pointed that in Indian culture, marriage is believed to be part of the treatment for mental illness and the mentally ill. In such scenario degree of suicidal incidence rises further.

For women attempters and completers especially in India, Rao et al. (1989) believe that they are more submissive, docile and non-assertive. These traits have been built into their psyche as a result of which they find themselves unable to deal with their negative feelings adequately. Among the stresses, the marital ones appear to be the most common. The hostile environment in families is compounded by problems of a difficult husband and dowry demanding in laws. They feel helpless, as they fear losing their husband's sympathies, and often, they do not have anyone to turn to. This results in the choice of suicide as a way out from psychological pain, anguish and suffering. According to Kumar (2004) for the effective prevention of suicide, one should concentrate on attempters. It is because they have a very close resemblance to completers. Every case of suicide-attempt needs a thorough psychiatric evaluation and appropriate intervention at both psychological and pharmacological levels depending on the nature of problems.

It is depicted that only 10% of the people who attempt suicide will go on to complete and die by suicide. However, 80% of the people who die by suicide have made a previous attempt. Chances are that suicide-attempt survivor will not attempt again but h/she is also at an increased risk for dying by suicide. The first six months after attempt are especially critical, and the person remains at an elevated risk for the entire first year (Bryan et al. 2012).

Mental disorders, especially mood, personality and substance use disorders, underlie the vast majority of completed- and attempted-suicides, and provide the primary context for suicide and suicidal behavior. Mood disorders, frequently co-occurring with other psychiatric and medical diagnoses, are the most commonly found diagnoses in psychological autopsy studies of completed-suicides for both men and women, across all age groups. In an extensive review of studies of family history and risk for suicidal behaviors, Wagner (1997) reported finding consistent evidence that negative parenting and physical and sexual abuse were associated with later adolescent suicide-attempts. Family violence and physical and sexual abuse have been associated with completed- and attempted-suicides among young people, and can act as distal or proximal risk factors (Brent and Perper 1995;

Shafii et al. 1985). Proximal factors like recent, severe, stressful life events, for example, the death of a spouse, other profound interpersonal loss or rejection, loss of employment, being diagnosed with a terminal illness, may act as precipitants of suicidality in vulnerable individuals (Moscicki 2001).

When a person attempts suicide or when dies due to suicide, the event turns traumatic affecting everybody. Among all, the most affected are family members facing variety of emotions. Members often feel shock, angst and pain, and find themselves surrounded with questions like why it has happened to their family? why they are not able to recognize signs? why they have not shared the difficulties or problems with each other? In the case of suicide-attempts, since person survived, family members have advantage to reflect upon with the attempted person.

For the family dealing with suicidal death, the process of coping with the loss is more intense as physical and emotional feeling overpowers their healing process. They express anger towards the deceased person, to themselves or others. There is also a sense of guilt and self-blame for the loss of loved one as they try to explore the reasons behind the act and what they missed and how could they have helped in saving life. There is also a fear of repeated suicide in the family. Many intense feelings of the family members may diminish over time, but there may be some residual feelings that may never truly go away and some questions about the deceased may forever remain unanswered. Family and friends feel tremendous guilt over suicide, and worry about what they could or even should have done to prevent the death. Over time, many survivors come to terms with this guilt, but many express that even years later, they wonder if there was something they could have done to help. As suicidal act is surrounded with stigma and shame, most people find difficult to say that the person died by suicide as they worry about others' judgments, or dread their potential questions (Totten 2008).

A person's suicidal act negatively affects the surviving people. However, the effect would differ according to the person's relation to the household. Impact would range differently in terms whether the act was of a spouse, parents, siblings, children or relatives. For instance, for a woman, the sudden death of spouse would automatically mean disruption of personal relations, slipping her into taking up the family responsibilities fully. Her status changes from being dependent to economically engage for the family. Similarly, there are high chances of behavioral problems developing as well as the issue of parental control in bereaved children due to one of the parent's suicide.

Not all suicide survivors develop complicated grief and suicidal risk, and require additional help for their bereavement (Jordan 2001). Support and immediate help at the early phase of suicide bereavement however may be useful as a stress management strategy. To identify the features, which make individuals vulnerable to or protected from, developing severe psychological distress or future suicidal tendencies following bereavement by suicide is most important (Wong et al. 2007).

About study

In western region of India, Gujarat stands second to Maharashtra in showing most loss of lives due to suicide. Major contribution of suicides in the state of Gujarat is from Saurashtra region followed by the north and south Gujarat regions. Central Gujarat's contribution is not high but within this region, Vadodara district reports high proportion of suicide. Data also shows increased incidences of suicide among various risk groups in terms of age, gender, marital status, etc., in both urban and rural areas. Table 1.1 shows the number of suicides and suicide rates in Vadodara.

Despite high statistics, hardly any systematic study has come up in the academic arena on the state or on Vadodara. One of the significant studies looking at the suicide scenario was by Bhagat (1994), which however focused only on the suicides by females. Her study was based on secondary data sourced from reported suicide cases (for the year 1988) in the well-known newspapers, published in different regions of Gujarat. It brought out important facts about female suicides such as their socio-demographic profile, causes for suicide and methods adopted.[8] In the last few years, studies in the state also showed certain patterns or characteristics of suicide-deaths but they were from medical doctors and mostly based on post-mortem medico-legal autopsies (Kumar et al. 2011; Pathak and Sharma 2010; Prajapati et al. 2013; Tanna et al. 2015).

Considering the lacunae of studies on the subject of suicide, we undertook this study to understand the enormity of the problem in the state of Gujarat largely and Vadodara in particular. Specifically, we tried to understand both apparent and non-apparent circumstances behind suicides. Our main concern was to know about

1 The status of suicide in Vadodara
2 Major contributing factors that make people to die by suicide
3 Specific patterns or trends in suicidal attempts or death

Table 1.1 Number of suicides and suicide rate in Vadodara

Years	*Number of suicides*	*Suicide rate*
2011	193	10.6
2012	208	11.4
2013	206	11.3
2014	225	12.4
2015	219	12.0
2016	220	12.1
2017	216	11.9
2018	183	10.1
2019	218	12.0

Source: NCRB and SCRB data.

4 Differences or similarities between the suicide-attempters and -completers
5 After-effects of suicidal act on the survived person, on his/her family and on deceased family

Any study, especially the qualitative study, on suicide is difficult as it covers the sensitive and ethical facets. Our empirical work applied the psycho-social autopsy (discussed in detail in Chapter 2) method to understand and discuss the dynamics of suicides. The method enabled us to state that one cannot doubt that suicide has biological or psychiatric causes, but the sociological approach rightly explains the contributory factors for such causes in relation to social settings, social forces and social imbalance.

Methodology: approach, setting and design

Leonard (2005) stated that a conceptual framework for studying the phenomenon of suicide must include both the interpersonal and intrapersonal perspectives, while at the same time not ignoring the interplay of biochemical, psycho-social and environmental constituents. From the interior of the suicidal mind to the exterior world that influences suicidal perceptions, the factors are far-ranging and inconclusive.

The study has used descriptive and diagnostic design to locate and highlight suicide scenario at micro level with the intent of understanding factors and circumstances responsible for suicide and its diverse impact on the person and survivors. Hence, our approach is rooted more in the framework of 'social-psychological perspective', which links a person's suicidal act to the interaction between social and psychological factors. It attempts to see the meaning and motivation, attached to suicidal act in relation to the influence of social variables, which could be summarized as in Figure 1.1.

Figure 1.1 interprets suicide as a social problem as its source is rooted externally to the social order and social institutions. As a part of society, individual is conditioned to exhibit behavior and play a role, which is acceptable to societal norms and values. Any deviation from it is viewed to be unacceptable and against the practiced norms. In such condition, people's lives and their behavior are always surrounded with community conscience at conscious and unconscious level. In life when they come across adverse life events or situations due to social forces, the risk factors become crucial and they suffer various issues. Such issues result in mental stress and anxieties. Crises and events sometimes also locate them as standing against the moral and social conscience with the feelings of regret, guilt, distressed, pain and so on. Fear and pressure of mental dilemmas makes them vulnerable to take their lives by suicide, which for them is a solution to overcome fear, and an end to all the problems and difficulties suffered due to crisis. For some the action could be immediate, while for others it could be delayed to the extent of their bearing capability exceeding the mental pressure. It is to note

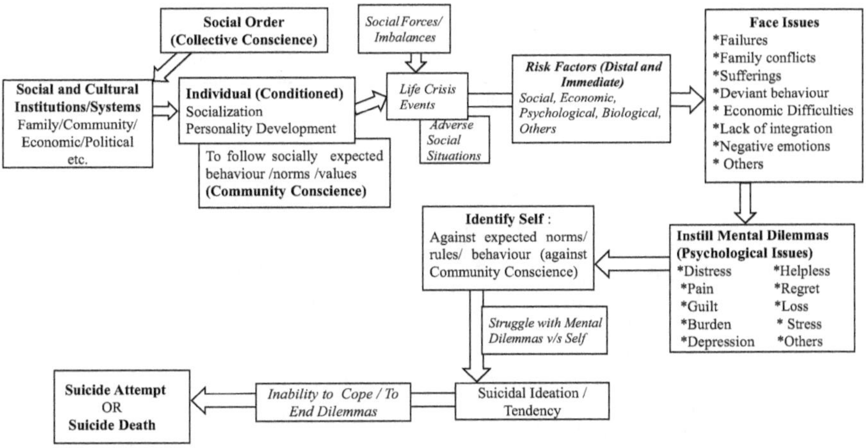

Figure 1.1 Socio-psychological perspective to suicide.
Source: Interpretation by the Authors.

thatprocess of socialization and personality development also affects how a person would deal with the life-problems, mental traumas and proneness to suicidal behavior. For instance, an aggressive or impulsive personality would be more vulnerable to suicide and would respond to self-harm instantly to hostile circumstances. Similarly, suicidal ideation among married couples would be high if the marital bond is burdened with conflicts, violence and non-responsible behavior.

This study was initiated in August 2016 and was completed in December 2018. The study went through two phases: first, the collection of secondary data on suicide-deaths in Vadodara rural and urban to identify the suicide scenario in the state as well as study population, and second, conducting the empirical study.

Secondary data collection

For the first phase, data was accessed from three sources, namely, State Crime Bureau (SCRB), police station records and hospital records. For SCRB and police station data, we met DIG-Gandhinagar (SCRB – Cell), Commissioner of Police (CP), Vadodara rural and urban. For hospital data (selected for the empirical cases), we met Medical Superintendent and Medico-Legal Officer. This sufficed the purpose of maintaining research ethics and legality in data accessed from relevant offices.

There are 27 police stations in the Vadodara district jurisdiction. We requested each police station to provide us information of reported 10–15 suicide cases from 2015 to 2017, which accounted to 231 total cases. The characteristics of these cases are presented in Table 1.2.

Table 1.2 Characteristics of registered suicide-death cases in Vadodara

Characteristics	*Numbers (%)*
Gender	
Male	168 (72.7)
Female	63 (27.3)
Total	231 (100)
Age group	
Not mention	28 (12.1)
Below 18 years	14 (06.1)
18 to 25 years	55 (23.8)
26 to 35 years	54 (23.4)
36 to 45 years	35 (15.2)
46 to 59 years	32 (13.9)
60 years and above	13 (05.6)
Total	231 (100)
Mode of suicide	
Not mention	31 (13.4)
Hanging	85 (36.8)
Poison	70 (30.3)
Self-immolation	23 (10.0)
Drowning	18 (07.8)
Self-injury	01 (00.4)
Others	03 (01.3)
Total	231 (100)

Source: Police Station Records, Vadodara.

It is evident from Table 1.2 that in terms of gender, the Vadodara follows followed national trend with males more being at the risk of ending their lives by suicide. Among 231 cases, more than 70% suicide-deaths were of males. This presents opposite results of three surveys held in pre- and post-Gujarat formation that highlighted suicide being a women phenomenon (Bhagat 1994). Age group suggests most of them belonging to young (18–25 years) and middle age (26–35 years). Similarly, in terms of suicide modes, poison and hanging was used by the most, followed by self-immolation and drowning.

Primary data collection

For the detailed empirical analysis of suicide cases for the study, we identified one of the prominent government hospitals. From their First Information Register Report (FIRR), we listed out 100 cases that were brought to the hospital after their suicide-attempt for the period in between 2015 and 2017 (there was overlapping of some cases in both hospital and police records due to norm of hospitals informing about such cases to police stations). We prepared sample design for selecting our cases based on the variables that included demographic details (gender, age and occupation), marital status and causes behind suicide. After scrutinizing the 100 listed cases, we finally ended completing the study with 49 cases. We had to drop some of the selected cases due to field issues such as change of address, problem in locating address and non-participation of the person. The final 49 cases included 13 individuals who attempted suicide but survived and 36 individuals who died in their act of suicide. To provide an account of the life history and circumstances of 'the suicide act' especially that lead to death, we relied primarily on the household members with whom the person was staying. In case of those who survived, interaction included the person who attempted suicide as well as the members of the household. The informants were mainly parents, siblings, in-laws, spouse, etc. Clinical psychologists have conducted all the interviews.

The choice of the research method employed to conduct research is grounded strongly on what is sought to be known, the thrust from which the researchers wish to be known and the depth with which they wish to dig into the details (Njie and Asimiran 2014). As reported earlier, considering the nature of suicide phenomenon loaded with personal, sensitive and ethical, a socio-psychological autopsy is important, for which qualitative case study method seemed most appropriate. Soy (1997) describes case study research 'as a way to bring understanding to a complex issues or event. It also excels in helping to explain an experience or add strength to what is already known through previous research (p1)'. In addition, case studies are useful for assessing the value of a therapeutic approach, especially when relevant variables cannot be manipulated in a prospective manner (Kazdin 1982; Stake 1995). Further, as it involves participant-observer relationship, it has greater access to groups or situations that might be more intimate with the researcher, which provides access to more revealing details. It is more exploratory, descriptive and explanatory (Stake 1994; Yin 2003). Use of case study not only unearths rich and useful information but also situates it in context through analysis for the best possible meaning.

Use of case study method provided us an insight into the events, accounts and socio-psychological status of individuals along with reconstructing of hidden links of relevant contexts, enduring stressors and precipitating factors for the question of 'why' someone would take their life. As a part of case study questions, we developed and used a check list-cum-interview schedule.[9] It covered the open-ended information on the following domains:

- Personal details
- Family details
- Medical/psychiatric details
- Socio-psychological details
- Personality and lifestyle
- Account of suicidal behavior

- Recent events (prior to attempt/death)
- Effect of suicidal attempt or death in the family

Before taking the interviews, investigators explained the objectives of the research study to the informants to ensure their willingness and create a comfortable setting for them to share information. All interviews were held at their homes. In some cases, multiple visits were made. All the responses once gathered were sorted, coded and analyzed into different themes (the thematic details are in Chapter 3).

Plan of the book

The next chapter describes about autopsy method used in debriefing about causes of death. It gives detailed explanation of psychological-autopsy and sociological-autopsy for identifying or layering up the influences of sociological and psychological factors of suicidal acts, regarding the circumstances of suicidal individuals. Further it discusses the application of the psycho-social autopsy in suicide studies, and deals with key procedures in the psycho-social autopsy method and their execution in our study. The last part of the chapter points out the process and some of the methodological challenges faced while completing the study at the level of planning, accessing statistical data, approaching case-narratives, conducting field interviews and involved ethical concerns.

Chapter 3 is based on empirical cases, unearthing interpretative understanding of suicide. It throws light on how suicide and self-harming behavior of individuals are largely surrounded by stress along with negative thoughts and feelings about themselves with the perceived inability to cope. The chapter unravels suicide based on different dynamics through qualitative narratives of 49 cases. These narratives bring out socio-psychological dimensions of suicide allied with the conflict between social structures and individuals in terms of integration, regulation and cognitive vulnerablility. Reactions and repercussions after suicides are also discussed. Surviving suicide-attempts can be physically and emotionally exhausting. Many people have trouble discussing about the act out of guilt, embarrassment or hurting members. This, in turn, could leave a person feeling isolated or abandoned. The chapter discusses some ways of dealing with suicide as experienced by our case narratives. The last part summarizes key dimensions, interlinks of reasons behind suicide, deducing general trends, features and leanings.

Chapter 4 is an extension of Chapter 3, and it correlates some of the cases discussed in it with few sociological and psychological theories. Though our study is confined to a particular micro space, the inferences drawn from these cases can be related to the theoretical conceptualizations, thus providing a broader framework to the interpretations. It attempts situating the case inferences empirically as well as theoretically as a pan-human phenomenon. It gives insight about the macro aspects of economic and political turmoil on the rate of suicides. Based on secondary data on suicides at different socio-historical circumstances, it attempts to see the connectivity between the two in Vadodara, Gujarat and India.

The last chapter attempts to look at way forward in dealing with the suicides. It asserts concern for treating suicide as a public health issue by acknowledging its seriousness and need for the appropriate efforts to prevent it. It also explains suicide prevention approaches and various interventions at length. Contours of long-term policy implications with reference to the possible role of various stakeholders in suicide prevention are addressed. The chapter ends by briefing out mental health legislations in India and revision in the Mental Health Care Act 2017, by proposing some changes in various sections of the Act.

Notes

1 The words 'victim', 'commit', 'committing', 'committed' were commonly used while referring to suicide by a person. Lately, suicidologists, and mental health professionals argue for avoiding these terms, mainly because, suicide is no longer a crime but a mental health issue that needs treatment. The appropriate terminology suggested includes- 'die/died by suicide', 'ending/ended life by suicide', 'take/took one's own life', 'death by suicide', 'suicide', 'completed suicide'. (Beaton et al 2014; WHO 2008). We have avoided the terms commit/committing/committed, victim and followed the new terminology.

2 World Health Organization (2017). *Depression and other common mental disorders: global health estimates.* Geneva: WHO (http://apps.who.int/iris/handle/10665/254610, retrieved on 25 March 2019).

3 Prior to Durkheim, Charles Mercier in 1783 first identified statistical evidence showing the steady growth of suicide in the modernizing countries of Europe. Jean Pierre subsequently observed that suicide rates tend to rise during periods of rapid social change and in periods of economic depression. In 1881, Thomas Masaryk, foreshadowing Durkheim, argued that the rising suicide rates apparent in various European countries was the result of modernization and the dissolution of traditional institutions and moral controls, especially those connected with religion. He contended that religions that had strict rules and firm beliefs were better at reducing suicidal tendencies than religions that encouraged questioning and protest (Giddens 1971; Lester 1994. Cited in Maskill et al. 2005: 8).

4 It is a social condition, where there is a disintegration or disappearance of the norms and values common to the society. People living in the period of anomie typically feel disconnected from their society. It is because they no longer see the norms and values that they hold dear reflected in society itself, leading to the feeling of non-belongingness and not meaningfully connected to others. For some, this may mean their role or identity no longer valued by the society, thus fostering the feeling of lack of purpose engenders hopelessness, encouragement to deviance and crime and so on. An anomic society has few or no moral regulations. Being a less socially regulated some people can be encouraged to expect too much from life and become liable to greater frustration when their expectations are not fulfilled.

5 http://www.worldatlas.com/articles/countries-with-the-most-suicides-in-the-world.html. Retrieved on 4 February 2019.

6 Initiated in 2002, India began the Million Death Study, a mortality survey on the causes of death in 1.3 million nationally representative households in 6,671

areas. Non-medical staff conduct verbal autopsies, which are structured interviews including a half-page narrative in local language of the family's story of the symptoms and events leading to death. Two physicians independently assess each death to arrive at an underlying cause of death. The study has thus far yielded information that substantially altered previous estimates of cause-specific mortality and risk factors in India (Gomes et al. 2017).

7 The definition includes both a genuine suicide pact, extended suicide (assisted suicide followed by suicide) and murder suicide in which the killed and victims have a strong emotional tie with each other before the act, with the feeling of oneness being important. This suicide mostly classified as *johshi* – mutually consented lovers suicide – and *oyako-shinju*, i.e., parent child suicide with subcategories: mother–child suicide, father–child suicide and family suicide.

8 She carried out her analysis on the 1064 cases (465 – rural and 599 – urban). Her study revealed that most cases came from Saurashtra and Kutch (west) followed by Panchmahal, Vadodara and Bharuch (east). In terms of districts, maximum suicides were in Rajkot and Vadodara followed by Bhavnagar and Jamnagar. Caste wise (excluding unknown) maximum cases were from other backward castes followed by upper, middle and scheduled castes. Most women were in the age group of 21–25 years and 26–45 years engaged in some kind of work and were married. Major causes of suicide were mental and social torture from in-laws, conflicts among couples, suspicion/extra-marital affairs.

9 For details see Annexure 1 (Checklist-cum-Interview Schedule).

2 Psychological and sociological autopsy

Making the paradigm explicit

Suicide is an unnatural death. When someone ends life deliberately, s/he leaves behind several questions to ponder upon mainly about the reasons or causes for such drastic step. This also holds true in the case of self-harm as in suicide-attempt. The answers to the reasons in both cases lay on identifying the contribution of influences of psychological and sociological factors. This assessment known as *psycho-sociological or psycho-social autopsy* (PSA) attempts to build up a person's psychological state and social circumstances prior to the attempt of death.

The term 'autopsy' derived from Greek word *autopsia* is a method dating from ancient times and means 'to see with one's own eyes' (Dumbrava et al. 2010). Autopsy in simple terms means examining or debriefing a body after death and determining cause of death. It has been in use since the seventeenth century. Ancient Egyptians were one of the first civilizations to practice the removal and examination of the internal organs of humans in the religious practice of mummification. In medical field, the term is commonly known as post-mortem and is used when there is non-clarity about a person's death and needed to figure out exact causes and the way it happened. Legally, autopsy is called for when someone dies in a suspicious, unusual or unnatural way (Sabrina 2018; Siddamsetty et al. 2014).

In the field of medicine, autopsies can enhance our understanding of diseases and how we die, contributing to the critical medical knowledge. Similarly, through autopsies, forensic pathologists have identified public health emergencies, such as the anthrax terrorist attacks or other lethal infectious diseases, as well as public health hazards and suicides. Most of us think of autopsies in relation to homicide cases, but there are other ways in which autopsies can provide evidence for legal action. For example, if an autopsy determines a death to be the result of a work or environmental hazard, it may lead to compensation for family. If an autopsy reveals evidence of medical malpractice, it may be the grounds for a lawsuit. Autopsies can also be an important way for families and loved ones to seek reassurance or peace of mind after demise of a person.[1]

The concept of PSA finds its root in psychological autopsy (PA), which is derived from the forensic autopsy as practiced in forensic psychology.

The American Psychological Association (APA) defines forensic psychology as 'the application of clinical specialties to the legal arena'. This definition emphasizes the application of clinical psychology to the forensic setting. Cronin (2009), who has written a well-known textbook on forensic psychology, defines it as "the application of clinical specialties to legal institutions and people who come into contact with the law" (p. 5), again emphasizing the application of clinical skills such as assessment, treatment, evaluation to forensic settings. This is considered a narrow definition. The broad definition of forensic psychology emphasizes the application of research and experimentation in other areas of psychology (e.g., cognitive psychology and social psychology) to the legal arena. This would include applying results from studies in areas such as cognitive psychology to legal questions (Ward 2013).

Looking at the works in this field, the practice of forensic psychology or the most frequent duty of forensic psychologists is that of the psychological assessment of individuals who are involved, in one way or another, with the legal system. Therefore, although it is necessary to have training in law and forensic psychology, a forensic psychologist must possess clinical skills like clinical assessment, interviewing, report writing, strong verbal communication skills and case presentation. These skills are important in setting the foundation of the practice of forensic psychology, and forensic psychologists can perform tasks such as threat assessment for schools, child custody evaluations, suicide-attempters' evaluation, counseling services to victims of crime and suicides, the assessment of post-traumatic stress disorder, the delivery, evaluation of intervention and treatment programs and so on. Forensic psychology has grown with great speed in the past 20 years. Forensic psychologists work in many different legal environments, writing reports, giving testimony, doing direct treatment or working with therapeutic communities (ibid.).

In self-study of dead body, forensic experts carry out forensic autopsy (or medico-legal autopsy) which determines the cause, mode and manner of death. They are generally performed, as prescribed by applicable law, in cases of violent, suspicious or sudden deaths, deaths without medical assistance or during surgical procedures. Forensic science involves the application of the sciences to answer questions of interest to the legal system. Medical examiners attempt to determine and provide answers to questions about the identity; the time of death; the exact cause of death; and what, if anything, preceded the death, such as a struggle.[2]

Concept of psychological and sociological autopsy

Psychological autopsy

Incidents of some deaths need certain kind of evaluation. The typical case for evaluation is of PA which is done when there is some doubt as to whether death was accidental, self-inflicted or malicious and if the deceased played an active role in his/her own demise. Mostly relevant in cases of self-inflicted death, i.e., suicide, it throws light on the mental state of deceased person, their personality and thought processes during the time of the act (Canter 2000). The principle of PA is based on the meticulous collection of data that are likely to help reconstitute the psycho-social environment of individuals who died by suicide and thus understand the circumstances of their death (INSERM 2005).

Edwin Shneidman, a director of the Los Angeles Suicide Prevention Center, is credited with coining the term 'psychological autopsy' along with other directors Norman Earberow and Robert Litman in late 1950s.[3] It involves a thorough and systematic retrospective analysis of the decedent's life, with a particular focus on the identification and assessment of suicide risk factors, motives and intentions present at the time of death, with the goal of enabling a determination of the manner of death to as high a degree of certainty as possible. To look for information either supports or contradicts a mental condition consistent with suicide (James 2008). One of the major contributions of it has been to introduce the psycho-social context into decisions about the cause of death since examination of post-mortem remains to tell only what lesions the patient died with, not what he died from (Weisman 1967).

Contributions to understand suicidal death through PA have been made over a period of approximately 40 years which could range from an essentially informal attempt to reconstruct the thoughts of the deceased to a much more thorough exploration of everything that is known about him/her. However, there are still no standardized procedures that have been agreed upon for making them, but where more systematic methods are employed they have commonly involved obtaining information from interviews with survivors of the deceased and archival sources (Canter 2000).

As an assessment tool, the PA has evolved through a number of iterations. Initially, Shneidman (1976) developed a list of 14 areas of inquiry, which include:

1 Identifying information for victim (name, age, gender, address, marital status, religious practices, occupation and other details)
2 Specific details of the death (including the cause or method and other pertinent details)
3 Brief outline of victim's history (siblings, marriage, medical illnesses, medical treatment, psychotherapy, previous suicide-attempts)
4 Psychiatric and death history of victim's family (suicides, cancer, other fatal illnesses, ages at death, mood disorders and other details)
5 Description of the personality and lifestyle characteristics of the victim
6 Victim's typical patterns of reaction to stress, emotional upsets and periods of disequilibrium

7 Any recent (from last few days to last 12 months) upsets, stressors, pressures, tensions or anticipations of trouble
8 Role of alcohol and drugs in the overall lifestyle of the victim and his/her death
9 Quality of the victim's interpersonal relationships (including physicians); fantasies; dreams; thoughts; premonitions; or fears of victim relating to death, accident or suicide
10 Changes in the victim's habits and routines before death (hobbies, eating, sexual patterns and other life routines)
11 Information relating to the 'life side' of victim (upswings, successes, plans)
12 Rating of lethality
13 Reactions of informants to victim's death
14 Assessment of suicidal intention, i.e., role of the victim in his own demise

The proposed criteria were not that dissimilar to the framework that might be used by any physician in preparing a medical case history; however, the major difference was on its focus on range of information about the person. It focused on the corroboration of varied range and variety of sources of information about the deceased in terms of their typical actions, especially reactions to stress, their interpersonal relationships, their thought processes and their experiences surrounding the death. The procedure is basically based on the assumption that people close to the deceased can provide accounts of both historical and recent developments and behaviors of the deceased. The procedure ensures that the bias inherent in any one source of information does not distort the whole picture (Canter 2000).

In contrast to the Shneidman PA criteria, in the late 1980s, the Centers for Disease Control established a list of 22 criteria, called the Operational Criteria for the Determination of Suicide (OCDS) to assist forensic investigators for certifying a death as a suicide. These criteria are based on a definition of suicide as "death arising from an act inflicted upon oneself with the intent to kill oneself" (Rosenberg et al. 1988). The OCDS used a more scientific approach in their retrospective review of deaths, with an eye towards creating an assessment instrument that was reliable and valid with the goal to develop more accurate suicide statistics that could assist in policy development and research efforts to lower suicide rates (Scott et al. 2006). Shortly afterward, in 1991, suicide researchers (Jobes et al. 1991) developed the Empirical Criteria for the Determination of Suicide (ECDS). This instrument combined the OCDS criteria with additional criteria garnered from the prevailing literature to produce the 55-item Death Investigation Checklist. Using empirical methods, researchers established the ECDS by selecting those items that best correlated with self-infliction and suicidal intention. The resultant is a 16-criteria instrument[4] that contains a scoring system that produces total scores for self-infliction and intention (Scott et al. 2006), which are:

1 Pathological (autopsy) evidence indicating self-inflicted death
2 Toxicological evidence indicating self-inflicted harm
3 Statements by witnesses indicating self-inflicted death
4 Investigatory evidence (e.g., police reports, photos from scene) indicating self-inflicted death
5 Psychological evidence (observed behavior, lifestyle and personality) indicating self-inflicted death
6 States of the deceased indicating self-inflicted death
7 Evidence that decedent recognized high potential lethality of means of death
8 Decedent had suicidal thoughts
9 Decedent had recent and sudden change in effect of emotions
10 Decedent had experienced serious depression or mental disorder
11 Decedent had made an expression of farewell, indicated desire to die or acknowledged impending death
12 Decedent had made an expression of hopelessness
13 Decedent had experienced stressful events or significant losses (actual or threatened)
14 Decedent had experienced general instability in immediate family
15 Decedent had recent interpersonal conflicts
16 Decedent had history of generally poor physical health

There are four basic questions to be answered in the PA: *what*, *why*, *from what* and *how* has the subject died. There are, respectively, four constructs underlying the PA's strategy: precipitants and/or stressors, motivation, lethality and intentionality. Precipitants and/or stressors are immediate facts or circumstances that would trigger the last push for suicide. Motivation can be understood identifying the psychological reasons to die, rooted, in lifetime, in the subject's conduct, thoughts, lifestyle and personality. The degree of lethality is measured by the chosen method and its consequences. The assessment of the degree of lucidity in the planning, preparation and objectivation of the self-destructive action establishes the subject's intent (Werlang and Botega 2003).

The procedure of PA method involves collecting and analyzing all relevant information on the deceased. All applicable records should be reviewed, including medical records, psychiatric records, police records and autopsy findings. A visual inspection of the death scene via photographs is necessary, and a visit to the scene will occasionally be required. A thorough review of the decedent's writings in the form of diaries, journals, e-mails and internet correspondence is vital. In addition to reviewing records, structured interviews with family members, relatives and/or friends are necessary. Thus, a PA synthesizes data from multiple informants and records. When performed in a comprehensive manner, the method may take anywhere from 20 to 50 hours or longer to complete. The overriding principle is that the greater the amount of relevant data analyzed, the more accurate the investigator's conclusions are likely to be (James 2008).

It has been argued that in reconstructing a suicidal individual's mental state, suicidologists must conduct face-to-face interviews with everyone who knew the suicide person, including the suicide person him/herself. That is, how can someone know the state of mind of someone has never met? Psychological autopsies thus reconstruct the state of mind of the deceased though not entirely through their set criteria or principles of analysis (Douglas and Marci 1995).

Sociological autopsy

Suicide is peculiarly slippery construct, and the interpretative aspects involved provide an important focus on the broad view of the social context of suicide. While there is a wealth of research on suicide practice, there is much less from a sociological approach. Most sociological research on suicide has grown from Durkheim's work. Rooted in social explanation, his emphasis was the idea that it is the sociological, political, religious and cultural variables that have a greater predictive ability for high-risk subgroups and populations than the psychological variables. The central point of his analysis was preference over groups/structure than individuals (Slater 2005).

The 'Sociological Autopsy (SA)', as an impersonation of PA, has an admittedly sociological purpose, both encompassing the construction of knowledge about suicide cases and aiming towards reasonably objective judgments about the circumstances of suicidal individuals. This method is a qualitatively driven paradigm that explores the possibilities of sociologically oriented research on individual suicides. It emphasizes on individual suicide cases for generating insights into the social context in which they occur (Fincham et al. 2011), and achieved through qualitatively driven mixed research (Mason 2006).

Chatterjee and Bailey (1993) originally coined the term 'sociological autopsy' as a method for studying all broader social problems from a sociological perspective. The underlying assumption of this approach is that sociological variables are powerful determinants of suicide. While individuals make the choice to die by suicide, rates of suicide are higher among some groups of people, in some parts of the world and in some cultures rather than others. These factors are not solely attributed to individual choices, but are subject to them collectively, which affect group suicide rates.

Analysis of suicide is drawn on individual-level data which include, in most cases, the testimonies of several witnesses who knew the deceased well as well as data on the circumstances in which the body was found and the situations of the day of the act. SA thereby leaves room for a social focus on suicides. Recognizing the inevitably interpretive dimension involved in the act, it focuses on underlying social and psychological factors, which allows for case-based as well as variable-based analysis. The approach also retains the multidimensional complexity of individual cases rather than reducing any sociological analysis to a mono-causal interpretation (Scourfield et al. 2012).

Similar to PA, analyzing suicide through SA involves three basic elements that reveals knowledge about suicide cases and objective inferences about the circumstances of suicidal individuals. These include:

1 Details of the case through different sources:
   - i Suicide notes
   - ii Written witness statements as interviews with relatives and friends of the deceased
   - iii Interviews with eye witness
   - iv Pathology reports
   - v Psychiatric and psychological reports
2 Socially situating various detailed documents in a suicide discourse
   - i As deceased possesses different identities, *vis-à-vis* different relations or circumstances
3 Incorporating different accounts into an interpretation, which does justice to all

The SA emphasizes that the causes of suicide are, ultimately, to be found in the meanings and motivations of individuals. In order to understand why suicide becomes a conceivable option to somebody, it is necessary to examine the immediate circumstances they were in when they killed themselves, look at the experiences which led to them being in these circumstances and relate these two elements to the values and beliefs the person held which might support suicidal action. It bridges both interpretive and structural dimensions of suicide in suggesting suicidal behavior (Fincham et al. 2011). Such analysis contributes to our overall understanding of what suicide is all about, and what it means to the suicidal persons themselves, in their particular context, and may contribute to inform practice in suicide prevention (Heidi et al. 2012).

Application of PSA in research

Several scientific studies and publications highlight that PA in suicide cases has been useful as an instrument for clinical assessment and research. Over the years, it has shown broader applicability than simply determining the mode of death. For almost 50 years, it has been used as research tool to assist medical examiners, homicide investigators, suicidologists and suicide researchers, and as a forensic tool in the courts (Jacobs and Klein 1993; James 2008). It helped determine why a person had chosen suicide, in terms of their motivation, personal philosophy and psychodynamics, and why a person had died by suicide at a particular time. As such, it proved helpful in identifying and explicating proximate causation, determining the role of a variety of factors in bringing about a suicidal death. From a clinical point of view, in some ways this retrospective method to reconstruct the mind of the deceased is more objective and less controversial as the person conducting PA has had no prior contact with the suicide victims and the informants, thus removing any kind of vagueness (Douglas and Marci 1995).

According to Ebert (1987), the PA serves at least four purposes. In addition to clarifying the mode of death in equivocal[5] cases, the PA may determine why a death occurred at a particular time. The PA may also obtain data that may be useful in the prediction of suicide and the assessment of the lethality of the suicidal person. Another purpose of psychological autopsies is to provide therapeutic value to survivors (Young 1992). According to Schwartz (1997), the therapeutic value of a PA could be understood in terms that, though it is conducted for forensic purposes, it can incorporate many therapeutic elements. Some of them include empathetic listening, the ability to join with family members, building trust, compassionate sensitivity to multicultural issues, debriefing and crisis interview skills, knowing when to ask questions and when to listen.

The first authors to use the method of PA did so for medical and legal reasons, when the causes of death were ill-defined. Today, the method is increasingly being applied to suicide prevention, crisis intervention or research both to improve existing knowledge and identify subjects "at risk" of suicide (INSERM 2005). It is used to gain an understanding of the psycho-social antecedents preceding deaths of other populations (like sudden unexplained deaths of psychiatric inpatients and prisoners) and also in gaining a clearer understanding of living people in order to better predict their actions in hostage situations and forensic settings (Oliver et al. 2007).

The method revealed itself potentially useful in at least two different areas, i.e., in the identification of risk factors with clinical and/or preventive goals in mind and in research on biological markers and genetics with a view to improve current knowledge (INSERM 2005). PA's application over several decades had generated the valuable research data about suicide and informed about prevention efforts especially on the preponderance of suicides with the presence of mental disorders (Cheng et al. 2000; Conwell et al. 1996). The first generation of such research found that more than 90% of the individuals who completed-suicide suffered from mental disorders, mostly mood disorders and substance use disorders (Berman 2000; Simon 2002). The second generation of research has employed it in risk factor research, with appropriately selected case-control designs, and is able to estimate the role of various psycho-social risk factors involved in a suicide or other death (Appleby et al. 1999; Isometsa 2001). Performing formal suicide risk assessments in patients at risk for suicide is endorsed by overwhelming clinical consensus; PA is therefore generally accepted in the mental health field more rigorously (Simon 2002).

Another potential use is its clinical utility as therapeutic tools in helping surviving family members better understand the tragedy and begin the grieving process (Begley and Quayle 2008; Owens et al. 2008). It is not uncommon that surviving family members need a better understanding of their loved one's suicide before they can continue the grieving process. In addition to referral to helpful support organizations, the PA may help provide families with the answers they need to find meaning within the tragedy (James 2008).

Use of psychological autopsies, however, has its own doubts especially due to its retrospective nature. It is stated that due to several reasons the quantity and quality of data provided by the informant can be influenced in the absence of the studied object (Werlang and Botega 2003). For instance, either informants could exaggerate the presence of psychiatric symptomatology because of guilt or they may minimize the persons' psychiatric problems due to stigma or idealization. In addition, the information could be incomplete as it is limited to only what the informant has shared (Douglas and Marci 1995; Shaffer 1988). As for interviewers, they may have specific expectations about the types of most probable disorders in a person dying by suicide. They may adhere to specific events for finding explanations of how the death occurred. They may have difficulties to deal with discrepancies between informants, due to their training and experience.

In order to assess the reliability of the obtained information, many studies propose to perform a second interview with the other informant, or with the same informant, but conducted by other technician (precision), or other interview with the same informant and technician, after a time interval (stability) but all these have their own limitations. The other way of validating the obtained data is comparing them with the information reported in the personal, medical, police, school and other document records (Beskow et al. 1990; Clarck and Horton 1992; Jacobs and Klein 1993).

In addition, researchers have also consistently pointed out the main problem in conducting PA studies is in obtaining cooperation for interviews from friends and family of the deceased (Shafii et al. 1985). Suicide is a multidimensional phenomenon and considered to be a crime and sin, more specifically as a crime against oneself. Although the stigma attached to suicide has persisted, the recent trend has been to view suicide less as a sin and crime, and more as an unfortunate consequence of mental illness and social disorganization (Litman 1980; MHCA 2017). Blame still appears to be an issue in suicide. The responsibility for suicidal deaths has shifted to persons deemed in a position to cause a suicide, either by specific acts on their part or by neglecting their duty to protect the suicide person from self-harm (Douglas and Marci 1995). Such factors influence the cooperation of willingness of family members or other related persons to share information about the suicidal person.

Suicide risk factors vary among different populations. The investigator should consider special nuances of the deceased, such as age group, mental health diagnosis, gender and other factors that may allow for a more precise consideration of risk factors associated with that group (Houston et al. 2001; Pirkola et al. 1999; Simon 2004). Some person may display unique, individualized behaviors suggestive of increased or decreased suicide risk that will be known only to close social contacts or treating mental health professionals (Simon 2004). It is thus argued that those who conduct PAs should stay up to date with the evolving psychiatric and suicidology literature. It is important to learn as much as possible about the distinct risk factors such as depression, bipolar disorders (Marangell et al. 2006; Owens et al. 2003), as well as patterns of reactions to past stress and those who are not receiving mental health care services (Hamdi et al. 2008; McGirr et al. 2008).

Despite confined in its boundaries, PA has proved to be beneficial for the masses with its systematic method to understand the psychological and contextual circumstances preceding suicide and has been beneficial in government inquiries into major public suicides in legal contexts. In addition, it also plays an important role in suicide prevention and crisis intervention (Majid et al. 2017).

With reference to SA, Klinenberg (2002) used it in his study of deaths during the 1995 Chicago Heat Wave. His 'social autopsy' approach sought to enhance knowledge on suicide from individual-level public health research on the 739 heat wave deaths by focusing on a particular area and the impact of social deprivation on individual deaths. He linked isolation of elders living in a predominantly African-American neighborhood to a degraded physical environment and the fear of crime, which caused these people to stay indoors leading to their death. His analysis was however criticized by Duneier (2006), who pointed his work of committing the ecological fallacy by extrapolating to individual circumstances from area-level data. He came out with his own findings and argued that many deaths due to heat wave in the area were not of elders and many had drug or alcohol problems, which Klinenberg ignored. Klinenberg (2006) however re-asserted his claims about people dying alone because of ethnographic evidence.

Specifically, in relation to suicide, Slater (2005) used it to study the firearm suicides including measurement of key indicators among the older adults in the USA. Focusing on the political, economic status and violence with the gun access revealed that the gun culture, gun policy and gun access have affected the suicide rates among elders, the firearm suicide rates among the general population and overall suicide rates of the country.

It is well documented that compared to women, more men die by suicide. While understanding suicide in men through the approach of SA, Scourfield et al. (2012) attempted to locate suicides among them with reference to their gendered identities and gendered practices. Studying 100 cases of suicides, they suggested that suicide in men has its relation to the men's economic life or status and breakdown of their intimate or family relationships. Both factors are the principal trigger for suicides as most of the individual cases pointed were about the difficulties of financial problems, debt, occupation stress, relationship failures, losing child-custody battle. Sense of failing masculinity image due to these co-related aspects was also the underlying hidden cause. Honor, shame and manliness all require public affirmation. Scourfield (2005) has highlighted the tension that can be produced when a gap between aspiration and reality in suicidal men becomes overt and recognized, rather than submerged or socially embedded, and a life marked by a loss of masculine honor is not seen as worth living.

Analysis of the 100 suicide cases by Fincham et al. (2011) brought out the social circumstances of suicide. They identified various overlapping issues as a reason for suicide, which included family and interpersonal relationships, work and finance, physical and mental health, drugs and alcohol, intrapersonal distress and crime with most frequently being family and interpersonal relationships and signs of intrapersonal distress. The study also indicated that the social circumstances surrounding suicide varied quite markedly according to the age and sex of the person. In terms of age, it reflected young people in crisis with suicides more related to adolescent issues (love, family attachments, peer pressure, etc.), mid-life gendered patterns (suicidal circumstances reflecting changing roles and responsibilities associated with life-course) and older people in decline with suicides more closely associated with physical illness and other losses.

In the field of suicidology, the SA framework adapts the PA model. While latter tries to understand the suicidal mind better through retrospective investigation of the intention, the former seeks to see the same in a sociological context. Combined together as a Psychological-Sociological Autopsy or Psycho-Social Autopsy model they present a methodological case for empirical research for comprehensive understanding of the individual who made a choice to die by suicide. Moreover, empirically its use shows that individual suicide has meaning and can be explained when it is put in the social context or circumstances of his/her life history, which would otherwise be lost or remain hidden. In addition, its qualitative nature makes it uphold the multidimensional and multifaceted reality of suicidal act. This psycho-sociological view both favors the social contextualization of individual suicide stories, enriched by the clinical focus, and allows the formulation of analytical categories to find traits that lend unity to isolated suicide cases (Minayo et al. 2006).

Key procedures in PSA and their adaptation in present study

The research tool of PSA could become more mainstream than it has been in the past or currently, with the continuous development of the fields of forensic and investigative psychology or of suicidology as an academic discipline. As a method of conducting qualitative inquest, it follows certain methods, which we followed and adapted as per the context of in our research:

- *Identifying suicide case*

  The first step is of gathering statistical data on the verified suicide cases. Sources like medical, hospital or police records are important as they serve the purpose of identifying the death as suicide legally and medically.

  For our study, police records and government hospital information were the main sources to identify the suicide cases. Since police records generally had the information on suicide-deaths, approaching government hospital allowed us to include cases of suicide-attempts. We also met psychiatrist/clinical psychologists for identifying cases, but due to medical ethics, we did not get the cases from them.
- *Case study design*

  Case study design is an inclusive method of qualitative research. It has its ability to investigate cases in-depth where the focus is on answering to 'how' and 'why' questions. Its essence is that it tries to illuminate a decision or set of decisions: why they were taken, how they were implemented and with what result (Schramm 1971). Case study facilitates a holistic perspective on causality because it offers the possibility of investigating causal complexity where there are many relevant factors but few observations and over which the investigator has little or no control. Additionally, it supports the retrospective investigation of events and the specific contexts in which they are activated (George and Bennet 2005). In case studies, documents, interviews, observations and secondary analyses are the main data sources; researchers are urged to make greater use of documents, interview the right people and make observations more objective. The concern of case study is not to exclude what it cannot command, but rather to avoid omitting some detail that might turn out to be important in explaining what happened in the situation being studied (Schramm 1971). It is important for the investigator to be passive in case study research as s/he is much more of an observer than an experimenter and remember that, even in a multi-subject case, each case must be treated individually and then cross-case conclusions can be drawn (Shuttleworth 2008). Before one start on the main cases, it is recommended to carry out a pilot study to explore both substantive topic and method issues. This can help to sharpen the focus of research as well as ensure about the effectiveness of the intended field procedures (Yin 2009).

We too followed the procedure as a way to know more about the complex issue of suicide through the socio-psychological reasoning. As mentioned earlier, prior to final interview with the cases, we first undertook a pilot study to assess our approach and methodological challenges. It helped us in reframing our schedule and the ways to minimize field encounters.

- *Ethics, sensitivity and informed consent*

  Incident of suicide is personal and sensitive, and involves ethical issues. Studying about it means collecting information about the deceased from near ones. There are many ethical considerations to be taken while designing and carrying out PSA as it places emotional demands on participants (Murthy 2010). While interviewing surviving family and friends, the investigator must consider the survivors' reactions. Ideally, the investigator should have adequate clinical experience to be able to handle survivors' reactions with appropriate sensitivity. For research purposes, a two- to six-month interval between the suicide and the interview is recommended (Beskow et al. 1990; Seguin et al. 2007). Currently, there is no clearly agreed method for initiating contact with survivors; however, it is suggested that investigators performing psycho-socio autopsy should have proper address and/or phone numbers of the potential interviewees. They should inform them about the purpose, their participation and consent as well as the preferred time/place of their visit. The evaluator should not request the individual to complete a detailed personality questionnaire of the deceased. Such requests are likely to result in negative reactions from interviewees, thereby potentially jeopardizing the communication of valuable information (Beskow 1979).

  We kept in mind the ethical issues involved in the subject of study. We selected those cases for interview where the suicide-attempt or suicide-death occurred at least eight months or above (one to two years maximum) prior to our research, thus keeping the recommended time interval between the incident and the interview. We collected their addresses from the hospital records, and in some cases, we contacted them over phone before meeting personally. Being a subjective and sensitive issue, we did our research with the informant's right to consent. We interviewed those people from our final list of cases, who gave consent to share the information. Clinical investigators carried a consent form that detailed about the objective of study; their willingness and consent are to be part of the study along with the confidentiality clause of the shared information. Before every interview, informants were asked to go through it (or verbally articulated), and once they agreed, interview was held.

- *Background and history of the case*

  Large amount of information as background history about the case must be collected in order to perform a PSA. Kind of information may range from personal information like lifestyle, relationships, any history of drug/alcohol abuse, known stresses, etc., to biographical information of birth date, occupation, marital or relationship status and to other secondary information like criminal record of the deceased or about overall family history. Once this information is gathered, one can begin to piece together story of a person's suicide.

While interviewing informants we included to incorporate these details. Our checklist-interview schedule had questions on these aspects (see Annexure 1).

- *Sources of evidences*

  Whatever methodology chosen, each requires extensive information gathering. Collateral records as sources of evidences should be reviewed whenever possible (Scott et al. 2006) and include:

  - Victim's psychiatric, medical, employment and academic records
  - Suicide notes
  - Personal journals, and computer hard drives
  - Other documents – police reports, toxicology reports, autopsy reports, insurance police records or the deceased's last will and testament
  - Witness statements

  In our cases, important sources were police reports, hospital records and witness statements.

- *Case study questions*

  At the core of the case study is the research questions for the interview. The structured interviews should have open-ended questions with the information about the trajectory of life events, childhood development, parent-child relationship, medical facts, personality traits, family background, personal relationships and so on.

  Our case study questions were open-ended and descriptive with the inclusion of the mentioned trajectories (see checklist).

- *Collateral interviews with persons close to the deceased person*

  Careful interviews with the decedent's family members and other relevant social contacts are considered an extremely important information source and are significant in PSA. Most experts recommend a structured or semi-structured approach to collateral interviews. Collateral interviews often reveal critical and/or determinative information about the decedent that cannot be obtained elsewhere. For instance, psychiatric illness alone is not enough to fully explain an individual suicide. Rather, a stress-diathesis model is proposed, in which the risk for suicidal acts is determined by the interplay of bio-psycho-social factors and situational variables (Mann et al. 1999). According to this model, a diathesis may be reflected in an individual's tendency to have maladaptive responses to stressors, such as acting impulsively. Such information is most likely to be obtained via collateral interviews (James 2008). Through these interviews involving the survivors-parents, spouse, children, friends and physicians the deceased's recent life events and emotional state can be reconstructed which would establish the explanations, intent or causes for the drastic step of suicide. While conducting interview it is important that examiner or interviewer should be sensitive to the language used and tone of the conversation. For instance, studies (Cooper 1999; Lobo and Bharati 2018) found that survivors preferred the term 'sudden death' to 'suicide' because many individuals interviewed did not believe or accept that their loved one's death was a suicide.

Our informants were the primary relatives, i.e., parents, siblings and those who were living with the suicide-attempters or -completers. In attempted cases, we made sure to seek answers from the persons involved as well as the close primary kin.

- *Range of data collection from family, friends and others*

  Information collected from those people who are directly or indirectly connected with the deceased would bring out lot of information about the person's daily life especially the personality. Such information is significant in understanding the thought process, intention and motive behind suicide.

  - Socio-demographic data about person
  - Socio-pathological data about person
  - Information on daily life, relationships about person
  - Behavior dynamics of the deceased
  - Information from police report
  - Information from hospital report

- *Contextualizing and discussing the case*

  Once data are collected, the process of interpreting is a challenging task. The goal of analyzing data is to get off the data and open inquiry to wider introspection of some aspect of the process being studied. For Yin (2003), developing case description is the primary emphasis of the case study as it explores the meaning from acquired information to understand the suicide-deaths.

  In discussing or contextualizing cases, themes and meaning surfaces, thereby reduce data into recognized patterned categories, explanations and meanings. Idea of contextualizing and analyzing case study results is to organize data into a manageable form and to construct a narrative around it enriched by empirical insights. The analysis of cases must present different perspectives on what happened? why it happened? and whether it could have been avoided.

  To present gathered raw qualitative data into meaningful way is a demanding task. In our case, we followed framework analysis to come at valid interpretations of the case studies. It consisted of several stages/ processes and can be presented as in Figure 2.1:

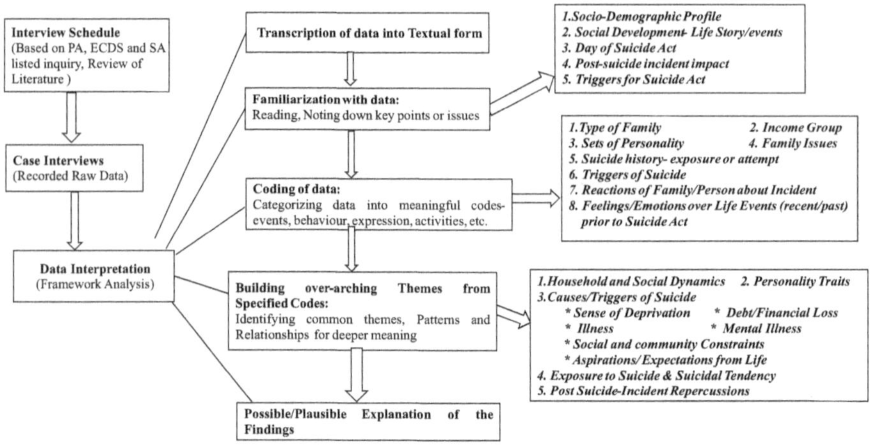

Figure 2.1 Data analysis of the empirical case studies, Vadodara.
Source: Intrepretation by the Authors.

As observed from Figure 2.1, the explanations of our findings were deducted after going through the systematic process of first getting familiar with each case stories. It involved noting down valuable information pertaining to their life history, personality, circumstances initiating condition for suicide, day of suicide act and repercussions on self and others. The information was then categorized into meaningful codes. Such categorization helped in binding different cases into certain common facts. Further step lead to marking out over-arching themes helping in identifying shared circumstances and issues across cases and possible explanations of the preceding and subsequent effects of suicide act. Following the analytical framework brought out certain form of patterned explanations behind the act of suicide such as different risk groups, situations and reasons. Arriving at possible explanations thus gave the meaning to the shared stories, told individually but merged together contextually.

Suicide research and methodological challenges

From the methodological point of view, studying about suicide is a meticulous task especially due to the issues of validity and reliability of the gathered data. There is always a concern for missing records (statistics of reported cases) and partial story (as in case of qualitative information). Operationally PSA though assists in learning about the phenomenon but is a complex and multidimensional strategy. Despite various concerns, careful collection of information from different sources could help in explaining condition of suicide in general and in reconstructing the circumstances, which leads people to want to end their own lives.

This following discussion sheds light on some of the methodological complications we endured at different stages in completing the study, especially in the context of information resources.

Challenges endured: planning, data and ethical issues

The foremost challenge was initiating the study itself. While shaping our study we brainstormed various thought processes like whether it is feasible to study such a complex issue. If issues are complex, how to proceed will also be an issue. Such thinking enabled us to first draft a working plan that involved listing out research questions, objectives, our approaches and our sources of information.

Primarily to connect with the larger context and maintaining the practicality and feasibility we sorted our broad research questions into simpler interpretations:

- What are the social conditions, situations and issues that compel persons towards suicide?
- Is it true to assume that different problems, life events build psychological issues (loneliness, depression, etc.), creating situation or circumstances for suicide?
- Why is it that under similar circumstances some end own life by suicide and others do not?
- Is suicide an act of inherent abnormal Is it an act of mental–self-destructive behavior/personality trait?
- Are deviant personalities more prone to suicide than non-deviant personalities?
- Is there a genetic link to suicidal ideation/behavior?
- What are the problems in identifying risk groups having suicidal tendencies?
- Do completers and attempters of suicide show any patterns in their occurrences?
- Is the link between individual personality, social circumstances, psychological issues and act of suicide linear or uneven in terms of cause and effect relationship?

Suicide could be seen from multiple dimensions. We adopted to understand it through the lens of social-psychological perspective with the proposition that social forces in terms of life crisis or events build up inner mental stresses and turmoil, prompting a person to take away life as a way to escape from such anxieties. With this approach, we wanted to locate suicide largely in a social context and were interested to know more about what makes person to die by suicide? what are the social context/circumstances? what kinds of pressure (within family/individual) leads to suicide? Through such queries, we wanted to bring out the background story of the person – before and after the final act of his/her suicide, considering that suicide incident is not 'an occurrence of the day' but 'series of issues aggregating together overtime for months, days or years'.

Nature, accessing and organizing secondary data

The next challenge was related to data in terms of its nature and access, both at the secondary and primary levels. To know about the statistical scenario of suicide we relied on NCRB annual reports as well as SCRB data; however, both had their own limits. We had to reproduce the information into tabular forms for our use from the textual reports, especially the NCRB data (up to 2015). While doing this we came across certain inconsistencies in the data (for our selected years), in terms of non-availability of information on some variables, and availability of information about the variables only for particular years. Like data on marital, educational and occupational status was available only from 2001 onward while there was no age-specific data for 2014 and 2015. There was also the issue of differences in information over years for the same variables. For instance, the variable of education, age and causes of suicides saw change of its categorization over the years. Up to 1991, the age classification was categorized in four groups with inconsistent age gaps but from 2001 onward, they were clubbed under five categories with the gap of 14 years between each category. It took us four months to sort out the NCRB data.

Even for the data at Gujarat state level (SCRB), we encountered problems. Unlike NCRB (whose data is available on website), to get it we had to follow official route with the series of meeting with concerned officials. With a brief note about purpose and need of the data, we first met Director General of Police (DGP), Gujarat, and then Director General (DG), Crime, Gujarat. Only after going through our project specifics, they allowed us to meet the office and personnel who could provide us the data. The office personnel asked us to give them the set of information we required in writing. Based on our specificity they forwarded us the soft-copy (in XCEL files). SCRB data was also challenging as we received data not for all the years we actually planned, and it was in *Gujarati* language. It was sorted into readable form by translating it into English, converting absolute numbers into percentages and desegregating some data into common variables or broad categories. For better analytical purpose of suicide scenario in Gujarat, the gathered data was categorized into major Gujarat regions. Such exercise helped in interpreting the meanings and speculations from the generated tables, especially about the common features and trends. Almost six months were spent in the whole process.

In order to know the suicidal deaths, particularly in Vadodara district, another set of data was sourced from the 27 police stations, by meeting Commissioner of Police (CP), Vadodara-City, and Superintendent of Police (SP), Vadodara-Rural. We asked them to give us the details of 10–15 reported cases (during 2015–2017) from each police stations under their jurisdiction. Concerning the nature of information, SP-Rural asked us to file a Right to Information (RTI) application for the same, which we followed. We received the information in a period of one and a half month.

Challenges in field study

Processing field study

While visualizing about field component at the planning stage we reflected upon the suitable research method and chose to use case studies, especially owing to sensitive nature of subject. Moreover, we thought it would give us more in-depth understanding as well as the information about the circumstances (immediate and extended) prior to the individuals suicide act. While finalizing this method we were also concerned about how to approach people? how to dig out information? amount of time to be spared for each interview and question of reliability of shared information.

We prepared a checklist of circumstances that lead to suicide and an interview schedule with broad talking points. A sample design was made in line with the analysis of various risk groups as observed in the secondary data. We decided to go for a pilot study with the prepared checklist and interview schedule of two to three cases. It was planned to take final interviews with three sets of people, i.e., persons who attempted/completed suicide, and their families, their neighbors and friends.

The next step was the task of identifying cases for our fieldwork for which we shortlisted key resource stakeholders, namely, psychiatrists, NGOs, hospitals and police stations. These were selected as they are the agencies who would be approached by suicidal person, family or others in terms of treatment, care and reporting about the incident.

We first approached a leading trained medical psychiatrist. He is in charge of the De-addiction Department and Psychiatry Department, Government Civil Hospital, Vadodara, besides running his own clinic. He also runs a Suicide Prevention Program in the city. We asked him to share the contact details of his patients for conducting field interview. However, due to ethical issues (confidentiality between patients and doctors), he was unable to share the list of cases. But he suggested us to visit the Government Civil Hospital (the one he is associated with), to get the cases, as it gets on an average four to five suicide cases per day. We accepted his suggestion and met Medical Superintendent and then Medico-Legal Officer (MLO) of the Civil Hospital who allowed us to access their Medical Record Registers (first information report of all kinds of cases that come to hospital) for identifying suicide cases. Going through 6 registers (out of 20) for 2016, we listed out 100 cases of suicide/self-harm. We had to drop important cases due to incomplete reporting in some, and in others the written information was not readable. After going through both hospital and police stations case lists we finalized 100 cases for in-depth interview.

Before the final field, we conducted a pilot study that made us to reflect on important issues regarding our work. First was our interaction with the pilot cases as a researcher. They thought that we are either social workers or medical professionals. This is obvious considering these disciplines overpowering presence in suicide research. This was evident, as two pilot cases responded, that 'such kind of details (i.e. about suicide) could only interest doctors and social workers mainly because they are concerned about the problem and could also offer helping hand'. The other problem was with the prepared schedule in terms that some questions were straightforward, which should not be the case. Similarly, some information was important to know but not properly presented in the schedule.

The outcome of the pilot survey was that we re-designed our schedule as well as the way to channel our questions based on the PSA and psychosocial harm assessment areas of inquiries (Jobes et al. 1991; Shneidman 1981). The new schedule covered the open-ended details/information on the domains, such as personal, family, medical/psychiatric, psycho-sociological details, personality and lifestyle details. It also covered behavioral aspects (addiction, response to bad events, behavioral attitude, mood swings, etc.), history of suicide-attempts and the aftereffect of suicide incident in the family. It thus helped in doing a SA of our cases.

To avoid the subject-discipline dilemma, we hired three clinical psychologists for conducting field study. We first held meeting with them so that they would get a thorough idea about our study, our approach and kind of information required. They were first asked to interview one case each and report to us with the information. This turned out to be beneficial for reasons:

- The information they gathered was more inclined towards a medico-psychiatric interpretation (this is because of their professional expertise). We reminded them about our focus and the way the case could have been interviewed keeping in mind a holistic approach. They were asked to revisit the same case and update missing information. The second visit filled the earlier gaps along with new information.
- It helped us in taking care of what the informant expects from us. For instance, based on their queries, we prepared a list of documents – letter of organization, identity cards for interview team, consent letter of participation and brief letter about our project and sponsoring organization. It was made to the point to explain and show these documents before each interview.
- We decided to include different sets of people but limited our interviews only to the family. It was felt that including neighbors and friends was not a feasible option due to time and logistic constraints. This,

however, gave us a 'one-way narrative', and the 'larger' part was missing. Also in cases where the apparent cause of suicide was love affair and marital issues, we were able to get the responses from the family of attempters/completers but not that of the others involved (lover, spouse, in-laws, etc.).

- We planned to interview various stakeholders who directly or indirectly deal with the subject matter of suicide like psychiatrists, social workers, religious leaders, NGOs. We wanted to know the views of the professional experts on suicidal trends and tendencies but we could not.

Conducting interviews: dilemmas of research team and interviewees (empirical narratives)

1 **Problem of tracking cases:** We prepared the list of final cases with their address based on hospital and police records. However, interview team faced problem in locating some of the cases at the mentioned address. It was found that the household had shifted their residence after the suicide incident. Even neighbors were unaware about the new address. When team tried to enquire about the suicide occurrence, neighbors showed inhibition saying 'we don't know'. Few cases had to be dropped due to distance, especially those which were far away from the center of the city or those residing in nearby villages. This restricted our study to be city-specific.

2 **Ethical concerns:** Before taking the interviews, interview team first explained the idea/purpose of the study to interviewees. They took their consent and ensured confidentiality. This established their willingness to participate besides creating a comfortable setting about the expected conversations and information out of the interviewees. On agreeing about the participation, interview was held at home as per the convenience of interviewees, which ensured their ease and privacy over shared narratives. Each interview lasted for about one and half hour, though in some cases, it took slightly longer.

   Certain cases demanded more attention than that of the others and resulted in multiple visits. They mostly included cases where interviews in first visit were discontinued mid-way due to participants' uneasiness to continue further or due to presence of member that was controlling the interview. In latter case, it was made sure to revisit the household, in the absence of that 'controlling member'.

3 **Reassurance:** Consent and willingness to participate by the interviewees took time. Even after yes, the informants (especially the family members of attempters and completers) were more concerned as to how it would be useful. Many did not find any meaning as to why they should even share their stories or failed to understand the benefits they would get out of it. Once they were reassured about the importance of such kind of studies and how it could be useful to others, directly or

indirectly (if not them) they somehow eased out their apprehension and shared their stories.

4 **Time interval:** We made sure to follow the ethics involved in the research studies on suicide, particularly the time interval prerequisite. We finalized cases where the suicide-attempt or suicide-death occurred during eight months to two years maximum prior to our research, thus maintaining the time interval gap. We were sensitive enough while interviewing people as suicide is a subjective and intense issue. We were skeptical of instigating the emotional gates of person and family that they had shut after the incident.
5 **Attentiveness to information**: Talking about suicide is emotive, and being attentive to the person sharing stories was a challenging task. Making note of each small detail while also giving equal attention to their expressions and emotional outbursts was significant. It also implied our seriousness and importance of their information to us. After initiating the interview, they were allowed to lead the discussion while full attention was paid to their narration, body language and gestures. Since writing and observation were supposed to be done simultaneously, it was slightly difficult to synchronize both initially but it was achieved effectively.
6 **Managing the interview:** Persons who attempted suicide and survived chose to speak in the company of other household members. The presence of family members in few cases somehow controlled the narration. The interruption of family in between made them to speak in a very precise manner as the interruption had an undertone of intimidation and taunt. Because of their professional skills, interview team overcame such situation and tried their best to involve the attempt-survivor more in the conversation. In some cases, few members (non-informants) kept on coming in between while the conversation was on, but did not share anything. They kept a regular check on the discussion. Only few of them were welcoming and open to tell the story about what had happened and how they had felt and are struggling with the loss.
7 **Reluctance in response:** Despite the recent development of decriminalizing suicide and de-stigmatizing mental illness, people feel difficult and uncomfortable to disclose anything related about it as it is considered private and personal occurrence. This notion very much influenced our interviewees (self and family members) as they showed sign of discomfort, apprehensions and reluctance in responding to our questions. Such signs existed because of fear and anticipation of 'private becoming public' with an inference of them being judged negatively. Once interviewees developed trust and confidentiality, they finally opened up and responded to the questions.

Building up of rapport through multiple visits also helped in showing our sincerity to the subject and a genuine interest on our behalf to know about their story, struggles and aftereffects of the suicide incident. Taking care of members' comfort in terms of when and where to meet further reduced their reluctance.

8 **Reaction to response:** The interviewees questioned us the significance of shared information. They were apprehensive about the visit, as they had never expected anyone to visit them with such inquiries. They hardly believed that someone would be interested to know about the person who chose to self-harm, other than police or legal officers. In suicide-death cases some felt that talking about the dead person was not going to bring them back in their lives; hence, what is the necessity to tell about them to strangers.

9 **Reliability of shared information:** It is almost impossible to bring out complete facts about important risk factors or underlying mechanism behind suicidal act especially, if it leads to death. In the case of deceased, sources such as suicide notes, medical records or interviewing family members or close friends become useful. However, obtaining information from the family members brings in the issue of reliability and validity. Hence, after initial averseness, interviewees opened up and told the suicide stories but it cannot be negated that shared story might be just a part of the whole story. It is so because narration depended on members' willingness of what to share and what not to share. Nevertheless, from the collected narratives we were able to sieve out some form of social reasoning behind the person's act of suicide.

10 **In search of help:** In some households, person's suicide has created financial difficulties either due to the loss of earning member or due to debt burden of the person. In few of the households, it was sensed that they shared the story with a hope of some kind of help in return. They asked for helping them out financially or legally.

An interpretative understanding of suicide phenomenon was important to us as it brings out broader analysis to the problem of suicide. Such an understanding involved generating information from those who had went through the process of suicide in terms of attempt or a loss to life. Based on our empirical insights, we can highlight some elements, summarized as in Figure 2.2, that we feel played an important role in creating difficulty in seeking facts and insights on suicides at micro level.

As per Figure 2.2, it is evident that firsthand information on suicide is difficult to grasp mainly because of social perception towards the phenomenon in terms of it being a household issue that involves the question of sensitive and private element. The notion of social stigma to mental illness also creates difficulty in accessing information on suicide as mental illness was seen something that needs to be discrete and concealed. In case suicide incident was known and if someone enquires about it, household always maintain to disclose what is apparent and already recognized.

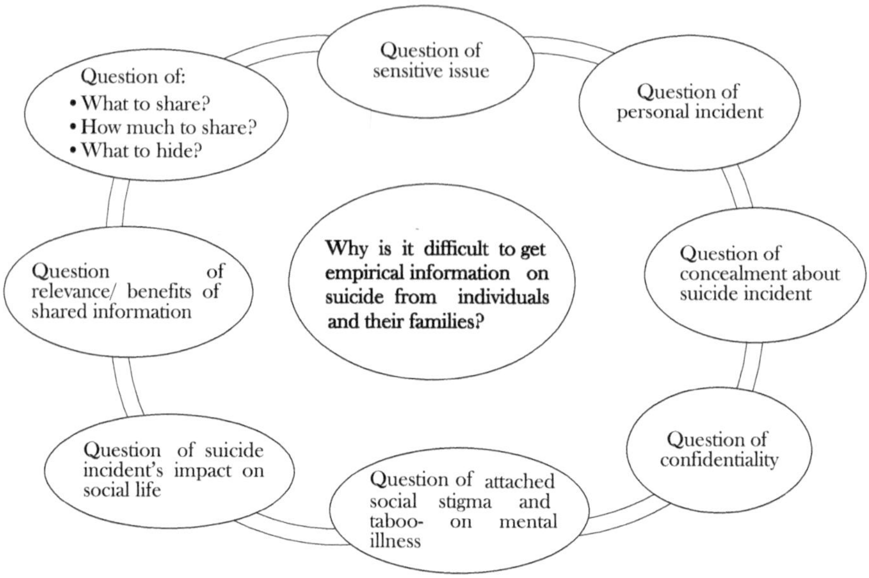

Figure 2.2 Reasons for the difficulty in accessing empirical insights on suicides.
Source: Intrepretation by the Authors.

In collecting relevant and meaningful information behind people's decision and motives for suicide we too faced the difficulty in digging out information. However, with prior preparedness and anticipation, we handled some difficulties while the others we controlled during the process.

Notes

1 Retrieved August 13, 2019, from, https://www.pbs.org/wgbh/pages/frontline/post-mortem/things-to-know/autopsy-101.html.

2 Various forms of autopsy or post-mortem examination are as follows: (1) Medico-legal autopsy: done in the Department of Forensic Medicine on request from police or investigative officer (IO) of the case (generally Sub-Divisional Magistrate). The doctor conducts a full and complete post-mortem to find out the cause of death and other relevant questions from the IO. For this, the consent of the relatives is not required. (2) Pathological autopsy: done in the Department of Pathology on request from the relatives/members of deceased. In these cases, the doctor conducts a partial autopsy of the organ or cavities where the pathology is suspected to find the cause of death. (3) Virtual autopsy or virtopsy: it is an alternative to a traditional autopsy, conducted with scanning and imaging technology. It involves application of imaging methods for non-invasive documentation and analysis of relevant forensic findings in living or dead persons. It also involves imaging methods used in clinical medicine such as computed tomography (CT) and magnetic resonance imaging (MRI). It can be used in cultures and situations where autopsy is not tolerated by religion or rejected by family members (Dikshit 2010; Dumbrava et al. 2010; Thali et al. 2007).

3 It was developed in approximately 1958 because of the Los Angeles County Medical Examiner's Office consulting the Los Angeles Suicide Prevention Center for assistance in distinguishing drug-related accidental overdoses from suicides. This collaboration laid down the basic principles for the PA procedure. Refined over the years since the PA has become a best practice post-mortem procedure to reconstruct the near- and long-term causes of an individual's death by suicide or to ascertain the most likely manner of equivocal death that is left undetermined by a medical examiner or coroner.
4 Investigators of ECDS tested its accuracy by asking 70 medical examiners to apply the criteria to 126 deaths that included suicide and accidents. The ECDS was found to have predicted 100% of the previously certified suicides and 83% of the previously certified accidents (Jobes et al. 1991).
5 An equivocal death is one in which the manner of death is questionable, or the circumstances surrounding the death are otherwise unclear.

3 Demystifying suicide

Insights from primary research

In this chapter, our focus is to present an understanding of the processes and causes associated with suicide or self-harm by placing them within micro region and larger social context through the narratives of 49 case studies. These narratives recognize suicidal tendencies and actions as socially constructed option. They are the result of emotional psychology, but are the determinant of the pathology of relationship shared by a person with the social environment (family, community, etc.) that induces, perpetuates or aggravates such behavior.

The chapter explores the suicidal acts of case-study narratives under broad themes highlighting underlying forces, contexts and risk factors behind their decision for suicide. It highlights the reactions of suicide incident and its repercussions on the household and its members. It also discusses some aspects of attempt-survivors and bereaved members in dealing with the suicide. Finally, it summarizes key responses of the case-study narratives to the larger context.

Unraveling the dynamics behind suicides: evidence from case studies

Underlying forces behind suicides as observed from case studies suggest that suicide is a product of several elements to which an individual is exposed to over time, some affect them in real time while others, though, present remain concealed in individual's socialization, personality, social conditioning or regulations. Because of some reason if individuals find themselves or their actions going against the desired social behavior expected out of them (either from family, society or other member), they become vulnerable to negative feelings towards their life. If not handled properly such feelings instill suicide ideation or self-harming. Such explanation could be illustrated as seen in Figure 3.1.

As per Figure 3.1, one can assume that society instills collective sense of right and wrong among its members through social ordering of its social institutions such as family or community. This collective social conscience enables individuals to weigh their persona and actions as per the standard

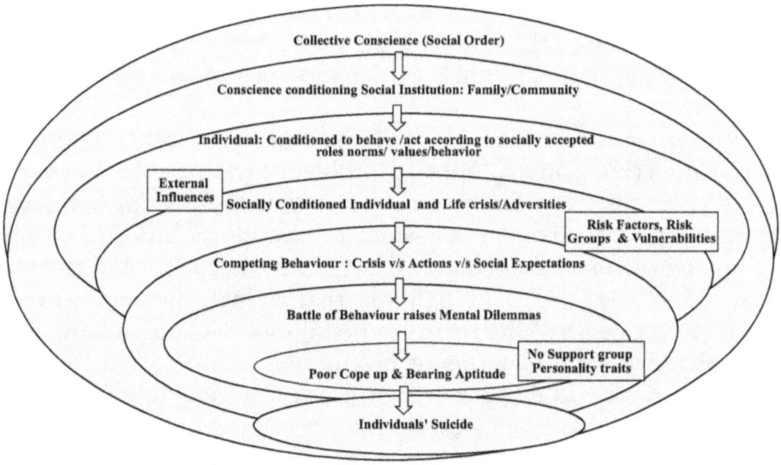

Figure 3.1 Dynamics behind suicide act.
Source: Intrepretation by the authors.

norms in order to remain socially acceptable. Such conditioning remains with the persons consciously and subconsciously that develops in shaping up their personality and attitude towards life, and dealing with its problems. So when various risk factors create life-crisis in an individual's life, they become vulnerable to sets of social and psychological issues. This is also the time, when they might remain thinking about their actions and social expectations as going against each other in the view of life-crisis. The situations raise mental dilemmas surrounded by the feelings of unhappiness, deprivation, guilt, shame, depression, hopelessness and so on. If individuals cannot overcome such feelings due to poor cope up ability, non-adaptive personality and timely support then they finally end up in taking their own life thinking that it is the only way to end all the miseries and stress aroused due to life-crisis. It is to note that the life-crisis could be because of their own action or by others or independent to individuals' will.

However, it is important to note that some suicides may be merely, an impulsive act, done to either threaten or seek attention from others. Such suicides may not fit entirely as per the above illustration (in terms of adverse social event or unacceptable social behavior), yet they might be traced back to the way in which they are conditioned by their families. For instance, there is a link between person's suicide to his grown-up years in a family environment with too much pampering, and non-adaptive nature to any harsh realities and refusal of any kind to his/her demands or wishes. Such socialization by family fuses hostility in a person when one finds the demands being not fulfilled unlike other times. Similarly, a person killing oneself just in a fit of anger also shows the way family overshadowed his/

her anger issues as normal in growing up years rather than taking them seriously, as a suicidal risk or as an abnormal behavior which could create issues in his/her personal life in multiple ways. At the same time, some suicide cases may not have any valid explanation or the linkages as per above illustration.

The interpretation of the case-study narratives[1] largely identified contexts and underlying motivations of problems and perceived causes that triggered their suicide. The inferences from their stories also extend our understanding of the reasons for suicide beyond one's normal visibility, thus showing the inner facts and diversity in the accounts and their implications[2]. Moreover, they also highlight that though suicide is always the act of preferring death to life there is a possibility of certain characteristics having collective form in terms of origin, set patterns or social settings but with a variation in degrees or significance in each individual context. The ensuing discussion includes the findings of case-narratives put forth in broad themes and sub-themes that created space and acted as triggers for their suicide.

Household and social dynamics

Household composition and economic status

Family patterns are conceptualized in terms of one's family composition of which the household is one of its dimensions. The household is a residential and domestic unit comprising of one or more persons living under the same roof and eating food cooked in a single kitchen (Shah 1973). The bond that ties the individual to his family, the range of the influence and authority that the family exercises makes the family not merely an institutional structure of our society, but also gives it a deep value (Mishra et al. 2012).

In terms of household composition, majority of our cases (29) lived in the nuclear settings with total household members between two and five persons. Twenty persons belonged to extended households with composition of more than five members. In few cases of extended household, the members comprised three generations. In both kinds of households, members whether married or unmarried resided with their parents (surviving parent or both) and siblings (mainly males) or other relatives. In addition, one finds commonality of more cases of suicidal-deaths than the suicide-attempts in both household types.

The economic status suggested that most persons belonged to the middle class (32) followed by the lower income group (12). Only five people were from upper-class economic group. These classifications were broadly based on the observations of their residence, household infrastructure, number of earning members and nature of their employment in the household. Of total 36 suicide-completers, 24 belonged to the middle class, 9 to the lower-income group and 3 to the upper class. Similarly, out of total 13 suicide-attempters,

8 belonged to the middle class while 3 from lower and 2 from upper class. The economic scenario of the person him/herself and of the household implies that middle- and lower-income group could be the risk factor for high suicide occurrences. This assumption could be substituted with the police records for Vadodara district (city and rural) that showed 356 suicides in 2014 and 391 suicides in 2015 of those with the annual income of less than five lakh (SCRB 2014, 2015). According to NCRB, in Gujarat, those who died by suicides during 2014–2016, 77% had the annual income of less than one lakh. In 2017 and 2018 it was 70% and 73.4%, respectively. Likewise, during 2014–2016, those with the income of one lakh to less than five lakh annually accounted 23% and about 27% in 2017–2018. It is to note that Gujarat's share was higher to that of India for income group of less than one lakh for these five years (70% during 2014–2016 and about 66% in 2017 and 2018). For the other income group India's proportion remains in between 27% and 30% (NCRB, Yearly reports).

Level of social integration

Examining the level of attachment security explaining the social dynamics of an individual is important while understanding suicide (Sheftall et al. 2013). Suicidal person's early experiences in family/social settings depict their level of attachment. This process does not merely view the internal representations of relationships influencing an individual but also throws light on the interpretation and understanding of those relationship across a lifespan. Since every person would have a different pattern of attachment, therefore, they had different ways of dealing and coping with stressful life circumstances defining the differences seen in the expression of suicide-attempts (Bowlby 1969, 1980, 1988; Brennan et al. 1998).

To the several explanations of individual's level of attachment, it is generally argued that disturbed/insecure social and family bonds or attachments increase the individuals' vulnerability to suicide-attempts (Lizardi et al. 2011). However, secure and stronger attachment could also become risk to suicidal ideations in certain conditions for an individual in short or long term. Stronger attachment in terms of pampered, over-dependence and/or indulgent behavior in family settings influence an individual's social world; despite being arbitrary in nature and rather invisible, it plays an inherent role when an individual faces a crisis. Their level of engagement subconsciously makes them end life by suicide, either leading to their death or survival as a suicide-completer and -attempter, respectively. In our narratives, this kind of risk was found in the six cases who had the strong family integration. These persons were brought up in an environment where they seemed to be highly pampered and loved by family members. The attachment between them was so high that they were highly dependent on the members of family for their actions and life's decisions. For instance:

Case of Razia,[3] 25-year-old female

Razia, attempted suicide by hanging and died. The reported cause of her suicide was marital conflicts and health issues. A closer look at her early and later life experiences unveil the link of her suicide to various other internal things centering her life. As a single child, her parents took to showering her with extreme love, care, and compassion. She was brought up in a family where she hardly faced any undesirable responses/situation; on the contrary, her family supported her and fulfilled all of her needs and wishes. Unfortunately, after marriage, her social world changed drastically. She found herself in a family with an absence of pampered environment in which she grew up. On being part of the institution of arranged marriage, she was left muddled in a world with conservative in-laws who created issues over trivial matters. Since the beginning of her new marital life, she faced taunts, disrespectful behavior, and intense arguments, sometimes even involving taunts and rash comments passed on her parents and biological family. On facing such a situation, she instantly developed insecurities about herself. Feelings of helplessness, sense of failure on playing the role of wife despite all her efforts further instigated a negative atmosphere. Though her husband had no issues with her, the tension between them due to in-laws took a toll on her and increased her insecurities. The diagnosis of her reproductive health problem depressed her further, as it meant more taunts from in-laws since the problem was related to fertility issue. However, the issue of fertility ended with the medical treatment and she gave birth to a baby girl. Despite a new entrant (baby) in the family, her insecurities persisted due to the strain and tension-filled relationship shared with her in-laws. Such strained relationship even after adjusting in so many ways since the beginning of her marriage lead to perceiving of her married life (of six years) in a saddened and upset state. The thought of self-harm culminated in her due to relapse of another health issue along with an argument with her husband over their daughter on the day of act. In order to release her frustration, stress or seeking attention from the marital family she attempted to harm herself by hanging that however turned out to be fatal and led to her demise.

Case of Anant,[4] 22-year-old male

Anant was the only child of his parents and was pampered all his life while he was growing up. Most of the time, his family fulfilled all his needs and wants. They never pressurized him into doing things which they wanted him to do rather they made him to live in freedom and choose his studies or career. He was married with a two-year-old daughter, but he was not concerned to take up a job and be responsible to his own family. He was instead dependent on his parents for monetary support. It was observed that his father was a

> dominating and authoritative figure who played a significant role in all the household decisions. With no active role, he was immature in understanding his responsibilities as son, father and husband. Moreover, his upbringing made him stubborn and impatient. This behavioral trait reflected upon in his inability to accept 'no' or his tantrums and anger attacks if he was not given things he asked or wished for. He attempted to kill himself by consuming poison just because his father rejected to buy him a bicycle of ₹ 17,000 immediately when he asked for it. His family averted his suicide with the timely action and he survived.

In cases of Razia and Anant, both grew in a similar pampered environment, but the suicide expressions were entirely different with different emotions and feelings. In Razia's case, the suicidal death of her makes us believe that it was not only a result of marital discords and health issues (as it was reported) but intrinsically it was also due to her need for approval and acceptance from her new family similar to the environment in which she grew up. In terms of the interpersonal theory of suicide, in individuals, feelings like lack of the reciprocity in care and love and the absence of belongingness usually give rise to a desire to die. Razia developed such feelings as she was unable to feel the belongingness or attachment to her marital family due to tensions and problems between her and in-laws. As a daughter-in-law, despite all her efforts to make them happy further increased her non-attachment. In relation to her, it can be said that when the need to feel wanted and connected to others was not met, the person develop an insecure attachment and social disconnection. Such feelings endure to act as a source of risk for suicide-attempts over a period (Joiner et al. 2005; Van Orden et al. 2010). From social-interaction perspective, her suicide could be correlated to her disturbed social interactions in the marital home in terms of degree of reciprocity (giving and receiving), interpersonal role conflict and interpersonal frustrations.

In case of Anant, the underlying factor of suicide could be traced back to his behavioral pattern and growing up years. His demands were fulfilled without delay and/or hesitation, as he was the only child of his parents. He was also not used to hearing 'no' from his parents on his any kind of demands. Further, his parents never questioned him about his life decisions, in any manner; he was brought up in a secured social world, and he remained quite attached to it. Hence, when his demand for buying a cycle was not promptly yielded by his father and instead was met with the rejection, he felt upset. His nature of being stubborn, impatient and angry also aggravated his low and upset mood. Seeing that the response to his wish was not accepted immediately and was rather scolded by father, he consumed poison to harm himself. In his opinion, he did so in a fit of anger, whereas his father believed that this was an impulsive act as he was used to having all his demands met by him instantly without any refusal. Associating his suicide-attempt in relation to attachment theory, one may trace back his action to his early childhood experiences where the parent was actively receptive to his needs and wishes or emotions. On experiencing, non-receptive behavior from them to his demand of purchasing bicycle unlike in the past resulted in extreme frustration and disconnectedness, alienation and hostility in his subconscious mind.

Family conflicts/abusive behavior/alcoholism

While understanding the narratives, one uncovers various underlying social variables that actually contributed to the decision for their suicide. Some of these variables turned out as explicit causes while some remained unnoticed despite being effective in nature. The annual NCRB and SCRB reports on suicide-deaths had highlighted various socio-psychological causes of suicide, the prominent of them being 'family issues or problems'. Statistics do not define it precisely but one could assume that it more or less refers to 'internal family-conflicts or fights'. These conflicts in the long run leads to suicidal ideations, thoughts and, eventually, suicide-attempts.

Family conflicts or abusive behavior existed among ten persons (three attempted and seven completed cases). The conflicts were not only limited between couples and in-laws but also between siblings and other members living with the person. Three persons were abusive towards other family members rather than them facing it themselves. For instance, a 50-year-old woman showed signs of mental disorder before her suicide, turned abusive towards her husband and other family members. Quite a few times, she fought with them unnecessarily and chose to hit them.

The association between alcoholism and suicide is established by various national and international studies (Behere and Behere 2008; Ponnudurai et al. 1986; Schmidt and Lint 1972). Alcohol use and alcoholism are high-risk factors for suicide but at the same time, the relationship between the two also underlies the interaction of intervening factors. People who are alcoholics may represent a further reflection of his/her impulsiveness and impaired capacity to cope with stress, recurrent feelings of failure, isolation, hopelessness, depression, separation and little orientation to future (Burge et al. 1995). A Finnish study by Heikkinen et al. (1993) focused on the role of life events and social support claiming that life events play an important role in the act of suicide. Family discord, financial problem and marital separation among the alcoholics act as risk and precipitating factors. Moreover, individuals with alcohol or drug abuse problems often die by suicide due to alienation from friends and family, therefore availing little or no social support system. In our narratives, the link between suicide and alcohol was found in five persons, of whom two survived the attempts while three lost their lives.

Case of Neel,[5] 30-year-old married male

Suicide attempt by Neel could be traced to internal conflicts between him and family members due to his alcoholic behavior. He lived with his family in slum quarters and was from lower socio-economic status. He was working as a rickshaw driver since the age of 17 years. He did not own the rickshaw but was driving it on a daily rental fee. While growing up, he fell into the bad company and since the age of 15, he started consuming alcohol and got habituated. He married his girlfriend hailing from a different caste despite the opposition and disapproval of his family. Soon after marriage, he became a father of a son. He used to consume alcohol regularly with his friends and returned home in an inebriated state. His mother and wife were not happy with his drinking habit. They would tell him to stop but he made no efforts to quit. There would often be fights and arguments at home due to his drinking problem. Such fights or arguments occurred mainly when he was nudged to go to work regularly so that he can add money to household expenses and can also save something for his son's future. His habit of drinking did not let him go to work regularly as he would either stay at home or move around unnecessarily with friends of similar habits. His alcohol problem made his mother feel bad, and was concerned, especially for his marital life. She showed concern stating, "My son married someone's daughter and brought her to this house and now it is our responsibility to make sure that she is happy otherwise, the community will point fingers at me for my upbringing". Neel also had a history of Diabetes Mellitus for which he was constantly under medication. He did not interact much with his family and mostly, chose to keep things to himself lately. His communication with them was mostly during the time of quarrels. His alcoholic issue and irresponsible behavior also caused a strained relationship with his brother. On the day when he attempted suicide, he chose not to go for work but when his mother and wife pressured him, he went and returned after few hours. On coming back home, he did not talk to anyone, went inside his room, and consumed pill of various kinds, most of which were expired. He was already semi-inebriated due to alcohol and after taking these medicines, he lost consciousness. His family found out his state and took him to the hospital where he was given first aid. After receiving aid and gaining consciousness, he ran away from the hospital without waiting for doctor's advice. He did this, as he got worried about the consequences of his actions and did not want to be in the eye of the police or the doctor.

In his opinion, he attempted suicide due to his current living conditions and the constant nagging and disagreements with his family. He wanted the family to stop interfering, commenting upon it and to let him live his life as he wanted. However, his mother was still hopeful that he would come back to his senses and will begin behaving responsibly, once he quit alcohol. There appeared to be many unresolved conflicts between him and the other family members due to his laidback approach to life, and his inability to support the family financially.

Case of Ved,[6] 38-year-old married male

Ved got addicted to alcohol since his adolescent years. He dropped out of eighth standard and began working as a daily wage laborer to add to the household income. In his adolescent years, he consumed alcohol occasionally, but later it became a habit whenever he spent time with friends, which occurred frequently. Whatever he earned, he instantly spent it on alcohol. Considering that both his parents were blind, he barely found himself under the supervision of his parents throughout his childhood and adolescence, who can keep a check on him and stop him from adopting such, hazardous habits. Moreover, his alcoholism led to the difficulty in finding a wife for him. He was finally able to marry a widow with a daughter from his neighborhood. His wife was unaware of his alcoholic nature and knew about it after marriage. Being a sole earning member, and no consistent job meant that he hardly managed to contribute to the household expenses and make ends meet. Every time he earned some money, he chose to purchase alcohol rather than giving it for home expenses. To manage household financially, his wife took a job with a packaging firm earning about ₹ 4,500 per month and later on, to improve the household finance, his elder daughter dropped out of school and began working as a housemaid earning ₹ 500 per month. Lately some months before his suicide attempt his family saw some change in him. He was keeping low and when asked about the reason he said that he wanted to become responsible and work sincerely. He also said that he was searching for a job (better than the one he was currently employed) but is not getting. Despite his efforts of looking for a decent job, he failed to get any which made him upset and saddened. In such a state of mind where feelings of irritation and being a burden on others was high, he chose to end life. One day he made his wife to go and visit her maternal home along with the children, which was not far away from their own house. He also told his mother to join them. Once they left, after some time he hanged himself with a saree. His wife came back after an hour, saw him hanging, and shouted for neighbors help. He was somewhat conscious at that time and was taken to hospital but he lost his life during the treatment soon after.

Case of Imran,[7] 35-year-old married male

The worries about his youngest son's health (pediatric illness since infancy) pushed Imran to drinking regularly, which was about two years prior to his suicidal death. According to his family, this habit started when he fell into the wrong-company of friends circle. In his inebriated state, he would become aggressive and angry towards family members. Later on when he becomes sober he would express regret over his actions. Sometimes, he also showed self-harming tendencies during his drunken state. He also stopped assisting his father in their tailoring shop regularly. He would rather remain in the house and lend a hand in the household work. To his drinking habit, he would reason with the family that, 'he drinks to get rid of his worries about his son'. Once in an inebriated state, he fell down in a gutter, near to his house and hurt his head. His family believed that his head injury changed his mental state (of which he was going through), even though he did not show any signs of behavioral or personality changes due to accident. One day in the evening, he closed his room, consumed poison (Baygon spray insecticide), and became unconscious. On smelling the strong odour coming from his room, his wife and sister-in-law pushed open the door to see him on the floor. He was rushed to the hospital where the doctor treated him. He lost his life on the fifth day at the hospital as his lungs developed an infection due to the poison.

Case of Deepak,[8] 38-year-old married male

Deepak was an alcoholic and died by hanging. He stayed with his wife and children separately. His parents lived with his brother few homes away. According to his family, he began drinking after he started working at the petrol pump. Initially, his drinking was occasional but later the frequency increased and stayed with him for the last ten years of his life. In this period, he tried to quit it many times. Due to his habit and no steady income, his family of four faced constant financial constraints that resulted in the necessity for his wife to work as a helper to an old woman. In the last few years of his life, he suffered severe leg pain from which he did not recover despite treatment. Moreover, doctor's advice of quitting alcohol and continuous treatment was not heeded; rather he chose to drink excessively in order to overcome the experience of intense pain. Due to the suffering of severe pain, once he tried to hang himself from ceiling fan but failed. Two week later after this incident, he was alone at home. His wife, father and children were away. He called his father, a railway employee and informed not to call him in the afternoon hours, as he will be sleeping. In the evening when his father called him and on not getting reply, he reached home and unlocked the front door. When he entered, he found him hanging on the ceiling fan hook. He called the police and his body was taken to the hospital. Doctor declared him brought dead. Before these attempts, Deepak also tried to kill himself in the past following an argument with his parents.

In above four cases, alcoholism was a common thread and considered a cause of their death. However, in all cases, the association of alcoholism was present with the other valid intervening factors. In the case of Neel, fights with family intervened with alcoholism. He became more argumentative which created fights in the family. He did not like any kind of interference from anyone on daily basis, especially someone telling him to quit drinking and to be more responsible. He wanted to live on his own without any taunts or bad mouthing. In Ved's case, alcoholic nature made him to neglect financial constraints that family was going through, as he would use earned money for drinking rather than spending it on essential household expenses. However, when he decided to change his behavior and became responsible for his family, he suffered setbacks. Considering that, his efforts of seeking good job went in vain with no positive result, he became frustrated, which ultimately became the hidden cause of his demise. Similarly, in the case of Imran, his youngest son's heart disease built up worries, and stress, which promoted his dependence on alcoholism, thereby imparting suicidal ideations to end his life. For Deepak, drinking was a normal habit, but when he suffered with the problem of leg pain, the intensity of it increased which fused with his way of coping up from unbearable pain. Since he knew that medical help was not of much use (as he was required to quit drinking), he felt helpless and viewed his remaining life as painful and burdened. He thought about suicide as a better means to overcome his pain. In all the mentioned cases, alcoholism was the risk factor that gave rise to other simultaneous issues such as family conflicts, non-performing of expected household duties and stress. These issues altogether intensified the conditions for suicide. As an option and non-frequent habit, drinking might give temporary escape from problems, but once it becomes a habit, it is harmful. Alcoholism develops individuals' inability to cope with life-sufferings in positive ways. It rather becomes cause for odd behaviors such as misconduct and suicidal tendencies.

Irresponsible/careless behavior

Irresponsible behavior and engagement in wrongdoings were observed in the two cases of suicide-attempters.

> **Case of Bhavesh,[9] 40-year-old male**
> Bhavesh was unmarried and lived with his widowed mother in a very small house. He would do odd jobs as a daily wage laborer. His mother was diabetic and was undergoing a treatment. He had two elder brothers, but they lived separately. They moved out from the house when their father was alive after they finished their education and started doing some jobs. The mother purchased two LIG flats on their name. The house in which she was living was for Bhavesh. He is not in talking terms with his brothers and whenever they met they fought. Lately, his brothers had stopped contacting him and the mother. Since mother did not keep well he himself looked after the household things like cleaning, washing and sometimes cooking. For living, he primarily stitches curtains and does other odd jobs. Paternal uncle sometimes help

mother and son financially and indirectly by providing food grains or other grocery supplies for the entire year. He attempted suicide because he was upset with his life. The reason being his concern for the mother. He was of a feeling that he was burdened with taking care of his ill mother as well as managing household. His siblings did not worry about her neither did they share the responsibility. However, in reality, such concern was not true. He was an irresponsible son and careless towards life. He never had a steady job, was addicted to alcohol and was involved in petty crimes. He used to gamble and lose a lot of money which he earned. He also went to jail for the case of purse snatching (incident occurred out of Vadodara). He refused to admit this crime and said it was his friend who committed it. For this case his mother had to travel far away thrice to arrange for the bail to release him. Even after this incident, he did not change his reckless behaviour. He got involved in few other crimes in Vadodara. Such indulgence made his mother more worried. Though he stopped doing crimes, he was still into drinking. On the day he attempted suicide, he had liquor with his friends. Since he wanted to drink more, he returned home as he had stock of liquor. In his intoxicated condition, he mistook the bottle of floor cleaner to be a locally made alcohol and consumed almost half a bottle. He became unconscious and collapsed. His mother saw him falling down and called 108 service immediately. He was taken to the hospital where after two days of observation he was discharged.

Case of Jignesh,[10] 35-year-old male

Jignesh seemed to be directionless in his life since his adolescent years. He dropped out of tenth standard and was sitting idle and not doing anything. His parents motivated him to take up a job if he did not wish to study further for his betterment. But he did not pay any heed to their suggestion. Rather than doing something, he started spending his time outside home with his friends and would come back late at night. According to his father, this period influenced his life negatively as he got engaged into bad habits such as drinking and gambling. He also started arguing with his parents and got irritated on trivial matters. Later on as an adult, he followed similar careless life with no interest in working and roaming with friends. For his financial needs he started asking money from his parents and on their refusal, he would threaten to leave the house. For two to three times he actually had left home, but eventually returned after three to four days. He also started harming himself by cutting his hand or consuming poison or pills for fulfilling his demands. His parents would rush him to the hospital where he would stay for a day and then run away or discharge himself against medical advice. This behavior of Jignesh developed a lot of tension and pressure on his parents. They eventually chose to give into his demands. His family suffered his threats for some time while also trying to make him

> mend his ways. But when they figured out that their effort is not giving any result and they are unnecessarily pleasing his wishes, they finally stopped saying anything to him and later on chose not to accept his demands nor support him financially. They felt giving him money meant he would waste it on alcohol and gambling. During this period, they also heard about his affairs with married women and later about his marriage to a tribal girl, though they never confirmed about it themselves. Fed up with Jignesh's threats and social activities his parents finally disowned him with the notice in newspapers, shedding away any liabilities on them if he does something to himself or anyone. Even after this, one night he came home in a drunken state and asked money from father to start some business set up. His father kicked him out with all his belongings and asked him not to return ever as his acts were demeaning their social status in the neighborhood. After this incident, Jignesh's parents never saw him, but they heard from others that he had two children from his tribal wife. However, he left his kids and wife for some other woman.

In cases of Bhavesh and Jignesh, both men were irresponsible towards their life and got involved into wrongdoings. Their habit of alcoholism further made them run away from taking responsibility of their families considering that the mother of Bhavesh was dependent on him due to her health and household economic condition, and in Jignesh's case, he had the responsibility towards his parents as being the only child for them. Alcoholism and irresponsible behavior intervened in their suicide-attempts: however, in one it happened during inebriated state, while in another it was meant as a threatening tool.

Loss of primary kin

The loss of primary kin recently or in the past affected and disturbed two persons. Disturbances indirectly related to their suicide as their loss created emptiness and loneliness affecting their life in different ways. For a 34-year-old man, missing of his father (in a country where he worked) during childhood was a huge setback, both in terms of the family's image in society and in monetary matters. Absence of father led him to take up household responsibilities at an early age, as mother's sole income was not sufficient to run the household. Since he took up the responsibility at a young age, he was compelled to take the role of a 'male head', symbolizing social significance and image in his community. Lately, finding himself torn between the huge debt/losses and maintaining the expected social role and image harnessed suicide ideations in him, which culminated in his suicide-attempt ending in death. Similarly, another 32-year-old man, who was the only child to his parents, the death of father and later separation from mother made him lonely and melancholic. His father's death separated him from his mother, as his maternal uncle forcefully took her away without providing any explanation for separating mother and son. With no financial source, he dropped out of college and managed his livelihood through private jobs. He was often fired from his job due to not meeting the targets. With no person to hear and share his life, he mostly felt lonely and sad, spending a lot of time alone at home. Loneliness and lack of family to talk or communicate built up suicidal thoughts. To end his lonesomeness by ending himself he attempted suicide, but through the neighbors' timely help he survived.

Personality trait dynamics

Each of us, as human beings, influences much that is within us and around us. Each of us has many psychological attributes: feelings, thoughts, motivations and the like. Our personality orchestrates our psychological qualities. Our sense of self help informs us on how to make choices from alternatives that may help us grow or that may harm us. The personality of ours slowly and persistently influences how we feel, what we do, who we are and how we influence the world around us.

Personality can be defined as a dynamic and organized set of characteristics possessed by a person that uniquely influences his or her cognitions, emotions, motivations and behaviors in various situations. It may also refer to the patterns of thoughts, feelings and behaviors consistently exhibited by an individual over time that strongly influence our expectations, self-perceptions, values and attitudes, which predict our reactions to people, problems and stress. In short, they play a prominent role in the way we interact with and interpret our environment (Kraiskopf and Saunders 1994; Winnie and Gittinger 1973).

Over the last three decades, the interest in the contribution of personality traits to suicidal behavior has increased. Studies have demonstrated consistent associations between personality variables and suicide ideations (Beautrias 1994; Brezo et al. 2006; Krueger et al. 2000). In the psychiatric/psychological literature, suicidal individuals have been reported to be impulsive, to have exaggerated interpersonal dependence, to be inhibited and to be sensitive to interpersonal rejection. In addition, such individuals often are excessively self-punitive, self-critical and perfectionistic; have increased neuroticism; and are introverted (Lester 1987; Shafii et al. 1985; Street and Kromrey 1994).

Freud (1953) believed that an adults' personality is dependent upon early childhood experiences and may be determined by the age of five years. According to him, the fixations that develop during this infantile stage contribute to one's adult personality and behavior. The ability of a person to resolve internal conflicts at specific stages of their life determines their future to cope and function as a mature adult.

By drawing reference from available literature and theories, our cases also demonstrate a linkage between their personality and suicidal act. All the persons showed specific personal characteristics or traits during the formative and growing years. As Freud said, these traits shaped their adult personality and expressed in various ways in their lives. The kind of personalities they acquired also influenced their actions and thought process when they faced stress and difficulties.

Being an introvert, non-expressive in communicating was a personality trait of 12 persons, while one showed the trait of an overbearing and non-adjusting personality. Two people had the traits of being stubborn, impulsive as well as aggressive or angry when things went against them. In another two cases, one was introvert and non-adjustive behavioral pattern, while the other had a trait of short-tempered personality. Anger, non-patience and non-adjustment issues were common among five people. In nine cases, persons exhibited combination personality traits of shyness, submissiveness and being sensitive. The persona of an extrovert with jovial and friendly nature was true in 18 cases.

Case of Amoli,[11] 25-year-old unmarried female

Amoli ended her life by hanging due to guilt over calling-off her engagement. She was brought up with love and care by the family and grew up to be very emotional and sensitive. She also had an introvert personality. She had one or two friends but her meetings with them was restricted to college hours only. She considered her parents as her friends. She was highly dependent on family and would never do her work all alone. Her brother and father were always available to help her. Even for college her father would drop and pick her up. If she wants to get something from outside, she would send either brother or father or in some cases would accompany them. Her extended families and relatives appreciated her submissive personality and homely attitude. Such responses further influenced her as she thought her behaviour and nature as ideal. Though it turned her to be a non-social person and vulnerable to hardships. Moreover, such personality made Amoli weak as she was not exposed to making adjustments with others or deal with opposing views and arguments. Such imbibed personality later on showed its repercussions when she was engaged. Amoli was engaged to his fiancé for almost six months but most of the time at this stage their relationship was filled with tensions. She would make big issues over trivial things whenever they met or spoke to each other and subsequent one or two days would go on sorting out things which generally happened from fiancé's side. One week before her suicide act, she was upset that her fiancé had not spoken to her since last two to three days. She fought with him over this issue and later decided to call off her engagement. She reported his family that she would not be able to adjust with him, hence wanted to end the relationship. After two days of this decision, she hanged herself in her room. Her mother and grandparents were at home at the time of the incident but unaware of when she took the step. Family felt that it could be due to her guilt of cancelling the engagement as it spoiled the family's image, which never happened in the history of their family. They felt so because one day before her suicide act, she expressed such feelings with the family.

Case of Hiya,[12] 24-year-old unmarried female

Hiya was an introvert personality. While growing up, she became less and less involved with people including her family. She used to remain aloof from the family and talked very less. She only responded when she was asked something or when it was required. She also made a point to not share her feelings and life experiences with them. This resulted in her being secretive and not really wanting to be answerable to anybody. She also developed anger issues. She would hardly mix in her community or neighborhood. Due to her personality, she had a selected set of friends. She had a boyfriend since her school days and both wanted to get married. Her family was unaware about this considering Hiya's secretive and non-sharing attitude. However, later on meeting the boy and his family they accepted the alliance and gave nod to their marriage. Parents of both side decided to meet on an auspicious day so that they can start the marriage ceremonies. However, before parents and kids could meet on the auspicious day, Hiya hanged herself. Since she kept things to herself, her family was clueless as to what led her to take the step as everything was going normal and her wish to marry her childhood friend was about to be fulfilled. They did not know the reason behind her suicide if she had fought with her boyfriend or was it for some other reason.

Case of Bhuvan, 38-year-old married male

Bhuvan hanged himself due to health issues. He was alcoholic. He was stubborn and aggressive since his younger years. He was also impulsive, would often make quick decisions without considering the outcomes, and would later regret about his hasty decisions. Due to impulsivity, he had attempted suicide two times, but he succumbed in the third attempt. Stubborn attitude also created a lot of conflicts and arguments in his married life as well as between siblings. Most of the arguments were centered on his drinking habit and his inability to take care of household duties.

Above cases as well as the other narratives suggest the possibility of link between personality traits and suicidal behavior. The predominant personality traits of a person include the ones who are either introvert, impulsive, aggressive, submissive, sensitive, non-adjusting attitude or extrovert and friendly; support the claim of influencing and directly having suicidal thoughts and attempt. Impulsivity/aggression has been reported as an important suicide risk factor of suicide ideation and is prominently seen in patients with conduct disorder, personality disorders, substance use disorders and bipolar disorders (Mann et al. 1999; Moeller et al. 2001). In our cases some persons had grown up with the personality traits of aggressiveness, short-temperedness and anger issues. These traits were more apparent, during few days before their suicide-attempt or death. At the same time, it is crucial to note that those who had personality traits of an introvert and extrovert nature were also equally susceptible to suicide.

Aspiration and expectation dynamics

Addressing the relationship between aspirations, expectations and stress to that of suicide, Merton (1957) emphasized that stress in an individual is generally a result of frustration because of person's inability to achieve what s/he aspires or wants from life. Seeking for ways to overcome problems but being unable to do so, an individual often feels overwhelmed by emotions of dissatisfaction and helplessness, leading to suicide ideations and suicide. In his opinion, suicide because of failures though seems to be an individual apathy, but is inherently related to the broader social norms, where failures are devalued and successes are praised. Aspirations to become successful in life, therefore, also imply aspiring for one's acceptance or praise in the system or society. On being unable to achieve much nor meeting own expectations, individual feels wrong about him/herself and chooses suicide as a way to escape such feelings. In such conditions, suicide thus turns out to be a social phenomenon, determined by deep-rooted social values of success and failures in the human psyche.

Merton's perspective was relevant in seven cases (one attempted and six completed). Their narratives detail out inner facts about their struggle in meeting aspirations, expectations from life, failures, fears and burden of social image. The disparity between their demands, wishes, wants and the reality made them to choose this path with the hope that it would end all the fears expected of the self and others. Cases in points are presented herein.

> **Case of Tanvi,[13] 27-year-old unmarried female**
> Tanvi took her own life by hanging. She was good at studies and after her twelfth standard (science) she decided to do engineering and completed her B-tech from Allahabad. She worked for a year in few institutes but was interested in studying further. Her friends informed her about the MBA course at IIM-Ahmedabad (IIM-A) as the best course and institute. She got highly motivated and as she was told it to be the best one in the country, she decided to do the course from the same institute and not from any other. With this goal of entering IIM-A in mind, Tanvi started preparing on her own for Common Aptitude Test

(CAT), a prerequisite for the admission into IIM and other Business schools of India. She wrote the exams four times, but in all attempts, she failed. Her ambitious nature to study nowhere else but in IIM-A could be linked to her stubbornness. Her personality made her such that once she set her mind on something, she would have to get it, no matter what she had to do for it. Because of this, she would often get irritated if someone scolded her or explained something that she should not be doing. This behavior played a significant role in her suicide. After failing twice in CAT attempt, her family asked her to do MBA from any other institute/college. But she was undeterred and was firm on her decision. She said that it was her goal to graduate from IIM-A only and would not settle for anything less. Her irritation made the family to not choose that issue in fear of disappointing her and allowed her to do as she wished. When she failed in the fourth attempt, she got angry and frustrated as her dream of being an IIM-A graduate crashed in front of her eyes once again. On knowing the result, Tanvi locked herself in a room the whole day (the day of result) and did not speak to anyone. In the evening, she came down, and reacted normally with everyone and later went up and slept. Next morning she did not turn up for breakfast. During lunchtime (around 1 pm), when she did not come down, her parents went up to see thinking that she is still sleeping. They knocked the door of her room but hearing no reply they pushed open the door and found her hanging from the ceiling fan above her bed. They alerted neighbours and called police, who took Tanvi's body to the hospital where she was declared, brought dead.

Case of Hemant,[14] 27-year-old unmarried male

Hemant died by suicide when he realized that his life was not going the way he aspired as his aspirations of a 'good and settled life' were not met. He belonged to a middle-class family and his educational background was in Mechatronics engineering. Since his childhood, he was serious about his life and the things he wanted to do and achieve. He saw himself leading a good life, a well-to-do job with great money and a settled marital life. Hemant also wished to renovate his house or if possible buy a new house, better than the one he and his family was staying, so that all could live comfortably. After finishing his education, he began seeking for a job to fulfill his wishes. Meanwhile, he received the information that many of his friends were planning to go abroad for higher education and work, which would mean raising their social and income standards. He also decided to look at these options with the hope of being able to go abroad and settle down. He and his friends appeared in one of the competitive exams. The exam was necessary and must be cleared, in order to apply for a visa and to get admissions in various universities in any foreign country. Unfortunately, most of his friends cleared the exam but he could not as he was short of a few marks of the required numbers to pass it. He was disheartened over failing in this exam and further got depressed when he saw his friends leaving him and the country to continue their studies at selected universities abroad. Hemant also wanted to go like them especially with the hope to earn and make money easily and was prepared to do hard-work for. When his dream didn't materialize and felt apart, he began questioning himself and his life. He kept on pondering about why he failed in exam even though he had studied from an English medium school and was much better than few of his friends who managed to go abroad. His parents consoled him and made him understand that he could do well in his life and fulfill his dreams by being in India. He just had to look for good job. Almost after two months of this episode, he started looking for a job. He got one good opportunity and was happy, but it was short lived as the department of the company he was posted in had shut down. While searching for another job, soon he received a call from the company about his selection. But this good news was also momentary, as the company never called him with further joining details. He was not happy with the things going on in his life, but he kept looking for a job, though failed in finding a satisfactory job of his choice. In the process, the failures that he was experiencing, first, failing in exam and second letdowns in job, made him feel low most of the time. They also reminded him, these incidents being hurdles that shattered his aspired life. In such situation, his parents kept motivating him as much as they could but did not bring any major change in his thinking. To add up into his miseries, he saw all his cousins and friends doing well in their respective lives. This again erupted in his mind to compare his life with them. He felt that he was much better than his cousins and friends in terms of his knowledge of things like computer, conversing in English but still far behind them without any job. Unlike him they are placed better and making their parents proud. Even on his marriage front, Hemant felt unlucky, as he was unable to find any good proposal. He started relating all the things comparatively, in terms that – no job means his inability to buy a new house, which in turn meant no marriage, as a girl would like to marry a settled boy and live in a good house. All these thoughts were building in him since six months prior to his suicide, making him depressed, resentful and mostly low. It was worsened in the last 15 days leading up to his suicide death during which he was disinterested in self-care. In these days, he started feeling that because of him, his parents are upset and suffering and to stop their sorrow he thought it was better to die. For this, he planned a trip to *Amarnath* and thought of ending his life by jumping from height but canceled it at the last moment. To lift up his mood, his father even told him to go and buy a bike (₹ 1,00,000) which he craved for a long time before six months. Riding it kept him alright for a few days, but soon the vicious cycle of negative thoughts began. The thoughts, affected his sleeping habit, as he was up all night and would sleep during the day. Constantly thinking about the failures, and not able to fulfill what he wished for himself and parents, one day when he was alone at home he hanged himself and died.

The above-mentioned two cases highlight that failures nurture negative thought processes in individuals affecting them to question their worth of life. Disturbance over failures drifts individuals away from built-up hopes, desires or ambitions, which they themselves or others expected from their life. A pain over not being able to live up to those hopes and aspirations makes them emotionally exposed to stressful thoughts and worries about the self, hence increasing their chance of ending life. Like in Tanvi's case, her continuous failed attempts in entrance exams for a prestigious institution instilled sadness and low self-esteem in her mind. The strain, stress and inability to accomplish her goal and adamancy to not step back from her decision of entering IIM-A as it would lead to embarrassment, and gags from peers and relatives had pushed her towards suicide. Similarly, in the case of Hemant, failing in exam to study abroad and work was a blow to his aspired dream of future life and settled marital life. The failure allowed him to think low of himself compared to others in his peer group and cousins. In both the cases, they had dreams to achieve something good in life that depended on the success of their educational or economic achievement. They raised themselves to believe about their ability to attain a higher level of accomplishments. However, the burden of real or anticipated failures turned their life upside down and in distress. They suffered from painful bouts due to perceived failure and the painful awareness of being deficient. In order to escape from the burden or facing any form of further pain and failures, suicide became an appealing way for both. Baumeister (1990) considers such acts to be an escape from 'painful self-awareness'. There is a fair amount of evidence linking suicide with negative views of the individual self. In studies of suicidal adolescents, for example, researchers frequently find that feelings of personal worthlessness and rejections are central factors (Bonner and Rich 1987; Tishler et al. 1981).

Mental sickness: depression, abnormal behavioral changes

Mental health is a state of well-being, whereby individuals recognize their abilities to cope with the normal stresses of life, work productively and fruitfully and contribute to their communities (WHO 2003). For all individuals, mental, physical and social health are vital strands of life closely interwoven. This interdependent relationship impacts one's mental health which is crucial to the overall well-being of individuals, societies and countries. However, mental health and mental disorders are not accorded the same importance as physical health issues and have been largely ignored, neglected or overlooked.

Mental disorders affect everyone, irrespective of age, gender, residence and living standards, even though some groups are at a higher risk for certain illnesses; only the impact varies (NIMHANS 2016). Furthermore, mental disorders are known to be caused by a complex interaction of biological, social, environmental, cultural and economic factors (WHO 2001). There are series of mental disorders that people may have, some of them include anxiety disorders, mood disorders, depression, bipolar disorder, schizophrenia, dementia and Alzheimer. Studies from developed and developing countries revealed that 60%–90% of suicidal behaviors were associated with some form of mental illness and/or substance abuse (Gururaj and Issac 2004; Harris and Barraclough 1977). This association could be contested, as it is untrue to say that all those with mental illness would die by suicide or all those ending their lives would be suffering from mental disorders.

Five persons (two attempters and three completers) in our study showed certain mental disorders that increased their vulnerability to suicide. In three incidences, family witnessed sudden behavioral changes among the persons, which made it difficult to assess the reason or cause for the disorder.

Case of Jay,[15] 32-year-old unmarried male

Jay was going through depression and experienced bouts of loneliness as he lived alone. He had no siblings, his father died and his maternal uncle separated him from his mother without her will to live with her son. This happened when he was still in college. Once, uncle took his mother, he never allowed mother or son to meet. After some months, Jay got to know that his uncle did it for the property of his father, which was on his mother's name. He was already upset with his father's death, and separation from mother disturbed him. With no mental, social and financial support, Jay found himself surrounded by problems and difficulties. With no stable financial source, he dropped out of college and managed his livelihood through private jobs. Due to his mental health, his performance at job suffered that lead him to seek and leave jobs very often. His life went into depression and he began remaining aloof showing withdrawal symptoms. This increased his vulnerability to the thoughts of self-harm, as he used to talk about ending life in formal conversation with his office colleagues and neighbours. One day, when he was alone, his mental state overpowered him and he drank poison but with timely intervention, he was saved by his neighbor. The neighbor had finally, adopted him as their son, and provided security, in order to liberate him from depression and start his life afresh. Jay now assist in the business of his adopted family.

Case of Namit,[16] 38-year-old male

Namit, was married and lived with his parents and siblings. He was a quiet and shy man and was friendly with selected few. He cleared his tenth standard but decided not to study further as he was not interested and started working. He got married at the age of 27, which was an arranged alliance, but after one year, he divorced his wife. According to Namit's sister, his wife was money-minded and of demanding nature that created problems between them as he was unable to fulfill her wishes. In addition, his wife also got pregnant and aborted the child without his knowledge and consent, which saddened him. Moreover, after abortion she straightaway went to her parents' house from the hospital rather than coming to her marital home. It is said that she did it with an intention of ending their marriage. Even after losing his child, he visited her and tried to reconcile with his wife. On noticing her reluctance towards continuing this marriage, he finally divorced her. After few months of Namit's divorce his family started to witness some changes in him. One day suddenly he went to a barber and had his hair cut short, which left his family perplexed because, since his younger days, he had a lot of attachment and love for his long hair. He took care of it, religiously and was particular and passionate about it. Family was also puzzled as he chose to visit a new barber, which was unusual as he had a fixed barber to whom he regularly visited since ten years. In the following five days after his haircut and up to his suicide, his family also saw him behaving strangely. For instance, Namit insisted his mother to take him to a particular temple, which was unusual of his behaviour, as he never went to any temple. Likewise, in his home, he began stomping around the floor loudly while walking and asking his family about his daily routines (bathing space, his clothes etc.). Sensing that Namit was behaving abnormal due to the 'evil eye', his family took him to a temple for *puja*, but even there, he behaved strangely. He purchased all the garlands from a nearby vendor and garlanded the idol, himself that was again uncommon of him. In the temple, he began asking for PM Narendra Modi's phone number from strangers. He also shouted at temple visitors as he thought someone has stolen his footwear by saying that he had a lot of strength and would punish the guilty. At home, he began to call people whose numbers he had gathered from the newspapers classified section as well as, to his friends and relatives asking them about Prime minister's number. His unsuccessful attempt in getting number made him scream and get angry over them, as they are not sharing what he was asking for. He mentioned that he wanted the number, as he wants to give his idea to Prime Minister that would eliminate the need for any soldier to sacrifice himself and can save everyone. His family tried to calm him down and wanted to take him to the hospital but he did not let anyone come closer or touch him. On the day of his act, he showed similar behavior, his extended family gathered considering that he needs help and would take him for the treatment forcefully. They remained awake until 2.30 am observing him; however, they found him hanging from the ceiling in his room at 6.30 am.

Case of Kantaben,[17] 50-year-old married female

Kantaben started showing abnormal behaviour two years prior to her suicide death, but it become more sudden few days preceding to her act. She was of reserved nature and belonged to a low socio-economic group. She was working as a housemaid and lived with husband, two sons, daughter-in-laws and grandchildren. Her husband was an alcoholic and most of the time was in drunken state but never engaged in abusive behavior. He worked as a peon in an office. He almost stopped working after Kantaben's death due to his drinking habit. It was reported by daughter-in-law, that everything was going normal in the household until two years ago, when Kantaben first started behaving differently. She would keep muttering incoherently throughout the day. She would talk non-stop, would laugh and have conversations even when she was alone. At this time, she would become abusive and would hit her husband or other family members without any reason or fault. She was also living with a thought that someone was out to hurt and destroy her. She would keep telling family that everyone surrounding her is talking about her. Moreover, she also doubted her husband constantly with a feeling that he was engaged in extramarital affairs. The regular appearance of such behavior made the family concern and they took her to the hospital. Psychiatrist prescribed some medicines based on her behavioral symptoms. The medications showed some positive results in terms of suppressing such behaviour. But when she stopped taking them after feeling better, the symptoms would return and she would start behaving illogically again. With all these abnormality, she was regular to her job, but her family asked her to quit it. They were worried for the reason that she could harm her employer in case her symptoms erupts in front of them. Since medications were controlling her behaviour, so when family forced her to take medicines, she would become abusive. Surrounding with behavioral disorders, one night, Kantaben poured kerosene on herself and set fire on herself. Hearing her scream, family and neighbors doused the fire but she succumbed to her burn injuries soon. She also tried to kill herself in the same manner before and when asked why she contemplated it, Kantaben told that already someone wanted to hurt her, so she wanted to do it herself rather than from anybody else's hand. Though, she survived in the first attempt, her second attempt became fatal and she cost her life.

Case of Savita,[18] 55-year-old married female
Savita from lower middle-income group lived with her husband, unmarried daughter and son. She was living with the mental disorder, but unlike Kantaben, she was suffering from it for the past 12 years of her life. She was being treated for her behavioural disorder and was into medications. Her father also suffered from the mental illness. Part of treatment also involved counseling, but she refused to go for it and was fine with the medicines. Before her suicide death, abnormal symptoms and disturbing episodes became more often. Her family found her reacting abnormal over certain issues. For instance suddenly she started worrying about the food items at home and kept saying that the food will finish and family will not have anything to consume next day. The fear made her stop the family from feeding the stray cows and dogs, which she used to do it normally. Family also saw her appetite getting reduced as she would skip her meal or eat very little. Other daily behaviours also changed such as she started sleeping excessively during the day and stopped bathing and taking care of herself. She also stopped doing any household work. This was an odd behaviour as she loved and felt happy to take care of her family's needs and doing household chores. Due to symptomatic behavior, Savita also began many frivolous fights with others. Just prior to few days of her death, she was also worried about the quarrels amongst her own siblings in relation to the division and distribution of property that was passed on to them after their mother's death. With all these issues, she started staying quiet, sad and used to stay aloof. On one particular day when she was alone at her home, she hanged herself. On the day of act, Savita had the last conversation with her son in the evening, but to her son it didn't had any pointers or inclinations about the step his mother would take. Her husband discovered her hanging body when he returned from office around eight in the night, by that time she was already dead.

The cases of Namit, Kantaben and Savita suggests that they all were suffering from the mental disorder of schizophrenia that affected their thoughts and behavior. The disorder caused distortions of reality with a person having auditory or visual hallucinations, behaving fearful and withdrawn towards circumstances and situations (MDMH 2011). As a common characteristic, all three persons showed disturbances in their behavior that involved fragmented or bizarre delusional beliefs about others or certain events. They were occupied with certain kind of hallucinations or the imaginative world with their own perception, affecting their life and behavior. Their death supports the assumption that suicide may become the common cause of death among people with schizophrenia. The link between the two might also strengthen the fact that prior to their suicidal deaths, all three displayed more signs of abnormal behavior. Their behavioral aspects also collaborated with the studies of Vijayakumar (2006) and Khan et al. (2005) where in the studies they identified the presence of psychiatric illness, stressful life events, depression and substance abuse, poor compliance and any recent interpersonal or economic loss as the risk factors for suicide. While showing the link between suicide and schizophrenia, Gupta et al. (1992) in their two-year follow-up study of patients who attempted suicide with schizophrenia and depression reported that more than 50% of the suicide-attempters had a personality disorder while 42% had neurotic symptoms during childhood and about 23% had a history of drug dependence. Mahla et al. (1992) in their investigation on attempted cases of self-immolation also found the association of their suicidal behavior with the presence of psychiatric and personality disorders. Jain et al. (1999) also revealed the diagnosis of depression, hopelessness and mild to moderated suicidal intent among suicide-attempters.

Financial risk dynamics

The importance of financial difficulties and debt in suicidal behavior is well recognized (Meltzer et al. 2011; Yip et al. 2007). In India, sudden economic bankruptcy and debt was an important risk factor correlated to suicide. Studies, especially in the farming community and the problem of agrarian crisis, have looked into this association more significantly (Behere and Behere 2008; Gill 2005; Ram and Singh 2017).

In our study, six persons were facing economic insecurity in the form of debt (4) and financial loss (2). Among them, one survived and other five died in the suicidal attempt. Their struggle to overcome the monetary burdens was the main reason behind their decision to end life.

> **Case of Krishna,[19] 60-year-old male**
> Krishna, a widower from lower socio-economic group was living with his married son and unmarried daughter. He lost his wife due to cancer, some years ago. All his family members were employed. He used to drive an auto rickshaw on rent but later started a *sev-usal laari* (food-street shop) of his own. His son was a daily wage labourer, daughter worked in a private office as a cleaner along with doing other odd jobs while his daughter-in-law worked as a housemaid. Few months before his suicide, he borrowed ₹ 30,000 from some lender, in order to pay the outstanding house-rent. In general, he did not mention any of his difficulties with his family members but he shared with them his difficulty in re-paying the debt. Dwindling income from his *laari* and his addiction to alcohol, further increased his worries as he was unable to pay the debt. When lender started asking him to pay the amount, his worries further raised. With the acquired stress and his inability to pay the borrowed money, on one fine day when everyone was asleep in the night, he woke up, went to the kitchen, poured kerosene on him, and let

himself on fire. With all the burns, he ran outside and started screaming which woke up his family and neighbors. They poured water on him and rushed him to the hospital where the doctors began treatment but were unable to save him as he succumbed to his burn injuries by the morning. His family is slowly paying off the debts.

Case of Vijay,[20] 43-year-old married male

Vijay also took his own life due to the burden of debt. He belonged to the upper middle class and lived with extended family in separate households. He completed his ITI diploma and joined the family business of printing press. His father started it, but lately, it was entirely managed by two brothers. He also began doing a side business of a real estate broker. He was a selfless and friendly man who was always ready to help his neighbors and friends financially and in many other ways. Few years before his suicide, one of his friends asked him some money, which he needed urgently and promised to repay soon. As he himself did not have the money his friend required, he sought to help him through private moneylender and arranged the amount (few lakhs), on his guarantee. The friend, however, failed to return the money to him on stipulated time. Moreover, he began to avoid his phone calls. In case he picked, he would give an array of excuses to avoid returning him money. Meanwhile, the lender from whom Vijay borrowed money began to ask him initially at a normal pace, but later lender resorted to aggressive follow-ups for recovering the money. To avoid these hassles, he started borrowing from his friends to repay the amount. He entered a vicious cycle, borrowing money from one friend to repay another friend and carrying the cycle. In between all this the friend for whom he actually borrowed the money from money-lender, showed no signs of repaying the money and kept on dodging the matter with more excuses. Because of this vicious cycle of debts, Vijay had to mortgage his personal house and his shop (without anyone knowledge) to pay off all the borrowed money to his other friends and the moneylender. With the mortgaged amount, he was able to pay only the interests while the principle amount kept growing. All the debtors started asking him to repay the borrowed money, by calling or visiting him at his office and house and harassing him. He was tired of answering to all the people he owed money and thought that he would never be able to get out of this cycle of debt. The stress and worry negatively affected his health and he suffered from a heart ailment. Due to constant worries, his real estate brokerage business also suffered. The poor printing press business also affected his household income. He did not inform his parents and brother about debt and mortgage, but they had some idea that he was under some difficulty. They came to know about the real issue when his wife told them that they were living at her parents' house, since many months. When the family tried to intervene, Vijay told half-truth, got frustrated and irritable, and refused to talk more on the issue. Just a few days before his suicide attempt, the calls from moneylender and friends increased. On the day of his attempt, he left home in the morning and purchased a bottle of insecticide, which he consumed on the sidewalk of the main street road. Co-incidentally, his brother-in-law was passing by and saw him drinking something when he called him he did not respond but fell down on the sidewalk. He rushed to him; saw the insecticide bottle as well as his seizures and frothing. Brother-in-law informed Vijay's father, called for medical help, and took him to the hospital. On reaching the hospital, he was given treatment but he went into coma. After two days, doctors informed his family members that Vijay had no chances of survival. They decided to take him off the ventilator and he passed away. The family wanted to take legal action against the friend, due to which Vijay actually ended up in this debt cycle. Since, they did not possess any written proof in the form of a contract about the money lent or suicide note where friend was blamed, they found themselves at a dead-end, unable to punish him for the abetment of their son's suicide.

Case of Parv,[21] 24-year-old unmarried male

Parv belonged to middle-income group and lived with his parents. As the only child to his parents, he had a normal childhood with good care and love. He was an average student but was not interested in studies. He studied up to tenth and then opted for ITI diploma course, but dropped out when he was in the third semester of his course and started working as he wanted to support his family. His father worked in a private company, but his earning was not sufficient to run the household. Parv did not find the option of studying and doing a job simultaneously doable, hence his decision to start earning looked better to him than studying. He got a job of salesperson at a mobile store, sometimes he also assisted in some minor technical repairing work in the office. His working hours was 10 am to 10 pm, which rarely gave him any time to socialize and to have a personal life like other people of his age. A year ago before his suicidal act, his father and mother fell ill in quick succession and were admitted to hospital. For their treatment, he borrowed money from four to five people (colleagues) interest-free. In order to pay them, he started borrowing money of smaller amounts (₹ 2000 to ₹ 5000) from his friends, without explaining his needs and urgency for the money. He repeatedly kept on borrowing small amounts from multiple friends repaying one another and thus, entered the vicious cycle of debt without even understanding the gravity of the situation. Gradually, his debts started increasing. Since, Parv's father was asked to take rest, he took leave from office and stayed at home. The presence of his parents at home made him all the more anxious as he did not want them to learn about his problem. The tension turned him to start smoking and making him to stay out of the house beyond his working hours. He would leave early and would come late in the night when his parents were asleep. He owed the debtors a total of ₹ 2.5 lakh. The phone calls from the borrowers started increasing and he found himself under a lot of pressure with the worries of how to repay them considering he did not have any kind of savings. On the day Parv attempted suicide, he received a call from one of the debtors when he was out in the market for some work. The talk over phone turned aggressive; since he was in a market, he purchased two bottles of insecticide spray and in a heated moment, drank one of it and fell unconscious. All this happened close to the police station; one police officer saw him lying on the floor and immediately took him to the hospital. On the way, he also informed his parents about the incident. His mother quickly reached the hospital. Parv underwent an extensive treatment for 12 days and was discharged after the medical advice. He was out of stress, as his family knows the truth and reason for his step. At the time of interview, Parv had left the old job and shifted to new one with a higher pay package. With the help of his parents and new job, he had paid half of his debt.

Case of Mohan,[22] 58-year-old married male

Mohan died by suicide as a result of financial loss. He was from upper middle class and lived with his wife, married children, and his wife's brother in a three-storied house. He worked as an accountant for fixed clientele besides doing a private consultation work earning more than ₹ 30,000 per month. His brother-in-law worked in a private firm. Few years before his death, he started a real estate company in collaboration with his cousin brother (maternal aunt's son). He invested a decent amount in this business, as he was interested in the estate market and wanted to continue it after retirement. He never shared any information about this business with his family. Only after his suicide, they got to know the details about it. They believed that the two brothers may have lost huge money in their estate business that made him upset and led him to kill himself. Other than financial loss, it jolted Mohan deep as he had hoped to make this business his future plan and wished to expand it. He started remaining depressed and spending time alone. He continued his daily routine and work as usual but limited his communication. On the day of his act, he went to temple, as it was his fasting day. He came home and went to his office (on the third floor of his house) to complete the pending work. He did not come down until afternoon and his wife assumed that he slept. In the evening, when he did not come downstairs, his wife asked her brother to call him for tea. He called his name repeatedly, but on not getting response, he went upstairs only to find him hanging. On hearing his scream, wife came up and was unable to respond. Neighbors gathered and informed police and emergency service. Medical team informed the family that he was already dead.

In the above four cases, financial risk in the form of debt or loss was the prominent reason behind their suicide. The risk built up pressure and stress in them and seeing their inability to pay back, they thought to escape from the ordeal by ending their life. In Vijay's case, his friendly and helpful nature jeopardized his life as he lost his savings and entered vicious cycle of debt that increased his mental burden and a way to his suicide. Mohan opted suicide, as he was shaken and unable to cope with the fact that the dream he longed for seriously had failed. The loss of money further added to his dilemma. Particular to these four cases, it can be stated that economic constraints, bankruptcy or debt trap results in life-crisis filled with insecurities and uncertainties, compelling many individuals to see suicide as their only option to come out from the uncertain situations (Kar 2010; Praveenlal n.d.).

Social and community conscience dynamics

Despite being a complex social issue, suicide is normally conceptualized as a medico-legal problem rather than as an issue of social concern, especially in the Indian context (Colucci and Lester 2013; Vijayakumar and Thilothammal 1993). Exploring the experiences and interactions of the individuals with their cultural and social environment is essential to acquire a wider understanding of suicide. Such explorations may bring out certain socio-cultural variables that might have a far-ranging impact on suicide.

It is believed that individual's behavior is deeply influenced by the way the social and collective life of a society is organized. As each society has its own set of rules, values and norms, it also has a constraining effect on individual behaviors (Fuse 1997). As the society draws lines and sets limits for its protection with possible norms, values, customs, structures and culture, they do possibly contribute to the suicidal ideations among its members. When persons are unable to express their thoughts, feelings and behaviors, and find themselves in complex and conflicting scenarios, the situations induce them for suicide, knowingly or unknowingly (Samithamby and Sathiyasegar 2015).

Sense of failure in fulfilling social responsibility

In our study also some aspects of social and community consciences, knowingly or unknowingly, became an inherent risk factor for the individuals' self-harm. The sense of expected social responsibilities and the failure in fulfilling them were embedded in the narrative of five persons. There was a burden of helplessness, restless and frustration for not playing the role of head of the household or as a protector effectively.

Case of Vitthalbhai, [23] **60-year-old married male**

Vitthalbhai was from middle-income group, worked as a construction contractor and was earning enough to sustain the family. However, he always had the feeling that he has shortcomings and is not doing sufficient for his family especially in terms of ample savings. The feeling erupted in him because his work was not progressing and showing any fruitful results. He would feel about how his family would survive once he goes away. This thought always haunted him thus giving rise to tension and stress. He felt that despite all his work for so many years, he was unable to gather huge savings, which his family can enjoy for leading a comfortable life or can help them at the time of crisis. This feeling became stronger when he was diagnosed with Tuberculosis (TB) and was admitted to the hospital frequently for treatment. His ill-health complicated his feelings as he was not able to work properly. The expenses of treatment were rather depleting his savings. Moreover, it affected his overall mood and behavior. He started feeling that he should have done more than what he did till now and was worried about his inability to save enough to help his children in their time of need. His failure in the responsibility of giving a secure environment to his family made him criticize himself and his achievements strongly, making him remain upset, and that aroused more concerns and fears. Being a reserved person, Vitthalbhai did not share his feelings with anyone not even with his wife and preferred to keep it all to himself. Lately, he also became receptive to the self-harm reports in the newspapers or in the neighborhood. He would often discuss about them in the gathering with friends or in conversation with family members. While struggling with all the negative thoughts he had built up in his mind, one day when he was alone at home he finally hanged himself and died.

Similarly, in the case of another male of 24-year-old (case of Parv), suicidal attempt was due to the stress of debt and his inability to repay it. However, the in-built reason was his concern for his parents and his expected role of caring and being responsible towards them, considering that he was the only son to his parents. He entered the debt cycle in fulfilling this role as he borrowed money for their treatment. He suffered from all the difficulties and harassment from the lenders but did not show his stress or pressure to parents, as it would hurt them. Keeping all the stress to himself, along with continued harassment he found himself frustrated and one day, he chose to consume poison to end his life. But timely intervention assured his survival. After disclosing the reason behind suicide-attempt, Parv's parents encouraged him to own up to the incident and put it behind. The duality of expectations and sense of failure could also be inferred from his mother's view who feels proud of his son. For her, whatever Parv has done (i.e., borrowing money that led to a suicide-attempt) was to fulfill his social duty as a son and to take care of his parents well-being.

Sense of guilt/shame over the events and impact on family/ self-social image

As an inherent reason for their suicide, four persons showed signs of feeling guilty/ashamed. They believed that their behavior insulted the family and risked their social image other than their own.

Case of Sneha,[24] 21-year-old unmarried female

Sneha who was unmarried attempted suicide as she thought her action had brought shame to the family. She lived in a slum with her parents and younger brother. She had two elder sisters who were married and lived out of Vadodara. Her father was a daily wage earner and mother worked as milk supplier of their locality and sometimes as a vegetable vendor. She studied up to tenth standard at a local government school and discontinued her studies thereafter. She started helping her mother in selling vegetables along with helping in household chores. Her maternal grandmother lived in another area in the city and she would often visit her and stay there for one or two months at a stretch. Her parents did not object as they assumed it as her love and helping hand to the grandmother. This was happening for almost three years. Once, while she was in grandmother's place, she suddenly came back home. When her parents asked, why she returned early, she did not give any reason. A few days later, a group of people living in the same area as her grandmother, came to the house and demanded to meet her parents. When Sneha's parents came, the group started yelling and, hurling abuses against her name. They told her parents about alleged relation between her and a boy for the past two years. The group were actually the relatives of the same boy. Relatives stated that it is because of the affair that she often visited and stayed at the grandmother's home. They pointed fingers at Sneha's character and even abused the parents saying that they encouraged her for this love affair. Her mother informed relatives that they were completely unaware about this and did not wish to do anything in this matter. Boy's relatives also, claimed that they had done a court marriage, but Sneha vehemently refused it. The issue was sorted there and the boy's relatives left, but only after threatening the family to make their daughter stay away from the boy. This whole episode made Sneha's father angry on her, while mother got upset and repeatedly told that she had insulted the entire family by her "wrongdoings". Harsh words and behavior of parents affected her deeply with a distressed mood. On the next day of this incident, Sneha did not join her mother in the work of selling vegetables. She rather kept on remembering the incident while feeling ashamed, and guilty. She did not talk to anyone and sat alone for most of the day. She would remember about boy's relatives yelling at her in front of everyone and that she brought shame and insult to the family. She felt that her family had to face the embarrassment in the neighborhood, due to her. On the consecutive three days, she again refused to accompany her mother by telling that she was not well and wanted to take rest. During these days too she mostly remained aloof and was thinking about the incident. On the fourth day, sometime later, when every family members left for their work (father to his job, mother to the market and brother to school), she picked up a bottle of phenyl and drank about a cup full. She started feeling uneasy and decided to lay down. At this time her mother returned from the market for some work and found her laying down on the floor. When asked the reason for resting down she informed that she had consumed poison. Hearing so, mother quickly took her to the hospital where she was kept for eight days under observation. When she became stable, she was discharged. While she was at the hospital, the boy with whom she had an affair got married to the girl selected by his parents. When asked about her suicide attempt, Sneha told that it was an impulsive one and done out of guilt. She felt bad about the parents' insults and a fear of facing them because of the ruckus incident by the relatives of the rumored boyfriend. She however regretted about the suicide step and mentioned not to repeat it. After a month of her suicide act, she agreed to meet prospective suitors arranged by her mother for the marriage. Sneha, said that she did not want to make her family suffer more due to her and wanted to follow what they had planned for her without any resistance. Her acceptance of marriage was more out of submission rather than free will or choice.

Case of Mahesh,[25] 49-year-old married male

The suicidal death of Mahesh was triggered because of his wife's extramarital relationship, which in his view contested his 'social image' in the society. He dropped out of school after tenth standard and started working as a labourer. He continued to be a daily wage laborer in the city till his death, but on days when there was no contract labor, he would go and try to find work in the neighboring villages. He married at the age of 18, with the girl chosen by his family members and soon became a father to a son. Mahesh was a calm, mature and honest man and had no issues in marital life. He was well known in the community and was helpful by nature. His married life of 30 years was going fine until the time his wife met a man (two years prior to Mahesh's suicide) with whom she got involved in a romantic relationship. Some person in the neighbourhood revealed about the affair to him, some months before his suicide. He got upset and confronted his wife. His wife confirmed about the relationship and asked him to give divorce so that she could start a new life with that man. This led to a fight between the couple. The next morning (after confrontation day), he woke up to see that his wife had left the house with all her belongingness sometime in the middle of the night. This act implied decision of her leaving him permanently. This incident came as a big shock that affected Mahesh in two ways: first, his turmoil on how his wife could leave him for another man after spending so many years with him, and second, thoughts of what society would say about him and her. As he was well known in the locality, he started being in stress thinking about the consequences of everyone knowing about his wife leaving him for another man. The emotional upheaval resulted in his downward spiral as he stopped going to his job and would sit at home all day. He also started drinking and every time when he was drunk, he would binge. He started withdrawing himself by not talking much with others and kept all his thoughts to himself. He also did not find pleasure in activities, which he used to love like visiting temple, meeting close friends or going to community gatherings. Gradually he stopped going out of the house almost, completely. He just wanted to completely pass out and avoid any form of social contact. This continued for almost two months. Being unable to make peace with the 'unacceptable crises' in his life, one evening Mahesh chose to end life by hanging. His daughter-in-law first noticed him hanging, raised an alarm, and gathered few people from the locality who called for emergency services as well as, informed the police. He was taken to the hospital where he was declared dead. His estranged wife was aware about his suicide but did not come for the funeral.

Case of Anand,[26] 34-year-old unmarried male

The fear of social image also led Anand towards suicide. He hailed from a family of the Patel community where social prestige and one's image are of utmost importance. His father got an opportunity from his workplace to go abroad (Dubai) for a few years as a part of his job. This opportunity brought great worth to the family as it helped them to grow financially besides gaining their social image in the community. Things were going smooth, until the day when his father went missing when he was going back to join his offshore office after one of his visits to his family in India. Legal procedures, in order, to find his father went on for a long time but nothing came out of it, but their savings reduced. This incident happened when Anand was 11 years, but the loss of father became a huge setback for the family, in terms, of one's image in the society and in monetary matters. After this incident, his mother started working at '*Gruh Udyog*' to run the household. Sometimes, family received help from mother's relatives. Since he was in school when father's incident happened, he continued his studies up to tenth and then enrolled in an ITI course. He wanted to earn early as his mother's sole income was not sufficient. Completing his ITI course, he joined a firm as a supervisor. His decision to work was also because of his father's absence, which steered him to take up the family's responsibilities at an early age. Despite so many years of father's incident, he remained equally disturbed all along, but tried to remain composed and was particular of not showing it in front of anyone while taking care of his family. He also, made it a point to get along with others and maintain good social ties and relations in his community and with extended family. Anand held a very good social image in front of others, especially in his own village. He wished to bring some kind of overall development in his village. While working at the firm, he also started a business venture of prawn farming with his maternal uncle in his village premises by pooling up finances. Since this was going to be an added income for him and his family, he took utmost interest in it. Shortly, after the culmination of this venture, the government sealed the water body that was in use for the farming business as it was a government property and legal permission was not taken before setting up the business. He had invested in the business by taking loans with the belief that his plan would work well. However, its closure resulted in financial losses as well as raised concerns about repaying the loan amount. Additionally, his uncle took away his financial support from the business, creating extra financial burden on him. As the farming business was shut down, Anand did not have enough income to pay off the debts or loan amount other than with his salary. He needed to pay back almost ₹ 2,50,000 and there was no way through which he could raise such a big amount. The situation created trouble as he was now supposed to run his family as well as clear his debts. He tried hard to make up for the setbacks but was unsuccessful. His mother was unaware about the loans he had taken, as he never discussed with her. In order, to pay back debts and loans, he first mortgaged the house in the village built by his father, but his inability to repay the money led to the seizure of house by government officials. This unsettled him because of the emotional bonding and a father's memory attached to the house. Sealing of house in village instilled in Anand the feeling of a substantial deterioration of his image in the village. He tried all his means to get the house back but got more and more into debts, which eventually led him to mortgage some part of his house in Vadodara. Due to debt burden, he even decided not to marry until and unless these financial issues settled down. It was so as he wanted to get married with a good image and not as someone loaded with debts. The financial issues went on for almost two years without any fruitful results. Problems worsened when Anand got to know that his extended family is getting aware of his mortgaged property and financial losses. This was probably the last thing that he had imagined he would ever have to face. Since he was so particular about maintaining his 'social image and prestige', he started feeling guilty about himself. He further, felt as if he was unable to handle the image of the 'head of the household' as a man in the absence of a father. While struggling with financial and social stress, few months

> before his suicidal act he received a letter that made him more tensed. He told his mother not to disclose to others about his whereabouts and workplace details. Probably the letter was about his mortgages and people might be in search of him to get back their money. Because of so much tension and stress, one day he informed his mother that he had some meeting and he would return late. Hence, mother came little late than her usual time from work, but on reaching home found all the doors locked from inside. After repeated knocking at the door and hearing no response, with the help of neighbors' door was broken. They found Anand hanging with the ceiling fan in one of the interior rooms. People took him to the hospital but he was reported dead. His mother was devastated by his action, as she never thought of his suicidal act. His mother still gets calls for debt clearance. Family has even written a letter to the bank stating their poor economic condition.

Above-mentioned three incidents seemed suicide due to love affair and financial debt but, inherently, all of them had the external reality of condition of 'bringing down persons social image', and belief of it being 'against social standards'. In Sneha's case, she was overpowered by the feeling of guilt and shame, which the incident brought to her family. A continuous nagging of parents especially the mother of how it was a great mistake and that it was her fault that the family had to face lifelong made her insecure and compelled to believe that she had brought humiliation and disrespect to the family's social prestige. Since her action hampered the family's reputation she wanted to end her life to cover up the entire stigma. In case of Mahesh, the departure of wife after living for so many years without him being abusive created depressive tendencies in him, along with the feeling of shame and guilt and a bleak view of the future. He was stuck in a dilemma of looking at this incident as an affront to his manhood. In Anand's case, more than the debts, probably it was his belief of tainted reputation in society that pushed him so far that he chose to take his life. Among all three, overthinking and worrying about the actions and its consequences due to stressful situations, and being unable to maintain one's false self-image formed feelings of guilt, shame and remorse. They all felt disgraced on facing reality, hence, chose suicide. Thus, the loss of hope, guilt, the absence of a choice and overpowering grief are few human conditions that may lead to suicide.

Deprivation dynamics

Feeling of burden or fear due to health issues

There were 12 persons occupied with the feeling of deprivation and burden. This was mainly due to their health issues. They were under heavy medication, had surgeries or visited doctors frequently prior to few months or days of their suicide.

Case of Rajubhai,[27] 80-year-old married male

Rajubhai took his own life because he was tired of the series of health issues and hospitalization process. He lived with his wife. He had two sons and two daughters. One daughter and her marital family was also living at the same colony. He was a railway employee and survived on his pension of ₹ 15,000. He lived his life well and was content with no complaints regarding anything or event. The only problem in his life was his health. Three years before his death he suffered from an eye illness of a recurrent blood clot which hindered his vision. To cure it he had to take 58 injections which was a very painful and expensive process (₹ 1,200 for each injection). Sometime later, Rajubhai suffered with prostate and underwent a surgery. He was facing a lot of difficulty during this period but survived all, due to his wife and family's support. His eye illness and prostate was cured but the experience had affected him psychologically. He started worrying and became more fearful about his health. He feared that his health would again deteriorate and cause him more pain and suffering. He was already tired of his previous illnesses, frequent visits to hospitals and medications further created issues. Moreover, his hospitalization made him scared. He did not wish to spend his old age in more pain than what he was already going through. He dreaded any other health issue. He constantly remained worried and would often say to his family that he cannot tolerate the pain anymore. Fear concerning his health had completely overtaken him. After few weeks of his prostate surgery, one afternoon he asked his wife to prepare tea for him while he went upstairs, poured some kerosene on his body and burnt himself. On seeing smoke, neighbors thought the house was on fire, they began shouting and alerted his wife who was in kitchen. On going upstairs, they found his burnt body laying down. He was taken to the hospital where he was declared dead on arrival.

Case of Meena,[28] 58-year-old married female

Burden of illness enabled Meena to end her life. She was illiterate, got married at a young age and bore three children. Her two daughters were married off and she lived with her husband, son and his wife in a small two-floor house with first floor belonging to her husband's elder brother. Her husband worked as carpenter on contract basis. She started working as a cook at a Jain temple after her son's wedding. She was very well-known in the premises and was appreciated for her cooking skills. For the past three years before her suicide-attempt, she was suffering from acidity and high blood pressure (BP) and was taking medication. In the last few months (leading up to death), she began to face many health complications. She suffered from the problems of gas and bloating and would constantly complain of a strong burning sensation in her stomach. She consulted many doctors but the problem remained as it was. The symptoms would come back after the course of prescribed medicines was completed. She saw no cure of her troubles despite meeting so many doctors and taking medicines. Rather multiple medical tests made her feel dejected. She started believing that now it was impossible to ascertain what was wrong with her, so there is no way that she would recover. Besides, her dependency on medicines grew, as after taking them she would do her work normally. Unhappy with herself because of her ailments, one day when Meena and her daughter-in-law were at home, she went to the market telling the daughter-in-law that she was going to get her medicines. She returned from the market and sat in the hall. Suddenly her daughter-in-law who was working in the kitchen adjacent to the hall heard some noise. On coming out she found Meena laying on the floor, frothing with the bottle of pesticide lying beside her. She immediately alerted the family and neighbors who called the medical emergency service. Meena was taken to the hospital, where after receiving treatment for two days, she eventually passed away.

Case of Ritesh,[29] 17-year-old unmarried male

Medical issues triggered the suicide of Ritesh. He lived with his parents and younger brother in a locality of the lower income group. He studied up to fifth standard and discontinued his education. He joined the neighborhood's small provisional store as a helper. His father worked as a daily wage laborer and mother as housemaid. In the past few months before his suicide, he had been facing medical issues. He was admitted to the hospital three times in the period of six months for the primary complain over high fever and body ache. In all the three occasions, after going with complete blood profile and other medical tests, no severe disease/illness was detected other than that of low hemoglobin. He was given many medicines after every discharge from the hospital. Ritesh started feeling distressed, and was bothered about his ill health. He was also very upset with the frequent hospital visits and the fact that no doctors could pinpoint as to what was wrong with him. On many occasions, he expressed a strong desire to stop his medications, as he was tired of taking them. He wanted some doctor to make a diagnosis so that he would know the reason behind his illness. Everyone made him run to lab tests but with no indication of severe abnormality of his frequent ailment. Struggling with no answer to the questions over his health problem, one day he went to his job in the morning and came back for lunch. Rather than following the daily routine, i.e., eating lunch and returning to the job, he instead stayed and hanged himself in the kitchen, only house-area with cement ceiling. His mother found his hanging body when she returned in the afternoon from her job. She screamed and alerted the neighbors who called the police and emergency services. He was reported dead on arrival at the hospital. Other than health issue, he had no financial or other personal stress.

Case of Sumanben,[30] 53-year-old married female

Sumanben also felt burdened and fearful due to her health hazards. She married in her late teens and had four daughters, all married. She lived with her husband along with his elder brother and his family. Her husband was carpenter and she worked as housemaid. To earn supplement income she also prepared artificial jewelry for idols/gods at various temples in her own and neighboring *pols* (lanes). In the months preceding her death, she started facing some difficulty in working, as she would frequently feel fatigued and had a feeling of malaise. She shared about her health discomfort to her younger daughter and on her insistence visited a doctor. Medical tests showed heart abnormality, which she initially informed no one but later disclosed it to younger daughter and sister-in-law. She wanted them not to tell about it to any other member as the house was busy with her granddaughter's wedding preparation. She did not want to give unnecessary stress to anybody on this good occasion. For Sumanben this illness was the new development as she was already living with other sets of health issues like diabetes and high BP. She had also been operated to remove the cataract in her eyes. Due to her heart problem, she even stopped going to her job. The family thought that she took leave for the marriage preparations. Sumanben was however, dejected with the diagnosis of the heart abnormality and was also tired of taking the various medicines prescribed by doctors for multiple illnesses. She would often say that the medicines were strong, and not good for health. She anticipated about the heart operation and further doses of medicines to cure it but fear over entire issues resulted in aversive thoughts about self which lead her thinking to end life. On the day of suicide, she woke up little earlier than the usual time. Her husband was busy in storing water for the housework while younger daughter was taking bath and other members were still sleeping. She went to the kitchen and set herself ablaze using kerosene; neighbors noticed her first and raised an alarm as well as called medical services. The uproar made her husband and other family members realize about the incident. They took her to the hospital, where she gave the statement to the police and doctors that she set herself ablaze as she was tired of her health problems and the medications. She passed away after 24 hours in the hospital.

In all the four incidences the trigger for their suicide was the diagnosis of various health issues and feeling of pain and prolonged medications. The illness affected their daily life and the sense of no cure to their pain implanted suicidal thoughts in them. Circumstances like debilitating diseases with no positive prognosis and the development of depression understandably lead persons to the active seeking of ways to end their lives. Among individuals, illness raises the feeling of their burden to the family along with the sense of unproductiveness. Such feelings influence their vulnerability to suicide (Van Orden and Conwell 2016; Van Orden et al. 2015). Physical illness may also interact with other psychological and social variables to promote suicide. The illness of a recurrent chronic nature may interact with depression and relapses may lead to hopelessness and despair, all of which may precipitate or lead to suicide (Baldwin and Jolley 1986; Murphy 1983).

Feeling of self-blame, rejection and failure

Awareness of self as falling on important standards can follow aversive states of negative affect among individuals. Seeing oneself as plummeting short of one's ideals, duties, obligations and moral standards produces dejection or agitation aggravates depressed mood, guilt and anxiety. These effects could become a reason for suicidal thoughts and ideations (Higgins 1987; Higgins et al. 1985). While showing the relationship between shame, guilt and suicide Hastings et al. (2002) argue that these two factors are significant contributors to suicidal risk. When somebody feels sense of shame, they feel isolated and cut off from a valued social group. This can lead to the feeling of a burden, causing a sense of one's liability and self-loathing.

Seven persons in our study (five completed and two attempted) were surrounded and living with the burden of self-blame, rejection or self-failure.

> **Case of Srishti,[31] 26-year-old female**
> Srishti, a divorcee was stressed with the thought of guilt and self-blaming over her short-lived marriage. She had an arranged marriage but separated within a year. She faced difficulties in her one year of marriage, especially from her husband's stepmother. She tolerated everything without sharing it either to husband or to her own family. One day her husband dropped her to natal home, with the intention of not taking her back and an indication of ending their marriage. Her family tried their best to save marriage, but finally resorted for divorce with mutual consent. During this period Srishti, remained upset over her rejection by the husband, along with a feeling of inadequacy and non-acceptance towards her by the marital home. The feelings made her uninterested to talk to anyone regarding her marriage or separation. After few months of her divorce, when her family discussed about her remarriage, she refused as she did not want to go through all the pain and rejection, once more. Moreover, remarriage talks made her feel bad about herself with a feeling that her parents want her to be remarried because she was a burden to them. Finally, the stress accumulated over

a series of events – end of her marriage, family's insistence to remarry, guilt of being a non-accepted member drove her to end life, by hanging.

Case of Aakash,[32] 24-year-old unmarried male

Aakash died by suicide over the guilt of blaming himself for the death of his fiancee. Since his schooling days, he was in a relationship with a girl, which continued even during college years. He was serious about the relationship and both disclosed about it to their family just three years prior to his death. On knowing about it, families from both sides did not object as they belonged to the same community. They decided for their engagement and wanted to meet on auspicious day to fix the arrangements and also about the wedding functions. But just few days before the decided date of meeting, his girlfriend killed herself in her home by hanging. The incident shattered and broke him emotionally. He started withdrawing himself from family. He would have crying spells and would often wake up in the middle of the night crying. Due to the incident, he also stopped conversing much with anyone. He was emotionally under a lot of guilt and could not think of his life without her. Aakash felt that he might have done something wrong or hurt her unknowingly, which might have motivated his girlfriend to end life by suicide. Self-blaming instilled suicidal ideations in him, as he would tell her mother that 'she is waiting for me in heaven', and 'I can't live without her even for a day, I will soon go and join her'. Three months passed and then one day he took his life. On the day of act, Aakash followed his regular morning routine. In the afternoon, he dropped his mother to a temple where she used to give voluntary services. His mother asked him to sit and listen to preaching, he agreed but as soon as the preaching started he left the temple. His mother thought that he has returned home, and asked her husband to go home for lunch. When his father reached home, he found the house door locked from inside, when no one opened after multiple knockings, he called his elder son with the spare key. The house was opened and his father went to his room assuming that he is sleeping and did not hear the knockings. But, as soon as he opened the door, he found Aakash hanging from the ceiling. An ambulance was called but on reaching the hospital, he was confirmed dead.

Case of Prashant,[33] 29-year-old unmarried male

The sense of rejection, failure, and self-blame overpowered Prashant due to life events that led him to take his own life. His family was into the business of jewelry and his father intended to see him take over his business. Since adolescence, Prashant wanted to do something big so that he could earn good money and live a luxurious and comfortable life. He aspired to establish his own business one day. Such being his attitude, he always showed a disinterest in joining the family business.

He was not highly educated and merely, held an ITI diploma. To do something on his own he began looking for jobs since he was ambitious, materialistically he had his own set of parameters for the kind of job he would like to do. The parameters included no struggle, non-willingness for hard work, quick result/output out of work engaged. His over expectation without struggle and lack of patience made him to overlook various opportunities. After much effort, he finally got a job based on his requirements in Anand, but unfortunately, he lost the job soon after because of an accident that fractured his right hand. The fracture was severe and required a surgery wherein a rod was inserted to assure the limbs function properly. As he faced difficulty in lifting heavy weights in his job, he had to discontinue it. Seeing the outcome of accident, he eventually landed at his father's jewelry shop to manage it along with him, despite disliking it. He was already upset over not being able to fulfill his long-lasting wish of doing something on his own and plentiful earning due to the accident, but he moved on and accepted his reality. He now wished to live a simple life with the hope of fulfilling the wishes of his parents. Meanwhile, Prashant's parents were looking out for an alliance for him, with the hope of finding a simple girl who could manage their house and family. For this, he along with his family had been to various marriage-*sammelans/melas* and had visited around 30–40 girls and met few of them personally for further discussions, but the outcome of these meetings were unfruitful. When he saw nothing coming out from the alliance-meetings he was attending, his expectations of leading a normal settled life again got jolted and he started feeling bad about himself. He began thinking that there was something wrong with him as he and his family had everything (like a settled job, own house etc.) that any girl would appreciate in a man. Prashant started relating the refusals from the alliances he met to the problem with his hand. His mind was constantly, occupied with the thought that due to his hand, girls and family do not consider him as potential suitor for marriage. The feeling of 'something is wrong with him' became stronger when a family *pandit* reaffirmed similar thoughts after seeing his horoscope. *Pandit* informed that his stars were not aligned in a desirable manner and that is why he was facing so much difficulty. Moreover, the *pandit* also mentioned that since he was born on the day of '*Amavasya*' (dark moon-inauspicious), his stars would remain like that and he would have to face problems/difficulties all his life. His own thoughts along with the *pandit's* statement kept his mind occupied with negative thoughts about himself and the things happening to him. He felt a lot of pressure, stress and emotional pain thinking about his unfulfilled wishes and rejections form girls. After few days of attending another *sammelan*, one day Prashant came back home from shop telling his father that he would soon return. He was alone at home at that time and hanged himself. His father came home for some work and found him hanging, as he was still conscious, he called people for help and was rushed to the hospital. Prashant was crying and felt guilty over his step. He received treatment at the hospital with family hoping of his survival. However, on same day in late afternoon, he passed away. Through suicide, he tried to overcome and escape his emotional stress. Ironically, after five days of his death, his family received a call from a family, to inform about their confirmation of the marriage alliance with him.

Case of Kuljeet,[34] 29-year-old married female

In case of Kuljeet, the suicide attempt was out of guilt and self-blame because of her infertility problem. She grew up in Punjab, completed her schooling up to class twelve and started helping her mother with household chores. At 21 years, she got married and moved to Vadodara. Her husband jointly with his father runs their transport business. She was shy, sociable but not very talkative. Two years after her marriage, husband's sister got married. As daughter-in-law of the family, she undertook all the responsibilities of marriage very well and in return received appreciation from all the elders. After few months, the family got the news that her sister-in-law was pregnant. This was at the same time when Kuljeet and her husband were also planning for a child. They had been trying for months, but not getting positive results. In-laws were not aware about their conceiving attempts yet. The news of her sister-in-law's pregnancy bothered her a lot because her own pregnancy plans were failing. As a cultural norm (daughter's first delivery happens at parents' home), the sister-in-law who was a few months into her pregnancy came to live with them. During this period Kuljeet showed withdrawal symptoms and kept a low mood, most of the times. In spite of her feeling upset, she did not express it to anyone, not even husband and continued to perform her household responsibilities. When her husband asked, she just said that it was because of work. Failed results of her pregnancy saddened her, which built up stress. She started feeling depressed that increased once she found herself to be surrounded with pregnant sister-in-law. In such state of mind, one day when she and her sister-in-law were alone at home, after lunch they decided to take a nap. When her sister-in-law fell asleep, she came downstairs and took a bottle of pesticide, consumed half of it and then went back for sleeping. After some time, she felt uneasiness and started murmuring. Hearing, the sound, sister-in-law woke up and got to know what she had done. She immediately alerted the family, calling everyone back home. They took her to the government hospital where she was admitted for three days. After primary treatment at the hospital for two days, family shifted her to a private hospital near their house where she remained for eight more days and on being stable, she was discharged. In the hospital, Kuljeet cried and told that she did not know what came over her that led to the attempt and confirmed not to repeat such act. The incident led the couple to consult the fertility specialist regarding their problems. According to the family, she had shown great improvement in her mood after meeting the fertility specialist.

As observed in the above incidences, Miller and Chabrier (1987) also pointed the link of suicidal deaths to feelings of guilt. They examined the content of psychotic delusions and found that suicidal patients more frequently were overthrown by feelings of guilt and sinfulness than other patients. A study by Hendin (1982: 139) also observed that guilt is central to the desire to end one's life. It was concluded after seeing it in the context of many suicidal alcoholics who felt guilty about letting people down, i.e., about failing to meet the positive expectations of significant others. In case of Prashant, suicide is a product of emotional pain due to collapse of dream and feeling of rejection by prospective alliances. In Shneidman (1993) view such pain is both intense and prolonged, combined with the feelings of hopelessness, numbness and results from the depression or in a state of anxiety with unexplained and unwanted emotions. When pain exceeds the individual's threshold to endure it, suicide seems to be the only way to rid oneself of it. In Kuljeet's case, the suicide-attempt was conclusive with the societal perceptions towards the infertile woman. Infertility is both socially and psychologically imposed taboo, particularly on a woman. In such a situation, many a times woman starts blaming herself for the inability to conceive. This self-blame grows when it is coupled with the views where identity or existence of the woman is dependent on her becoming a 'mother'. Therefore, when she suffers from the difficulty of giving birth to a new life, she feels dejected and that destroys her self-esteem by making her feel incomplete or inadequate. Thus, the driven frustration of inability influences the thought process of being burdened and discontent over life, thus willing to end it. Linking the relationship between infertility and suicide, Shani et al. (2016), in their cross-sectional study on 106 infertile women, highlighted that there are higher chances of them experiencing higher levels of depressive symptoms along with the symptoms of denial, social withdrawal, and self-blame coping strategies towards their life. Self-conscious emotions of shame and guilt hence seem to be important inherent aspects that increase the risk of suicidal tendency as they influence individuals' psychological adjustment and social behavior.

Feeling of hopelessness and self-imagined worries

Inherent factors of hopelessness towards life and overburdened with worries motivated two persons to end their lives, but both survived.

Case of Vidhi,[35] 21-year-old unmarried female

Vidhi attempted suicide due to anticipated worries. She was a graduate and worked with a company on contract that paid her enough for her own savings as well as her contribution to the household. She led a comfortable childhood and as the youngest child of three siblings was loved by all. Her father and brother had private jobs. Her father was strict and very particular with household matters. He would become angry if house is unkempt or shabby. She was religious, would visit neighborhood temple every evening and would organize/participate *bhajan sandhya* or *satsangs*. By nature, Vidhi was very perceptive and sensitive. Any conflicts at home, especially from her father, bothered her, raising more worries and concerns especially about herself. She would be preoccupied with such worries even if she had any conflicts with friends and would ruminate about the incidents while thinking of its various outcomes. She was a good and obedient student in school and college as well as a good worker to the company. She was about to complete her first year at the company and was waiting for the contract renewal. Before knowing about it, she started worrying with the tension whether it would be in her favor or not. Vidhi was afraid of the fact that if it was not renewed then she will have to stay at home all day without any work or money. She voiced her concern to a colleague who assured her that company would keep her because of her good job track. However, she was unable to shrug off the thought of life at home with no work. Her tension increased as the days of her contract renewal approached. Fears and doubts surrounded her. On the day she attempted suicide, she saw her father scolding mother over some matters, making her mother sad which made her very upset. This added more qualms to her anticipated emotional tumults. She was afraid thinking that if her contract was not renewed, she would remain at home and would face similar things from her father. On that day, after lunch, she along with mother and *bhabhi* went to their room for rest. After some time, she came out, consumed insecticide kept in the house and fell unconscious with froth coming out of her mouth. Coincidentally, her mother came out and saw the daughter laying down outside. She raised alarm and took her to the hospital where she was admitted for five days for treatment. On returning home, she got the news that her contract was renewed. Vidhi mentioned that her suicidal action was impulsive. She is now trying to manage her emotions in a healthy manner.

Case of Nehal,[36] 22-year-old unmarried male

Nehal attempted suicide due to the worries about his life and other events. He was living in a nuclear family with parents, brother and his wife. His father was into various small business and also involved in lot of political and social work. His mother ran a marriage bureau form her home while his brother worked as a hardware-repairing technician.

He was an obedient kid with a shy and introvert personality. He had a small group of friends with whom he met occasionally and would spend his time at home mostly. He was never interested in studies. He had to be motivated a lot to study for his exams. He failed in class twelve and later joined ITI. He was always fascinated by planes, trains and anticipated that his ITI training would help him in becoming a plane mechanic. However, his primary course at ITI was that of repairing cellphones. After completion of ITI diploma, he started looking for a job and gave interviews at various places. He was very selective, wanting a particular type of working environment with an expectation of high salary. If he would get the desired job, he would again raise his expectations higher, especially about the salary. Due to such nature, he could not stick to one kind of work and kept on changing jobs. Meanwhile, Nehal got worried about his future with the feeling of helplessness for not achieving anything in life until now. Additionally, being a sensitive and emotional person he was also worried about his 'social image'. He was bothered and felt that if he does not have good job or did not get married, the society would think there is something wrong with him. In this emotional turmoil, he saw his life as worthless and on few occasions, he told his parents that 'my life has nothing to speak about; it does not matter if I die also'. Another issue that disturbed him was that he might never get married. This occurred to him, as he was aware of few relatives/people who were unmarried and alone. Not having a serious romantic relationship, unlike his friends, also embedded this doubt in him. Bounded with these apprehensions, another incident happened with Nehal, which scared him and he decided to harm self. He lost his cellphone and was very upset. His family decided to buy him a new smartphone to make him feel better. The smartphone led him to be very active on social media resulting him in befriending a girl on Facebook staying in another city. Initially, both began to chat online for limited time, and after few days they exchanged their phone numbers and started talking over the phone. In the past one and half year (prior to his attempt), he started spending more time talking to the girl on phone. However, he never disclosed about this at home. One day, his brother asked his phone for making an urgent call to someone because his phone was not working. When brother did not return him the phone after 30 minutes, he got scared. He thought that his brother might have checked the messages/chats and found out about his friendship with the girl. He panicked and ran to the terrace, when family members followed him, he threatened them saying that he would jump off if they did not leave. His family members backed off, as they were astounded and scared. After some time, he came downstairs and asked for his phone. He was still scared and feared. He went to the wash area and consumed pesticide. His brother realized it and immediately, rushed him to the hospital. He stayed few days in the hospital for treatment and then returned. He stated that it was an impulsive and immature act. Nevertheless, currently, he is looking for a stable job and wants to settle down to fulfill his parents' wishes.

In both the cases, the persons were depressed with worries before their suicide-attempt. The worries were mostly self-imagined, erupted due to feelings of fear and hopelessness. Moreover, both showed a lack of self-esteem, along with a dominating family environment. The incidences that they faced on the day of their act raised their apprehensions, enabling them to escape from it through suicide act impulsively. In their cases, it could be stated that emotional state of worry, loneliness, sadness or feeling like a failure are the most common feelings reported by suicidal people for the period preceding the suicide-attempt (Bancroft et al. 1976; Birtchnell and Alarcon 1971; Maris 1981).

Other reasons for deprived feelings

The deprived status in the three suicide-completed cases differed in terms that they were not an outcome of any kind of emotional turmoil like other narratives over few years/months before their death. For instance:

Case of Rajshri,[37] 48-year-old married female

Rajshri was from upper middle class. He was married for 27 years and had a good life without any major problems. Her husband had a business of fabrication. She was very social and liked to be surrounded by people all the time. Due to this, she would look for occasions or opportunities to arrange family or friends get-togethers. She was a doting mother to his only son and was proud of his achievements. She would always tell others that she was lucky to have a small and happy family. Her happiness increased when her son decided to go to Canada for further studies. She made a routine of talking to him every day, once son moved to Canada. Seven months prior to her death, her son told about a girl he wanted to marry. She was happy with his choice and took charge of the wedding, as she wanted to make sure everything was perfect. Her daughter-in-law joined her son in Canada after two months. She bonded well with her daughter-in-law and would talk to her every day and discuss what their future plans should be. The day when Rajshri attempted suicide there was nothing that seemed different. It was the time of *Ganesh Utsav* since she was involved in arranging festivities in the society; was excited about the late night *aarti* (worship). She along with her husband attended the *aarti,* chatted with friends and then returned home at midnight. She changed into her nightdress, retired to the bedroom, and asked her husband to join but he said he wanted to stay up to watch some television. After some time her husband slept in the hall itself. When he woke up at 7 am next morning, he found the things like newspaper and milk pouches laying in the front porch of his house. He got worried, as this had never happened earlier. Rajshri would finish these chores by that time. He went to the bedroom thinking that she must be tired and still sleeping. But he found her hanging from the ceiling. He raised alarm calling out to his neighbors who informed the emergency services and the police. She was declared dead on arrival at the hospital. According to her husband, the only issue that cropped up on the incident day was that she wanted to indulge in some physical intimacy, while he was not prepared for it. He also mentioned that they had an active sex life and there had never been another incident like this when they had differences in sexual desires. She might have felt bad and dejected when her husband refused for the sexual intimacy on that particular day, as it was unlikely of him, compared to other times. Hence, in the bad mood, she impulsively acted to hang herself.

Exposure to suicide dynamics

The importance of understanding the influence that one person's suicidal behavior may have on another has received considerable attention during the past two decades. Ecological studies on suicide assumed that it may be 'contagious' as exposure to suicide predicts suicidality (Carroll and Potter 1994; Sonja and Colman 2013). Imitation plays a causal role in suicidal behavior, which had also influenced various suicide prevention recommendation and policies all over the world (AAS 1989).

Exposure to suicide could be in terms of the incident occurring in the family, peer group, neighborhood or history of suicide-attempts. Such exposure is long been identified as a risk factor and may increase the risk of suicidal ideation or attempts among individual, thereby uncovering the extent of its ripple effects (Pitman et al. 2014). Suicidal thoughts, ideation of dying and history of previous attempts are associated links to the risk of intent suicidality. In our study too, some case-narratives showed the link between exposure to suicide and their own attempt.

Seven cases had seen suicides from close quarters, viz., from family and neighborhood. For instance, Srishti (p: 100) was struggling with the life issues that involved marital conflicts, harassment and rejection. Few days before her suicide-attempt, she heard about the suicide of her paternal uncle. Since she had good relation with him, the incident took a toll on her. She would often cry and feel upset by remembering him. Her suicide took place after 15 days of uncle's death. Similarly, Savita (p: 85) who was suffering from schizophrenic symptoms was exposed to the suicidal death of her niece one year before her own attempt. Niece's suicide affected her severely, as she started worrying and thinking the reasons that made her to end life and came to believe that since she was saddened from life hence took the step. She related the situation to her own life, as she herself was also sad and upset over the death of her mother, and fights among siblings besides feeling depressed about herself with the notion of being burdensome to family members. Likewise, Meena (p: 97) had seen a suicide-death by a woman in her neighborhood due to health concerns few years ago. As she herself was facing health difficulties, so she associated the life of her with her own with a similar life of pain and health sufferings. Similarities, in their condition, overpowered her mental state and wished to follow the same pattern, i.e., terminating life by suicide.

Six persons had the history of previous suicidal attempts. Such as Neel (p: 69) attempted suicide previously by consuming poison due to fight with family over some monetary issues. He was also exposed to three-four suicides in his own locality. Like him, Imran (p: 70) also attempted suicide once several years ago due to his family not approving the marriage to the girl whom he loved. Deepak (p: 71) tried suicide twice, first by consuming poison due to fight with parents and second time by hanging due to his health malady. In Kantaben's case (p: 84), she attempted suicide twice during the years (prior to her death) by self-immolating herself but was stopped by family at both times. These two incidents happened when her symptoms were at peak and had an excessive bombardment of thoughts. However, in her third attempt, Kantaben finally succeeded and died by using the same suicide method.

Eight persons showed the suicidal symptoms, where prior to their suicidal act they were talking about death in their conversation with some of the family members. It might be because they were worried or got frustrated from the difficulties they were going through. For instance, 51-year-old Kakubhai was suffering from the pain in legs and stomach frequently in the last one year prior to his death. Despite undergoing surgery for ill-health, he did not feel better. He would often talk about his death or wished to die in order to overcome his illness days before his suicide-attempt. Finally, one morning he died by hanging himself. Similarly, a 22-year-old unmarried Mohit[38] told his mother one month before his suicidal death that he was going to die soon. He also mentioned that he would die by hanging. On hearing this, both had a conversation where mother convinced him to avoid such thoughts and focus on something else. After this mother did not find anything wrong and thought everything as normal. He himself neither brought out his feelings nor thoughts on similar lines again. After one month, he took his life in the same manner as he mentioned to his mother. It was observed that he was a reserved and sensitive person. He was also confused about his future showing worries over life failures and disturbed due to some meaningless incident.

Exposure dynamics to suicide in different ways highlights the inherent predictor of suicide vulnerability. In the cases where they heard about the suicide of close relatives or seen it in the neighborhood supports the hypothesis of suicide being contagious that could influence others to contemplate, attempt or die by it. For those with a history of suicide-attempts, the action is a strong predictor of future suicidal behavior including death by suicide as compared to others who did not have a history of suicidality (Brown et al. 2000; Joiner et al. 2005). Weiss and Scott (1974) in their study found that relatively few suicide-attempters had made major changes in their lifestyles within ten years after the attempt. Suicidal people may recover more slowly than the people experiencing other psychiatric crises, with them being more vulnerable to suicide relapses (Overholser et al. 1987).

After suicides: reactions and repercussions

Subsequent to any unpredicted event, there will inevitably be practical issues to deal with. One such event is the act of suicide. There is consensus within the suicide prevention field that there is no reliable method to predict suicide accurately. However, it is known that there are both warning signs and risk factors that help us to determine when someone may be at risk. Understanding the complicated legacy of suicide and ways to cope with repercussions can help to begin the journey of healing and acceptance.

Warning signs are things that may lead to suicide in the immediate future – for example, having a plan to die, resolving financial affairs or feeling an extreme sense of hopelessness. Whereas risk factors are associated with a heightened risk of contemplating suicide over the long term – for example, having previously attempted suicide, being socially isolated, having depression or being abused as a child. It is thought that the combination of warning signs and risk factors increases a person's risk of suicide. Protective factors, on the other hand, are those things that mitigate the risk of suicide. Recognizing protective factors can encourage hope among persons at risk; however, the presence of protective factors does not reduce the risk associated with the presence of severe warning signs. Instead, these factors can be used to support and encourage the person and can be highlighted as reasons why life is worth living (Perlman et al. 2011).

In suicide-attempt survivors, the time right after the attempt can be most confusing and emotional. In some ways, it may be even more difficult than the time preceding the attempt. They not only face the thoughts and feelings that led them to consider suicide, but might also be struggling to figure out what to do since they survived. In many cases, it is likely that decision to try to kill oneself came not suddenly rather it probably developed over time due to unbearable distressing feelings because of various stressful situations. As nothing else worked, suicide seemed the only way to get relief from the severe emotional pain. Since they survived, they can contemplate their action. It is advocated that attempt-survivors often feel embarrassed, ashamed or guilty for the reason that they had put their family and others through a difficult situation (SAMHSA 2015). The pain that led them to harm themselves might still be present but they could at least find the healthier and effective ways to cope with the aftermaths of the act. The time-period of coping might be few days or some months; the family members could play significant role in reducing their vulnerability and aiding the healing process. Finding ways to cope with conflict feelings and learning to live a healthy, productive life is the important part of recovery. It can be difficult to open up and accept help from others, but taking this first step is crucial for recuperating.

Death by suicide is sudden, sometimes violent and usually unexpected. An individual's suicide is often a solitary act. But each person who dies by suicide leaves behind 'suicide-survivors or bereaved members'[39] – people who've lost someone they care about and are left grieving and struggling to understand the reasons and learn to carry on with their lives (Cerel et al. 2008; Harvard Women's Health Watch 2009). The grief process is always difficult for their families but the process of sadness and mourning differs from those where the loss was due to natural death. In suicide-death, the families are plagued by the need to make sense of the death and to understand why the person made the conscious decision to end his/her own life. There are chances that some might understand the causes but they might still leave to untangle unanswered questions, which may include their own role in the sequence of events (Young et al. 2012).

A loss through suicide is like no other, and grieving can be especially complex and traumatic. Studies conducted on suicide bereavement focused on how it differs from bereavement by other causes, arising pathologies and how much the type of death effects the experience of grief and the subsequent resolution. For instance, studies found not much significant differences between suicide-survivor reactions to that of other types of bereavements (Barett and Scott 1990; Muller and Thompso 2003), some suggested qualitative differences (Van der Wahl 1989). Current literatures also highlighted the bereavement process involving different aspects, containing unique themes and as complex that involve longer time to move on (Bailley et al. 1999; Fielden 2003; Jordan 2001). These studies nonetheless suggest elements such as shame, blame, guilt and stigma being more present in the process of suicide bereavement.

People coping with this kind of loss often need more support than others do, but may get less. There are various explanations. In general, suicide is a difficult subject to contemplate. Survivors thus find reluctant to confide that the death was self-inflicted. When others know the circumstances of the death, they may feel uncertain about how to offer help. Grief after suicide is different. Nevertheless, there are many resources for survivors and many ways that one can help the bereaved (Harvard Women's Health Watch 2009).

Whether suicide comes without warning or after a long struggle with illness, witnessing suicide is never easy to experience, especially if it is directed to the death of a loved one. The analysis of the post-affect situation among the narratives suggests the diverse reaction of the household towards the suicidal act of attempters and completers.[40]

Feeling of shock and denial

Nothing can truly prepare a person for the news that someone close to the family has taken their own life. Whether someone else broke the news or person had the traumatic experience of seeing it on own, there is a sense of shock with feelings of disbelief and emotional numbness as one could not possibly think it as real.[41]

The response of shock and not being able to believe the truth on suicidal act of person came from 22 cases, all of suicide-completers. These reactions arose, as they never thought about such misfortune or tragedy coming their way. Members were not prepared, nor did they imagine the sudden loss of the person especially by suicide. For instance, in a suicide-completed case of Hemant (p: 79), family felt sad about his action. Denying the reality, they believed that he was not the kind of a person who would end his own life. His father believed that probably some spirit had possessed his body that made him to take the step. The reason behind such feeling was that some days prior to his suicide, Hemant had done his physical fitness test, a requirement for his trip to *Amarnath* (pilgrimage caves in Kashmir), which happened near a morgue room. Since his father had heard about the stories wherein spirits possess human bodies, so related it to his son's action. Otherwise, they failed to understand as to how an intelligent and understanding boy could take such a scary step to end life in the way he did.

Similarly, family of Mohan (p: 89) was in a state of shock when they found his hanging body. The reaction was because he was considered a mature man, tolerant to adverse situations. He taking such a step was nearly impossible for household members to imagine. Even after a year, his wife still feels restless and dissatisfied from his suicide. She did not get close, while his children had coped well with the difficulty and displayed mature stance.

The foremost reactions of family thus suggest the foremost reaction of the event as something that comes out unexpectedly with no warning, hence emotion of shock and rejection. The manner of death is hard to accept, as one knows person would not come back. Whatever the circumstances, finding out about a suicide is a deeply painful experience. Moreover, members may still ask – why did they do it? However, one may probably never know for sure the answers. This is the question that some families, especially of suicide-completed cases, have been bothered and seeking reasons since their loved ones' death.

An unwanted act

Family members of six suicide-attempters and nine suicide-completers felt the action as unwanted. According to them, the step was out of their own doubts that they developed by themselves. For instance, Kuljeet (p: 103) attempted suicide as she was not able to conceive. Being in a company with the pregnant sister-in-law, the care and love she was receiving from the family overpowered her will to kill self. However, it is to note that neither her husband nor in-laws ever brought out infertility issues to her. Rather in-laws were unaware about their plan of starting family. The incident made the family to make sure that topic of 'not having a child' be ever brought up in front of her either by them or by the outsiders.

Likewise, in an attempted case of a 38-year-old Manoj, his wife felt that the suicide-attempt was unwanted. To her, it was a result of his anger and suspicion on her for cheating him, which is untrue. In addition, Manoj's act of self-harming by cutting hands (more than once) after fights was not so serious that require severe treatment. He made such attempt to make his wife guilty, to take the blame on herself and to apologize to him. Defending his violent behavior, Manoj, however, said that he took such step to control and put sense into her of the expected obligations towards him. As he married her by going against his family's wishes, it was her duty to keep him happy at any cost and in any situations without questioning him.

Similarly, in Jignesh's case (p: 73) his family showed no emotions or sentiments about their son's suicide-attempt and considered it as unwanted. First time, they were scared and did whatever they can do, to make him happy and stress-free that meant fulfilling his unreasonable demands, despite facing capability constraints. However, when they realized that he was using suicide-attempt as a threat or blackmail, they stopped reacting emotionally. Rather, his habit made them to disown him. Likewise, in a case of 22-year-old Jigar (suicide-attempter), his father believed that his attempt was unwanted and senseless with no valid reasons (exam failure, fights, etc.). To him, it was an unfair blackmailing technique to scare the parents. However, his mother was disturbed and felt that it happened because he was not settled. Once he will achieve that (i.e., job and marriage), he will not think about such acts.

Feeling of regret, guilt and impulsiveness

Feeling of regret and guilt was among 13 cases, mostly of suicide-attempters (10). Attempters themselves felt about regretting their action and felt guilty of what they did. Some said it was not the intention, but it came just impulsively to them, maybe due to the situations they were in and thought process that grabbed them at the time of attempt. For instance, Nehal (p: 105) saw his action with guilt and regret as it occurred because of his fear over revealing his friendship with a girl, which the family was unaware. On knowing about his fear and step, his parents felt that he acted impulsively but it was because of the girl. They did not let him interact with any girls. Putting over his son's reaction, his father stated that 'modern girls take advantage of innocent young boys like my son and trap them'. Specific to his son, he also felt that 'kids nowadays do not wish to work hard. They rather find ways to easy money, for which they depend on their parents or other family members. They indulge in wrong activities and sometimes use suicide-attempts in their favor'.

In the case of Sneha (p: 92), she regretted and felt guilty of her attempt. In her view, she took the step, as she was embarrassed and ashamed over the incident (disclosure of her being in relationship with some boy) that shamed her and family by the outsiders. Her thought process at that time was filled with guilt-ridden emotions that routed her to self-harm and she did by consuming poison. Sneha's suicide-attempt further annoyed her parents, as they were already unhappy with her due to the affair-incident. They related both incidents with anguished feelings and ire towards her. To them, the attempt tarnished their social status in the community. They said that due to her they had to live with double stigmas – one, the humiliation and dishonor that she brought to their social life, and two, her attempted suicidal act. Parents' reaction or opinion over Sneha's suicide act validates the fact that in contemporary society, stigma over suicide persists and is thought to arise primarily from social distaste and disapproval, from associations of blame and shame and also from social unease (Chapple et al. 2015; Cvinar 2005).

In case of suicide-completers, their families felt the suicidal act being a result of an impulsive action. Since they are not alive, they were unable to understand the reasons completely, which allowed them to turn towards the act of self-killing. Like, in the case of Amoli, her family felt that she impulsively attempted suicide that caused her death. In their understanding, she took the step only because she would have felt that calling off her engagement might bring a bad name to the family. However, for them, the reason was redundant, as they would have accepted the decision without any problem.

Similarly, in the 17-year-old Hinal[42] case, family felt that their daughter died due to her impulsive act of suicide. She was worried with the anticipation of failing her 12th exams (she was in 11th standard and would write next year), despite being a good student and facing no compulsion from family over the expected marks/percentages in exams. According to them, Hinal heard about family's unhappiness towards her cousin's failure in the 12th board. This news made her nervous with anticipation over her own efforts. She lived in tense and fearful state with the discussion over what will happen to her in 12th standard – will she pass or fail? If she fails, what will she do? and what people would say? Her apprehensions took the life away. Her parents believed that if she had been alive she would have cleared her 12th with first division and would have been very happy.

Coping with the loss (in cases of suicide-completers)

Unlike the attempt-survivors, the families of suicide-completers go through certain different sets of issues towards the suicide news of household member. The loss curtails grieving or bereavement with different extents. Grieving the death of a loved one is an individual process. It can affect the family members either physically or mentally. It is stated that in bereaved stage a member wants to numb his feelings and might be tempted to use alcohol or other substances. But it will make things worse than being a solution (SAMH 2012). It is important that household members should focus on things, which helps to take one's mind off from mourning. Suicide prevention experts believed that bereaved can heal, but their pain is often underestimated. The stigma around suicide creates an additional burden.

Survivors of suicide-completers commonly experience a range of intense and distressing emotions. Shock, anguish, loss anger, guilt, regret, anxiety, fear, intrusive images, depersonalization, feeling overwhelmed, loneliness, unhappiness and depression are some of the common described feelings (Young et al. 2012). Sudden outburst of tears are also common in grief, triggered by memories or reminders of the loved one. Besides, many simultaneously even deal with the pressure to keep their loved one's suicide a secret or with the mistaken belief that they did something to cause their loved one's death[43]. However, not all people grieve the same way or for the same length of time. Dealing with grief is though essential in order to come to terms with the loss of member and move on with the life. The person who avoids grieving will eventually suffer from some form of depression or even physical problems (Worden 1991).

Coping struggle

In 13 cases of suicide-completers, the family was still struggling with the absence of dear ones and the way to cope with the loss. Like, the family, especially mother of a 22-year-old Kavya,[44] is yet to cope with the loss who hanged herself over some conflictual issues with her fiancée. Her mother was the one who discovered her hanging body. On seeing her, she was shocked and shattered. It was the second time in her life that she saw a close family member dying by suicide. First time, it was her husband who self-immolated himself (psychotic symptoms) and died, and second time, it was her daughter. Kavya's suicide happened two years back from the time we held interview; yet her mother and elder brother did not recover fully. They became quite emotional while narrating her story, with the multiple crying spells in between. Until now, they are in the pool of questions and seeking answers of what actually lead her to take the step. In their view, everything in her life was going well which negates them to accept Kavya's reality of taking such cruel step.

Correspondingly, in the case of Razia (p: 66), who hung herself over feeling of unacceptance in marital home, the parents are yet to come out from the feeling of loss. Since the girl shared a close bonding with her father, he was just not able to accept the reality that such an incident ever happened with his daughter. The grief was alive even after three years because of their granddaughter who stays with her father and stepmother. Razia's parents feel that the new mother would be keeping her nicely but later on when she had her own children, her love and care might be compromised towards their granddaughter. As one way of coping, Razia's parents give money for charity to various institutes in the memory of their daughter.

Death due to suicide brings suffering and difficulty into the lives of everyone who is touched by it. One faces unanswerable questions and wrestles with "Why? Why did this happen? Why did it have to come to this? Why couldn't it have been stopped?" But no matter what reasons there were for the suicide, in the end, it can never be completely explained.[45]

While the experience of coping with bereavement by suicide is subjective and unique for each individual, it is likely that there are common issues in the experience of coping during the aftermath of this type of loss. Theory generated in this area can inform both mental health practitioners and postvention services in supporting the bereaved (Stroebe and Schut 2001).

Acceptance

Family of four completed cases showed the gradual acceptance of loss, which happened mainly because the members were aware of the apparent causes that lead to their suicide. Family had witnessed the suffering and pain of these cases, hence the acceptance of death. The willingness of these four cases to die by suicide was perceived by their family as a way to escape and relieve themselves from the sufferings and painful life. For instance, in one of the male suicide case, family members though felt sad about the incident but handled with no strong emotions because they were aware of his behavior and his earlier attempts. Moreover, the fact that the recent suicidal act that became fatal happened in the inebriated and unconscious state also showed their non-emotional response to his action.

It is common for a person to feel relieved after a loved one dies when the loved one had been living in pain and suffering. For those who die from illness, the relief comes from knowing they are no longer in physical pain. And when a person dies from something like suicide or overdose, the relief may come from a place of knowing that their loved one is no longer struggling with emotional (and sometimes physical) pain.[46] Once the reality of the loss begins to sink in, over time, the waves become less intense and less frequent. For the most bereaved persons, the feelings gradually diminish in intensity, allowing the individual to accept the loss and re-establish emotional balance. The person knows what the loss has meant to them but they begin to shift attention to the world around them (Young et al. 2012).

People react differently to loss. Talking about inherent feelings of loss with someone might also help the grief-ridden members. People find that as they work through their emotions, it becomes easier to adjust to living with their loss. Talking about things and feel that they need to 'put it behind them and get on with life' is a learning way to accept that the person has gone and does not mean one forgets them in one's life. It is rather a way of healing with the loss.

Death as fate

In six cases of suicide-completers, family considered the death as fate. For them, the person's behavior and activities ultimately led them towards committing suicide. For case in point is Amoli's suicide about which her family feels that "it was something that was to happen and happened. Talking or thinking of the reasons about it would not make much difference". Such response was because they felt that by taking her own life she met with her fate. It was her attitude and behavior, which lead her to that stage. Amoli had anger issues along with being secretive and non-sharing personality. Such persona and temperament terminated her life, as she kept everything to herself without disclosing her problems or issues to others. The family felt that they could have sorted things if they knew much more about her personal life. It was Amoli's fate to die like that and she did.

In the same way, family of Hiya (p: 77) also coped with the loss by considering her death as fate. For them, she attained such death due to her life choices and behavior. Like the earlier case, Hiya also had a personality of being an introvert, short-tempered along with anger issues. She was about to get married to a person of her choice, which was initially resisted by the family but was accepted later on once they were convinced about boy's family background. Since Hiya hardly shared anything in detail about her relationship, family barely knew anything about the couple's internal matters. But they were aware of fights between them over petty issues. Family members, especially her brother, advised them many times the need to control anger and deal with patience. However, the advice was hardly heeded especially by Hiya. Family believed that her attitude towards not taking life and relationship in a mature manner lead her to kill herself. It was her fate that she did not put efforts to resolve her life problems, despite repeatedly told to correct it. Her mother felt that her suicide also questioned their social image in the community.

Regret over not saving life

In four occurrences family members felt that death could have been saved if the reasons behind their stress and frustration were resolved or if they had acted timely on their part. Like in Meena's case (p: 97), the main reason behind her suicide was non-identification of exact illness. Since no doctor was able to tell her the exact health problem that affected her daily functional ability and mental stress, she got frustrated. Upset over her state filled with severe pain, and no sign of being cured forced her towards suicide. Her family believed that if someone had found a cure for her health problems she would not have taken that step. Similarly, in the case of Rajshri (p: 107), the husband felt that her suicide could have been averted had he accepted her demand of sexual intimacy. There is a guilt in him for not going in for it that night. If he had accompanied her to bedroom, as she demanded on that day and talked to her, his wife would be alive today. He reported about carrying this remorse for the rest of his life.

Likewise, family of Vijay (p: 87), whose suicide was triggered by huge debt, felt apologetic and said about preventing it if they knew about his situation or if he had shared the difficulty with them. His father and brother felt a lot of guilt that they were unable to see the whole situation despite being so close to him. Vijay had told about his situation prior to his death but family did not consider its gravity at that time. They now realized that a serious consideration towards it could have helped him to come out of the situation through their financial aid. They were also angry with the lenders for their incessant harassment, which gave a final push to him to end his life. The debt amount Vijay had taken from moneylenders was high but after his death, they were doing their best to repay. They had also taken the responsibility of his son's education. They were hopeful that by supporting Vijay's son they were able to give him a better future, something that they could not do for him. It was also a way to reduce their guilt besides overcoming grief.

Family members in four cases reported that they could have saved life if they had provided an environment of security. For instance, a 21-year-old Meenakshi[47] died by suicide due to anticipated worries of her bright future that depended on her passing the college exam (as an external student). Her family was deeply upset over the unfortunate incident. Her parents were guilty of the fact that they could not give her the assurance of financial stability to help fulfill her dreams. Meenakshi was worried with the tensions divided between clearing the exams and doing a job without compromising to anyone. She was doing a job in order to finance her studies without troubling her parents. Moreover, part of her income was the contribution to household income in order to raise the family's economic status. Although upset over daughter's action and the reasons behind it, Meenakshi's parents felt proud of the fact that she was a responsible daughter and achieved much in her short life (education, job, goodwill from neighbors, etc.) and they were certain that she would have lived a long successful life if she did not ended her life.

Few families feared about the members' death and sensed their action but have been powerless to prevent it. They felt so due to their ignorance towards suicide symptoms such as change in person's daily routine, conversing about death with family members before few days or months of their attempt.

It is believed that loss of life through suicide encourages anger towards the person for leaving family with grief and on self for missing signs of suicidal intentions. Experiencing of intense reactions during the weeks, months or years after death including nightmares, flashbacks, difficulty concentrating, social withdrawal and loss of interest in usual activities is often seen among family members especially if a person has witnessed or discovered the suicide.[48] There would also be scenarios of – 'what if' and 'if only' – roaming in mind along with moods gripped by sadness, loneliness or helplessness.

To the issue of guilt by the family member of not having been able to prevent suicide of the loved person, Young et al. (2012) state that it happens as family-survivors are often unaware of the many factors that contributed to the suicide. In retrospect, they may have not been aware of before the event. Survivors will often replay events up to the last moments of their loved ones' lives, digging for clues and warnings that they blame themselves for not noticing or taking seriously enough. They might recall past disagreements or arguments, plans not fulfilled, calls not returned and words not said, and ruminate on how if only they had done or said something differently, maybe the outcome would have been different. Understanding that most suicide completers were battling a psychiatric illness when they died helps some survivors make sense of the death and can decrease the self-blame.

Loss of life and changes in household

Not only physical loss but a suicide-death also affects the bereaved family in different ways. It was reflected in the life of 12 persons. In three cases, the loss meant financial loss to the household, while in five it was mainly an emotional and social loss. However, in four cases the death brought loss of financial as well as of the emotional/social of a dependent member.

Since the person who ended his life was the earning member, the death resulted in household facing financial constraints. The difficulty was in the form of inadequate income in repaying the debts (those who had taken) and in running the household considering they belonged to lower or middle class. For instance, Anand's (p: 94) suicide affected the bereaved family financially as they were bound to pay the debt he had taken. This was an added burden to the family. His death affected his younger brother as he had to quit his studies to earn. His mother also works, whose earnings go on to household management, while whatever his brothers earn gets into paying debt. Besides financial issues, the suicide also created weakened social ties at their home-village that implies no social/interpersonal relationships and source of financial support from their social community. Studies of qualitative accounts have revealed the embarrassment over the disturbing nature of an unnatural loss or suicide and a loss of community support in terms of reducing help-seeking and perceptions of the support available (Bailley et al. 2000; Chapple et al. 2015; Cvinar 2005).

Transfer of household responsibility on other members of the house was found in five incidents. For instance, in the case of Sumanben (p: 99), her death resulted the household burden (work) shifting solely on her sister-in-law. The household also lost one of the earning members. In the cases of Ved and Deepak, financial burden to run the household came solely upon their wives. In Deepak's case (p: 71), his father had taken the partial responsibility (due to his pension) of taking care of his widow and children. They had registered for the 'widow pension' scheme and were getting ₹ 2,500 per month. His wife started working, as she did not want to be a burden on her in-laws. In Ved's case (p: 70), other than the job of his wife, the eldest daughter began assisting mother financially by working as a housemaid. In both these cases, men were addicted to alcohol, with no stable job and did not contribute much to the household.

Few households with financial constraints drove the family to seek financial or legal help (from the research team). Somewhere, it was assumed that by sharing their story they were hoping for some kind of assistance, which could help the family in a better way.

Distress among family members and kins

Depending on the living arrangement and relationship with the kins, suicidal step by the persons affected the members of the family differently. Among 49 cases, maximum, i.e., 21, were unmarried youngsters, 16 were married persons below 50 years of age and the other 12 are married persons above the age of 50 years.

i Distress expressed by spouse

Since many persons were married, the incident of suicide-attempt and suicide-death affected the spouse in various ways. The impact was mostly emotional but in some cases, it was also financial especially for women in the case of suicide-deaths, as it changed the household dynamics with newer responsibilities on them. For instance, suicide-attempt of Kuljeet scared her husband so much that he wanted to remove it from his memory. He became extra supportive towards her and more attentive to her moods. In case of Ved, his wife is struggling with bringing up their children with meagre income. She works in a firm and her daughter works as a maid to raise household income. But a part of their income goes in repaying the debt that they took for Ved's funeral. She felt that her husband never thought about their children and made efforts to save for their future. To her, he wasted money on alcohol and ruined the life of his children. Likewise, wife of Mohan still feels restlessness and dissatisfied over the incident. She has not gotten the closure. She reported about being in a state of disbelief and in a denial mode for a long time after she saw her husband hanging. Though the family does not suffer financially, emotional sufferings are still lingering.

ii Distress felt by siblings

In few cases of suicide-attempt, reactions of siblings were undesirable. Like, in Neel's case, who was alcoholic and irresponsible towards household responsibilities, his elder brother severed all ties with him after his suicide-attempt. He reported to register a complaint against him, claiming that if he takes the step again, the family should not be held responsible for his actions. In another case, the response of brother towards sister's suicide-death (he was one of the informants) lacked any kind of emotions. This could be because they thought that she brought such kind of death on her own. Her attitude and behavior made her meet with this fate. There were few cases, especially of men, where death resulted in shift of household responsibilities on the siblings.

iii Distress faced by parents and other members of kin group

All cases showed parents disbelief over their children's suicide act, as they never imagined something like this coming to them. Therefore, their first reaction after finding the incident was shock or denial. Some parents reacted aggressively to the incident in terms of blaming their children's attitude and behavior while some felt about not being aware of the problems and issues they were undergoing. If they would have known about the crisis, they could have intervened and avoided the incident. Some parents are still figuring out the explanations behind the step as for them their children were 'intelligent and mature to not take that step in their life'. In the case of 17-year-old Kshitij[49] who died by drowning, father believed that it was an accident. It is not possible for him to do so as he was afraid of water. They handled the loss by stating that 'his death was written at that place and that is how it happened. It was an accident and not a suicide'. Likewise, parents of Aakash (p: 101) were trying to deal with the loss. For them he was a jolly and friendly boy who would never think about taking his own life. However, they felt that he was strongly in love with his girlfriend, and could not think of life without her and so ended his life.

Attempt-survivors and bereaved-survivors: dealing with suicide

Suicidal act follows inevitably practical issues to deal with. One cannot underestimate the impact of personal factors like emotional regulation, cognitive responses, secondary stressors, coping style, access to support and resources in determining how a person responds to an episode of suicide. A suicidal person's thinking is paralyzed, their mood is despairing, their options seem spare of non-existence and hopelessness permeates their mental domain. In case of suicide-death, bereaved-survivors often seek to construct meaningful narrative in order to help them find peace and understand what happened.[50]

Our case study accounts manifested that the primary purpose of a suicide is not to end life but to end the enduring pain. In the control of despair and sadness, people battle an emotional agony where living becomes intolerable. It is argued that the most people who die by suicide have a significant depression that narrows down their problem-solving skills. Destructive thinking reduces optimism and opportunity of hope, and increases the feelings of helplessness. The depressive illness limits their choices to see or to hold on to the possibility of pain going away. Therefore, survivors of suicide-attempt often report of regret and are astounded about deliberating suicide, as visible in our cases.

Surviving from suicide-attempts can be physically and emotionally exhausting for a person. S/he would be troubled with the emotions of guilt or embarrassment. According to suicide prevention experts this, in turn, could leave a person feeling isolated or abandoned. Therefore, it is essential that one should not feel to cope with the suicide incident alone. Keeping back worries, the person should turn to family or friends to speak about their mental state. It is important that people who will be there to talk and willing to listen should surround people with suicide ideation.

Grieving studies have shown the distinctive bereavement issues that survivors of suicide-death go through. Families are prone to various sets of confused and perplexed feelings of the loved ones. Thoughts such as – *why did this happen? where they went wrong? why did they not see it coming? why god has punished them?* – surround their everyday life. Some often blame themselves as responsible for the suicide as well as feeling of anger and rage against the person for leaving them. Sometimes they show emotion of going against self for not preventing it. Many people struggle for years trying to make sense of the death and also making peace with the unanswerable questions.

As evident in our study, the incidence of suicide was a major emotional setback for the household members of suicide-completers. Most families who lost the person almost two years back from the time of interviewing them still had a difficulty in accepting the incident and the loss. Rather, they did display the unhealthy way of handling the issue. They were in a mode of denial about the death being suicide, instead claimed it to be an accident. Further, while sharing the stories, many cried several times, along with sharing the achievements (like awards, medals) and happier incidents (like photos, gift presents) of the dead person. Though families had settled back into their daily routines, it is assumed that they are yet to recover the loss in a healthier way. They are afflicted by the need to make sense of the death and to understand why the suicide-completers made the decision to end their life.

We need to note that in bereavement, people experience grief differently. The pattern can be affected by age, personality, family situation, previous experience and relationship with the dead person. Children and young people tend to grieve in bursts, and at other times look for reassurance and comfort in their normal routines and activities. They may also experience bad feelings and/or suicidal thoughts themselves. This implies that deceased's bereaved children and young people need ongoing attention, reassurance and support. It is not unusual for grief to resurface later on, after months or years in them after the death in the family. This can happen as they move through different milestones and develop as individuals. Coping with grief is an ongoing process, which can show up in different ways at different times.[51] Underlying structure of grief for survivors of suicide-loss is intricately complicated. For instance, there were few case-narratives where they had lost one of the parents in younger days, but the grief over the loss remains with them so integrally that it kept on resurfacing in their lives during crisis time and played a part in their suicidal thought process in terms of making them weak emotionally. Hence, it can be stated that in the process of overcoming the suicidal act of a family member, families also live with the challenge of putting themselves at the increased risk of suicidal symptoms such as complicated grief, frequent depression episodes, post-traumatic stress disorder and suicidal ideations (Crosby and Sacks 2002; Mitchell et al. 2004; Runeson and Åsberg 2003). Similar to the fact that suicide-attempt survivor is at risk of suicide in terms of repeating it; for the families affected by suicide-loss, bereaved members being equally developing risking suicidal signs and at risk of suicide-attempt is also factual (Krysinska 2003; Pitman et al. 2017). If their behavior or signs left untreated, the conditions can result in the prolonged suffering, negative health outcomes with fatal endings.

Despite mental illness having a neurobiological basis, suicide is still shrouded in social stigma with a common belief that death by suicide is sinful. Mental illnesses as a risk compel a person towards suicide ideations, but families pay less attention to seek help or treatment especially in India. Such persons are guarded against a wall of shame and secrecy. It happens because knowing about it invariably means risking social status as well as problems in getting a job or finding a spouse. It is due to this that those suffering from mental disorders do not seek timely psychiatric help either because of restraints from family or by self. Concealing it due to societal pressure indirectly increases their vulnerability to suicide ideation despite the likelihood of being medically cured. For case in point, few of our case-narratives showed symptoms of mental illnesses but the family hardly thought of seeking psychiatric help from professionals. Ignorance ultimately increased the possibility of their suicide. It was also observed that the negative perception of seeking medical help was not limited to the poor and uneducated households, but its spread is even among the educated and economically well off people. Like in one case, the person showed mental disorder symptoms but his parents took him to *Gurus* (spiritual/religious teacher) and *Ashrams* (spiritual hermitage) for the cure. They did not see the necessity of medical intervention by a psychiatrist. They opined that only people, i.e., *gurus* and *babas* (religious ascetics' monks) could help a person suffering from mental issues. A person facing any psychiatric illness or something as simple as emotional turmoil should be sent immediately to a preacher or a *guru*, as it is the only way to resolve. They were strongly opinionated against seeking medical help for mental illnesses. Such responses seems unpleasant as it merely threw light upon the family's (or people having similar thoughts) ignorance towards mental health and individual well-being. They did not realize that avoiding help meant their role in risking and abetting their son's life towards suicide.

Delay in treatment raises proneness of individual to suicidal ideations and tendencies as a way to escape mental troubles. Thus, if anyone is experiencing suicidal crisis, seeking help of mental health worker is of paramount importance. It is essential especially if one feels depressed or has recurring thoughts of suicide. This also holds true for bereaved member because unresolved angst due to loss of a close member can turn into complicated grief. Long lasting painful emotions can become severe with the symptoms of depressions and post-traumatic stress disorder resuming in their life. Medical intervention can make a huge difference in helping them through the crisis.

While dealing with suicide, both attempters and bereaved members also come across the question of opening up about the incident to others. They always wonder about what to tell people of such occurrences (those who are unaware). Some people might be open about this, but it can also be a difficult decision. Due to an element of stigma, openness can lead to misunderstanding and unhelpful attitude in others, making things difficult for the people affected by the incident or death. Sometimes people will speculate lot of things and could become judgmental without knowing the truth. Thus, it is better to tell the closest people and others who 'need to know'. Some people may be afraid or feel helpless. They might not know what to say to you or be worried that they will upset you, or they might avoid talking about it at all. However, those dealing with the suicide episode should try to accept outsiders' reactions and focus on coping with their own feelings. Sharing the story with others who are experiencing the same type of grief might help find a sense of purpose or strength.[52] The difficult task for them is to overcome the incident for which their coping mechanisms would differ as per time and state of affairs.

For the families of both attempters-survivor (including the person him/herself) and suicide-death, the phase after suicidal act is filled with a range of feelings such as regret, hurt, remorse, pain, sadness and so on. All undergo discomforts and yet learning to move on. Details over the unhappy incident would take time to ease out. It is important to deal with the issue in one's own way and time. Grieving in one's own timeframe is essential in order to feel hopeful again and envision possibilities.

Summary

In order to understand why suicide or self-harm becomes a conceivable option to somebody, it is necessary to examine the immediate circumstances they were in when they killed/self-harmed themselves. There is a need to look at the experiences which led to them being in these circumstances and relate these two elements to the values and beliefs the person holds which might support their suicidal action. It bridges both interpretive and structural dimensions of suicide in suggesting the suicidal behavior. Our primary research evidences had explored these dimensions thus deducing the social meanings of suicide and suicidal behavior. Evidences showed that suicide is essentially surrounded and dependent on social situations and conditions. Socio-cultural environment, relationships and other socio-factors determine the real-life situations of individuals that affects their consciousness, thinking and behavior, thereby compelling them towards attempt of suicide. Various factors and everyday social experiences of people make suicide as a plausible option (Staples 2012).

In the lives of our narratives, socio-personal factors such as family issues, life-fears, sense of burden along with medical and economic factors largely formed the conditions for them to live with psychological disturbances, stress and emotional turmoil. Their inability to come out from the disappointments and stress constrained them towards suicide. The mental upheaval made them to feel helpless and forced them to end their life as a rational choice and way out to escape from the difficulties that they had been going through. Notably, they acted suicidal not because of one-day occurrence of issues, rather it happened due to a series of suppressed thought process set over a period of time, which ultimately culminated into the bad/adverse conditions or mood on the particular day of act. The inferences also propose that the causal explanation to suicide does not exist in a linear way, rather they influence individual's suicide at multiple levels in interrelated or indirect ways with the combination of one or more risk factors. Case-narratives suicides, however, suggest a general cognitive pattern behind their action, which could be summarized as in Figure 3.2.

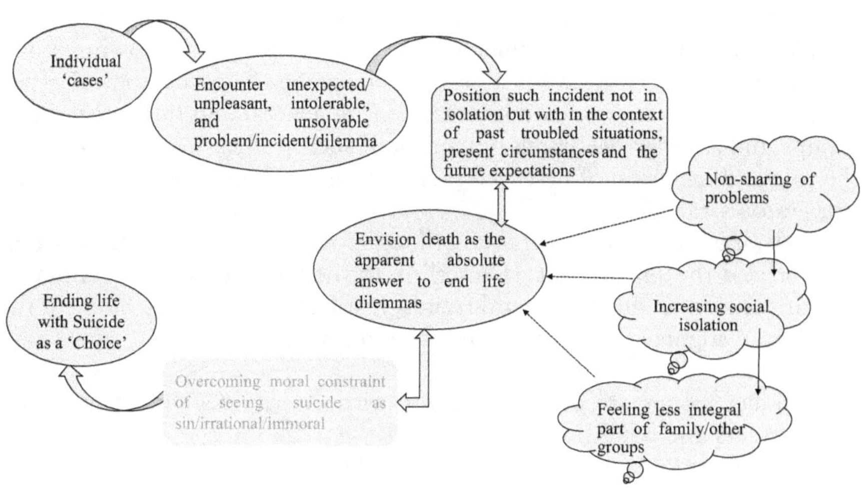

Figure 3.2 General cognitive pattern behind suicide of case-narratives.
Source: Intrepretation by the authors.

As per Figure 3.2, when surrounded with unpleasant problem/incident or crisis, case-narratives considered it as unsolvable and intolerable, an unpleasant issue in relation to past troubles, present context and future self-imagined anticipations. Self-anticipations and non-sharing of problems and mental agony increased social isolation and less belongingness to the others, thus weakening their sense of seeing their suicidal act as morally incorrect. For them, ending all the hostility they were surrounded with was possible only with the end of their life, hence attempted suicide, of which some survived, while others died.

The narratives also revealed that incidents of suicide has larger repercussions in the lives of those who attempted it and those who were affected by it. Suicide is unwanted and unacceptable life event in any household. Its occurrence brings in the series of sentiments such as disbelief, shock, denial, anger and so on that families live through. Sorrowfulness over the incident persists among the family members of suicide-attempters and suicide-completers, thereby suggesting their reactions and responses to suicide as commonly shared experiences. However, gloomy conditions prevailed longer in latter case because grief and bereavement period is extended. Yet it is to note that incident of suicide-death becoming traumatic would also depend on how the event is interpreted and processed by the bereaved-survivors/members, which in turn rests on the family members' knowledge about the risks that actually led to the person's suicide. The incident also changes the household dynamics in terms of shifting household responsibilities suddenly and new adjustments and sufferings.

In suicidology, the survivors of suicide-loss have been a low priority for researchers and clinicians whose main interest was to focus on the preventative work with the suicidal individuals (Salvatore 2010). Considering their suicide risk, the field of suicide bereavement research is growing; however, there remains a need for more knowledge on the psychological aftereffects of suicide grievers and its treatment in general and in diverse social groups and settings. Research outcomes of such studies would also justify the role and inclusion of bereaved members in any kind of national suicide prevention strategies.

Lastly, it is to note that our study though local-specific, explanatory reasons behind the suicidal act do interlink to the larger context or at macro level in terms of deducing general trends, features and leanings. Some of the common recognized patterns include the following:

- All age groups are prone to suicide with severity depending on social contexts and conditions.
- Suicide is more a product of family and economic issues.
- Certain personality attributes are more inclined to suicide ideation under socio-psychological pressure.

- Expectations and failures increases suicidal tendencies and its attempt.
- Long-term illness is a crucial suicide risk factor across age and gender.
- Presence of mental sickness in terms of depression, abnormal behavioral changes intensifies the suicide risk. Considering mental illness as some evil spirit or wizardry prevents timely medical treatment.
- Suicide is contagious as individuals' exposure to suicide and self-harm induces life comparison and their own risk to suicide-death.
- The impact of suicidal act (attempt or death) has unhealthy consequences on the individuals and households.
- Attached stigma to suicide and mental illness also increases suicide vulnerability.
- People with mental illness are in need of preventive help; however, they are unable to seek it. Non-acceptability of it as a 'disease', poor information of the available support and difficulty in accessing professional help (availability, cost, etc.) largely affects in pursuing preventive treatment.

Notes

1 In this chapter (and in others, when referring to case studies or case-narratives), persons who attempted suicide and survived are interchangeably referred as 'suicide-attempters/attempted-suicides/suicide-attempts' and persons who died are referred as 'suicide-completers/completed-suicides/suicide-death or loss'. For details of 49 cases of socio-demographic profile, see Annexure 2 (Tables A.1–A.5). All the names given to case studies are pseudonyms.
2 For more details, see Annexure 2, Tables A.6a and A.6b.
3 She died by suicide at night on 5 March 2015. In police/hospital record (PHR) the cause was family problem.
4 It was during the morning hours of 15 November 2016 that he attempted suicide but survived. PHR mentioned emotional blackmail as a cause.
5 He did the act during afternoon time on 8 January 2017 and survived. The cause reported in PHR was alcoholism.
6 He died in his suicide-attempt, which occurred in the afternoon hours on 13 February 2016. Alcoholism was the reported suicidal cause in PHR.
7 He died by suicide during evening hours on 19 December 2016. PHR mentions alcoholism as a suicidal cause.
8 He attempted suicide and died on 21 May 2016 at evening hours. PHR mentions alcoholism as a suicidal cause.
9 He attempted suicide at the afternoon of 16 November 2016 and survived after being under observation in hospital for two days. Involvement in crimes was reported cause in PHR.
10 His attempt occurred in the afternoon hours of 12 January 2016 and survived. Cause in PHR was family problems.
11 She hanged herself and died in the afternoon of 5 December 2016. Over-protectiveness was the reported cause in PHR.
12 She hanged herself and died in the evening of 10 May 2016. PHR mentioned love affair as a cause.
13 She hanged herself and died in the afternoon of 18 January 2017. Cause of exam failure was reported in PHR.

14 He attempted suicide in the afternoon of 8 November 2016 and died. PHR mentioned no job as a cause of suicide-attempt.
15 He attempted suicide by consuming poison during afternoon hours of 10 December 2016, but survived. Mental illness was reported in PHR.
16 He attempted suicide late night on 6 November 2016 and died. Family found his hanging body in the next morning. PHR mentioned mental illness and family problem as a cause of suicide-death.
17 She attempted suicide by self-immolation and died at night on 25 June 2016. PHR mentioned mental illness as a cause of suicide-death.
18 She attempted suicide at night on 9 August 2016 and died. Mentioned cause in PHR was mental illness.
19 He attempted suicide by burning himself at night on 16 July 2016 and died in the hospital next morning. PHR stated alcoholism as a cause of suicide-death.
20 He attempted suicide by consuming insecticide in the afternoon hours on 18 February 2016. He died in the hospital after two days. PHR mentioned aspiration as a cause of suicide-death.
21 He attempted suicide by consuming insecticide in the late morning on 27 October 2016. He survived the suicide-attempt post his difficult treatment at the hospital for 12 days. PHR reported debt as a cause of attempt.
22 He attempted suicide by hanging himself and died at afternoon on 18 February 2016. Loss in business was reported cause in PHR.
23 He attempted suicide during afternoon hours of 10 March 2016 and died. PHR mentioned TB as a cause of suicide-death.
24 She attempted suicide in the afternoon hours on 20 June 2016 and survived. PHR reported love affair as a cause of her attempt.
25 He attempted suicide at night on 15 January 2016 and died. Extra-marital affair was reported cause in PHR.
26 His suicide-death occurred at night on 26 February 2016. Financial loss was reported suicidal cause in PHR.
27 He attempted suicide in the afternoon hours on 10 January 2017 and died. PHR stated ill-health as a suicide cause.
28 Her attempt was at afternoon hours on 5 February 2016 and died. PHR stated illness as a cause of suicide-death.
29 He attempted suicide in the morning hours of 19 January 2016 and died. Sickness as suicide cause was stated in PHR.
30 Her death happened in the morning of 19 May 2016. PHR mentioned illness as a cause of suicide-death.
31 Her death happened in the in the evening of 15 December 2015. PHR stated family problem as a suicide cause.
32 He attempted suicide in the afternoon of 16 September 2016 and died. Love affair was mentioned in the PHR as a suicide cause.
33 His attempt and death was in the afternoon of 24 March 2016. PHR stated pampered child as cause of suicide-death.
34 She attempted suicide in the afternoon hours of 17 January 2017 and survived. PHR stated not having children as a cause of her attempt.
35 She attempted suicide in the afternoon hours of 24 January 2017 and survived. In PHR cause of death was unknown.
36 He attempted suicide in the morning of 9 January 2017 and survived. PHR stated family problem as a cause of suicide-attempt.
37 Her death happened in the early morning hours of 19 September 2016. In PHR cause of death was unknown.
38 He died in the evening hours of 30 July 2016. PHR mentioned mental illness/depression as a suicide cause.

39 Emerging suicide bereavement literature has proposed the term 'suicide-survivor', which describes a "person who has lost a significant other (or a loved one) by suicide, and whose life is changed because of that loss" (Andriessen 2009: 43; McIntosh 1993). Suicide-survivor was also originally used to include only family or relatives of the deceased; however, recent research now includes individuals who may not be related or closely linked with the deceased, but may have been in some way affected by the suicide such as friends, for example (Cutcliffe and Santos 2012, Cited in Ali 2015). Some researchers outline limitations of the definition and recognize that using the term 'suicide-survivors' can be confused with someone who has survived a suicide-attempt (Andriessen 2009). However, for the practical purpose of our study we followed the bereavement literature and used 'suicide-survivors and bereaved-survivors' interchangeably to describe the family members who lost their loved ones (primary kin) to suicide as widely used and accepted in the bereavement literature.

40 Post-affect reactions mainly constituted the views of informants who were present in the household at the time of interview. These informants were the primary kins of the case-narratives and lived with them. For detail responses see Table A.7, Annexure 2.

41 Retrieved April 6, 2019, from https://www.mayoclinic.org/healthy-lifestyle/end-of-life/in-depth/suicide/art-20044900.

42 She attempted suicide in the night of 25 August 2016 and died. PHR record mentioned aspiration and failure in exam as a cause of suicide-death.

43 https://www.mayoclinic.org/healthy-lifestyle/end-of-life/in-depth/suicide/art-20044900.

44 She attempted suicide in the afternoon hours of 11 February 2015 and died. PHR mentioned family problems as the cause of suicide.

45 Retrieved March 20, 2019, from https://www.familylife.com/articles/topics/life-issues/challenges/mental-and-emotional-issues/help-for-those-grieving-a-suicide/.

46 Retrieved March 20, 2019, from https://whatsyourgrief.com/grieving-suicide-death/.

47 She attempted suicide in the afternoon hours of 20 April 2016 and died. Aspiration as a cause of suicide death was reported in PHR.

48 https://www.mayoclinic.org/healthy-lifestyle/end-of-life/in-depth/suicide/art-20044900.

49 He drowned in the late evening hours, of 30 August 2016. His body was found after three days. The PHR stated unknown reasons.

50 https://whatsyourgrief.com/grieving-suicide-death/.

51 Retrieved November 18, 2019, from https://www.afterasuicide.nz/looking-after-yourself-and-others/coping-with-grief/.

52 https://www.mayoclinic.org/healthy-lifestyle/end-of-life/in-depth/suicide/art-20044900.

4 Pathways to suicide

Inferences and theoretical interpretations

This chapter is an extension of the previous chapter. Though confined to a particular micro space, the inferences drawn from the case vignettes can be related to theoretical conceptualizations, thereby providing a broader base to the interpretations and inferences.

Correlating the cases discussed with various sociological and psychological theories in detail, the chapter situates the case inferences empirically as well as theoretically. The impact of economic and political turmoil on the rate of suicide based on secondary data is also briefly discussed.

Inferences and theoretical interpretations

Cases discussed in Chapter 3 show the significance of the social environment, social relationships and other socio-psychological factors as the reasons behind suicide-attempts/-deaths. The following discussion will expand and relate such cases with theoretical underpinnings and studies, covering the social and psychological influence, meaning and suicidal behavior. It will refer to social-integration perspective, stress-strain theory, interpersonal psychoanalysis, feelings and beliefs about the world of individuals who end their lives by suicide as pointed in psychodynamic-cognitive perspectives.

Interpersonal theory

Van Orden, Joiner and others' (2006: 457ff; 2010) interpersonal theory reflects the cases of Razia and Anant who had issues of interpersonal behavior. According to the theory, the most dangerous form of suicidal desire is caused by the simultaneous presence of two interpersonal constructs: thwarted belongingness and perceived burdensomeness. The capability to engage in suicidal behavior is separate from the desire to engage in suicidal behavior. The model is depicted graphically in Figure 4.1.

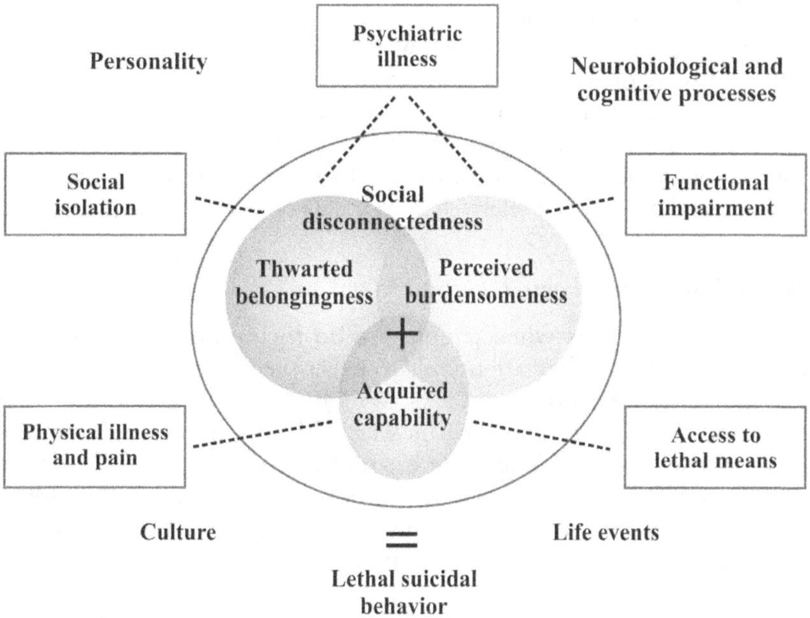

Figure 4.1 Assumptions of interpersonal theory of suicide.
Source: Based on Van Orden (2011: 234ff).

The three inner-colored circles represent the three key constructs posited to cause suicide according to the interpersonal theory of suicide. The five boxes represent key risk factors for suicide derived from psychological autopsy studies. The dotted lines from these risk factors to one of the inner circles indicate hypothesized psychological mechanisms (derived from the interpersonal theory of suicide), whereby these risk factors elevate the risk of suicide. All these factors and mechanisms are couched within the context of personality, neurobiology, life events and culture. When the fundamental need for connectedness is unmet due to social isolation, loneliness, low social support, functional impairment and so on the development of thoughts of suicide becomes implicit endangering individual's life.

Cases of Razia and Anant have all three key constructs: (a) social disconnectedness, (b) thwarted belongingness and (c) perceived burdensomeness. Both have risk factors of social isolation, physical illness and functional impairment. Razia was unable to feel the belongingness and perceived burdensomeness with her marital family. Anant had stubborn and mood-swinging personality that lead to functional impairment and social isolation even within the family.

People often face the urges, desires and natural tendencies that demand satisfaction. Giving in to such feelings is not always realistic, socially acceptable or even healthy. In order to deal with such challenges, people must exert self-control to regulate their actions. Very often, we need to delay gratification of these urges until a more appropriate time and place (Cheng et al. 2012: 129ff). Such self-management takes a great deal of mental effort, both cognitive and emotional. Some of these efforts require less willpower, while others demand more. Even relatively minor acts of self-control can take a toll.

Loss of willpower and ego depletion

Ego depletion happens when people use up their available willpower on one task. As a result, they are unable to exert the same level of self-control on subsequent, often unrelated tasks. Willpower is a limited resource. The idea behind this theory is that willpower is like a muscle which can either be strengthened or be fatigued. For example, if you exhaust yourself doing sprints, you will be less able to perform other physical tasks. Research has suggested that willpower and self-control are similar. If you use your available energy and reach a state of ego depletion, you will have less self-control when faced with ensuing tasks.[1]

Self-control is important, and having it is beneficial in a number of ways. People who possess high level of self-control may have better relationships and higher achievement levels (Gillebaart 2018: 1231). Those who lack self-control, on the other hand, can experience social conflict and poor academic performance.

In such complex scenario, many crucial functions of the self involve volition like making choices and decisions, taking responsibility, initiating and inhibiting behavior, making plans of action and carrying out those plans fail. Self-exerts control over self and over the external world. To be sure, not all human behavior involves planed or deliberate control on the self, in fact, recent work has shown that a great deal of human behavior is influenced by automatic or non-conscious processes (Baumeister et al. 1998: 1252ff).

The concept of ego depletion has taken some hard knocks in recent years. Reviews of research have suggested that the effect may be less powerful than previously believed. And an updated meta-analysis concluded that the ego depletion does not exist at all (Dang 2018: 645ff). Other researchers have proposed that ego depletion is not merely a result of draining limited self-control resources. Instead, they suggest that shifts in motivation, attention and emotion play a critical role (Evans et al. 2016: 291ff). A variety of factors can contribute to ego depletion and make it harder to control oneself and regain one's willpower, including:

- **Emotional distress:** If you are feeling emotional distress, your willpower will deplete more quickly.

- **Unfamiliarity:** It takes more energy to try something new.
- **Illusory fatigue:** If you think a situation will be mentally taxing, you will become mentally fatigued faster.
- **Choice:** If you are forced to do something, you will have less self-control than if you were allowed to make your own decision.
- **Cognitive dissonance:** Doing or saying something that contradicts your beliefs can diminish your self-control.
- **Age:** Older people may be more resistant to ego depletion than their younger counterparts.

If ego depletion leads to lapse of self-control, whereby we give in to temptations and impulses, then it can lead to all sorts of negative results such as "excessive personal debt, substance abuse, obesity, unplanned pregnancy, carelessness, crime and violent behaviour" (Muraven et al. 2000: 247ff). Let us discuss few cases narrated in the previous chapter.

In Ved's case, his alcoholic nature made him to neglect financial constraints that his family was going through, as he would spent his income in alcohol and not on household expenses. He has no self-exerted control over self as well as over the external world. His ego depletion led him into temptation to becoming an alcoholic. In the case of Neel, fights with family were intertwined with his being alcoholic. He became more argumentative with violent behavior. He did not like any kind of interference from anyone. In the case of Imran, son's heart ailment induced emotional distress. His willpower got depleted more quickly which led him to his dependence on alcohol thereby promoting the thoughts of ending life rather than controlling the situation.

Mental pain and perturbation

In the suicide literature, terms such as mental pain, psychic pain, psychological pain, emptiness, psychache, internal perturbation and psychological quality of life have been used to refer to the same construct. Shneidman (1993: 145ff) defined psychache as an acute state of intense psychological pain associated with feelings of guilt, anguish, fear, panic, angst, loneliness and helplessness. The primary source of severe psychache 'is frustrated psychological needs' (Shneidman 1996: 13). Psychache is the mental pain of being perturbed. Perturbation refers to one's inner turmoil, or being upset or mentally disturbed (Shneidman 1999: 287ff). Shneidman (1996) describe the 'psychache' pain as:

> Psychache is the hurt, anguish, or ache that takes hold in the mind . . . the pain of excessively felt shame, guilt, fear, anxiety, loneliness, angst, and dread of growing old or of dying badly.
>
> (p. 13)

From Shneidman's perspective, suicide is best understood as moving toward the complete stopping of one's consciousness and unendurable pain, especially when cessation is seen by the suffering person as the solution – indeed the perfect solution – of life's painful and pressing problems. 'Pain is the core of suicide. Suicide is an exclusively human response to extreme psychological pain'. The way to properly understand psychache is through the words of the suicidal individuals and not through a clinical diagnosis such as major depression. The words convey the source of the frustrated need and the degree of perturbation. Applying Henry A. Murray's 'need-press' theory to suicide, Shneidman maintains that suicide is virtually always triggered by the failure to fulfil some need, and the intensity ('press') of that need determines the degree of perturbation, which, in turn, leads to lethality.[2]

In thinking about the suicidal state, Shneidman further considered what conditions are necessary for an individual to become actively suicidal (see Figure 4.2). When stress (what Shneidman called 'press'), perturbation (agitation) and psychological pain are all at maximal levels, a perfect storm of psychache and suicidality can be created in the mind of an individual. It is at this point that an individual's lifelong coping patterns, presence or absence of perceived support mechanisms and reasons for living/dying come into play, influencing the direction an individual may take, spiraling into a suicidal state or countering a suicidal state as protective factors.[3]

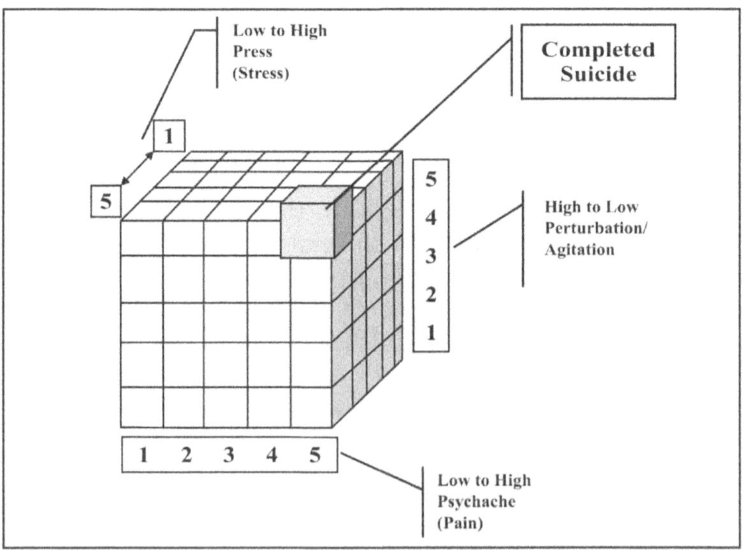

Figure 4.2 Completed-suicide: press/pain/perturbation.
Source: Based on Shneidman (1995; cited in Jobes 2006).

Table 4.1 Five clusters of psychological needs

Psychological needs	*Psychological pain*
Thwarted love, acceptance, belonging	Succorance, affiliation
Fractured control, predictability, arrangement	Achievement, autonomy, order, understanding
Assaulted self-image and avoidance of shame	Affiliation, defendance, shame-avoidance
Rupture key relationships and grief	Affiliation, nurturance
Excessive anger, rage, hostility	Dominance, aggression, counteraction

Source: Shneidman (1996: ff25).

Shneidman also suggested that most suicides can be categorized under one of the following five clusters of psychological needs (Table 4.1), which reflect five different kinds of psychological pain. Of course, these five clusters are not exhaustive; every suicide should be understood according to its own unique details and context.

Let us think about the case of Tanvi and Hemant narrated in Chapter 3 which highlights that negative thought processes in individuals due to failures affect them to question their meaning of life and ultimately loss self-control. A pain over failing to live up to the hopes and aspirations push them to great strain and stress. In order to escape from the burden, pain or failure, both of them chose suicide.

Social integration and social regulation

The key variables Emile Durkheim (1951) identified for suicide were social integration and social regulation. He had examined how these variables play out in relation to the four types of suicide that he had identified viz., egoistic suicide, altruistic suicide, anomic suicide and fatalistic suicide (refer Figure 4.3 and Chapter 1 for description on four types of suicides). Durkheim's influence was vast, and his was the first theoretical attempt to examine suicide in non-moralistic or judgmental terms. Ultimately, he attempted to "specifically identify types of suicide and ascribe reasons" as to why they happen (Selby et al. 2014: 290).

Durkheim argued that suicide can be a result of not only psychological or emotional factors but of social factors as well. Durkheim reasoned that social integration in particular was the key factor in suicide. As social integration decreases, people are more likely to end life by suicide. He emphasized that suicide depends on how different social phenomena controls individuals and affects social outcome as a whole. Destruction of social institutions, normlessness and anomie which result from social changes makes social ties weaker. In these crisis situations people become unclear about how to deal with problems (Durkheim 1951).

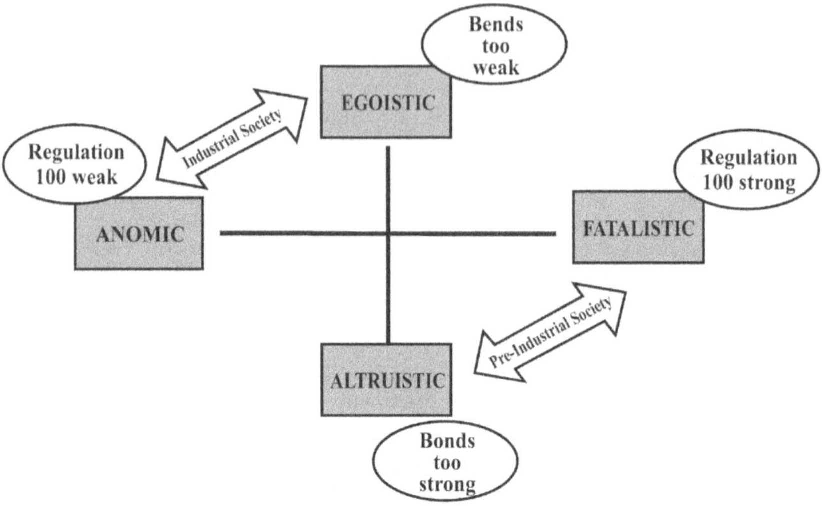

Figure 4.3 Emile Durkheim's social integration and social regulation.
Source: Authors' interpretation.

In the case of Vitthalbhai and Parv, social integration was comparatively good but worry and stress for social regulations affected their mental state. This stress converted into a sense of guilt and shame. In the case of Sneha, Mahesh and Anand, suicide seemed to have different reasons but inherently, all of them had the condition of 'damaging their the social image', 'broken social integration' and belief of it being 'against social regulations'. In all the five cases, there is a common thread of public humiliation. For Sofair (2011: 65), it acted as plausible tipping point to their private sufferings, despite their outward talent and dedication. Both betrayal and humiliation are mortifying experiences, and they may be ranged on a continuum of shame, pride and mortification as polar extremes. Sofair's concept of a 'tipping point' is of interest because not all persons who have been betrayed or humiliated would took their lives by suicide. Suicide occurs when psychache is mortifying and eclipses one or more realms of being.

Emotion dysregulation

Crowell et al.'s (2009: 495ff) theory of emotion dysregulation is often referred to as a "bio-social" theory, as biological and physiological elements figure prominently in an individual's responses to stress and emotion regulation. An afflicted person is characterized as experiencing intense emotions and an increase in sensitivity and even hypersensitivity in upsetting situations. These extreme emotional states are intense and aversive. Sufferers desperately attempt to manage their symptoms. Sometimes these efforts to cope or regulate the pain manifest as self-injury and in extreme cases result in suicide (Crowell et al. 2009).

Over the past several decades, research has focused increasingly on developmental precursors to psychological disorders that were previously assumed to emerge only in adulthood. This change in focus follows from the recognition that complex transactions between biological vulnerabilities and socio-psychological risk factors shape emotional and behavioral development beginning at conception. Since Linehan initially proposed a biosocial model of the development of borderline personality disorder, there have been few attempts to test the model among at-risk youth (ibid). According to current definition described by American Psychiatric Association (APA), personality disorders are characterized by persistent patterns of behavior that are rigid and pervasive and that emerge in late adolescence or early adulthood.

Borderline personality disorder, which is characterized by persistent and pervasive cognitive, emotional and behavioral dysregulation, is among the most severe and perplexing behavioral disorders. It is broadly defined by APA as features of emotion dysregulation, impulsivity, identity disturbance, problematic interpersonal relationships and suicidal/self-injurious behavior, among others. However, in spite of increasing evidence to suggest that borderline personality disorder can be identified reliably among adolescents, the clinical diagnosis of borderline personality disorder is rarely given before the age of 18, and there is a dearth of empirical longitudinal research with these youth (Miller et al. 2008: 969ff).

The literature on borderline personality disorder suggest a complicated process through which impulsivity and emotional liability are amplified within the family context. These processes result in numerous negative consequences, which in turn lead to emotional dysregulation, behavioral dyscontrol and impairing psychopathology among some individuals (Crowell et al. 2009).

The biosocial developmental model presented in Figure 4.4 is based on theoretical and empirical evidence reviewed below (ibid: 5), which suggests the following:

- Poor impulse control likely emerges early in the development of borderline pathology, and this may account for the overlapping biological vulnerabilities for borderline personality disorder and other impulse control disorders.
- The development of extreme emotional liability characteristic of borderline personality disorder is shaped and maintained by the caregiving environment and is based on characteristics of the child (e.g., baseline emotional sensitivity) and the developmental context.

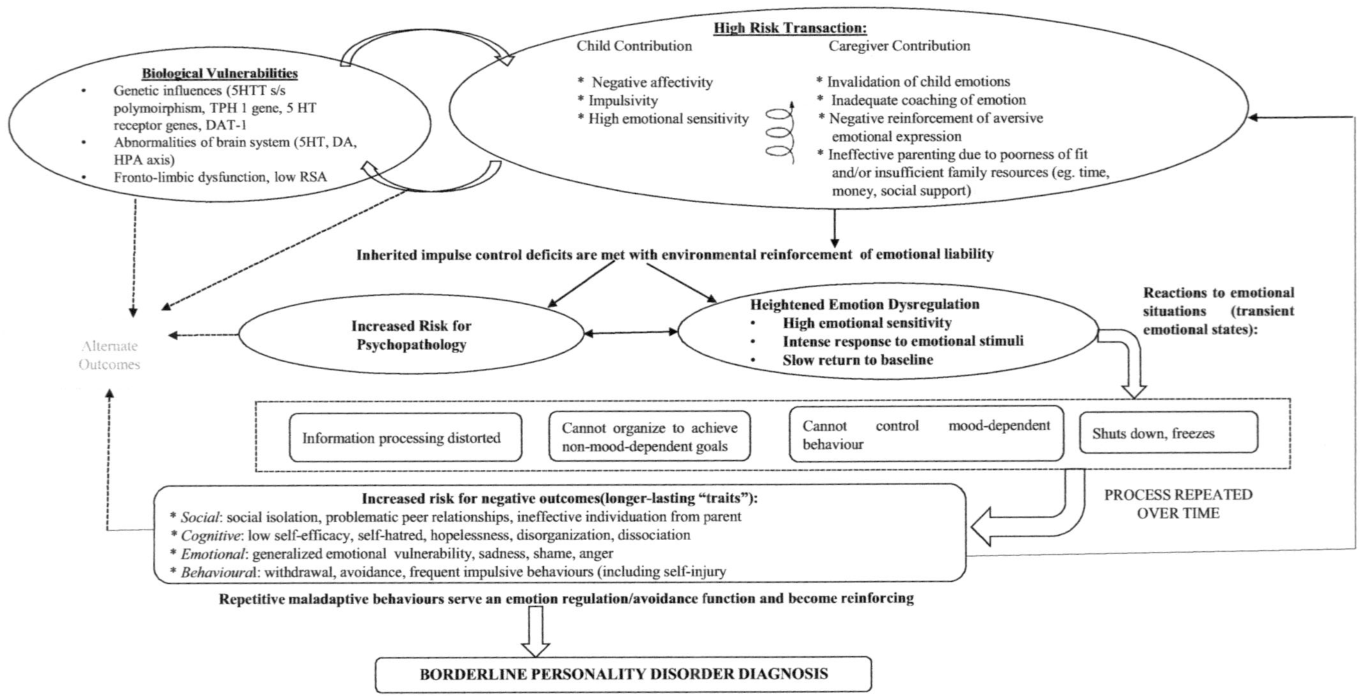

A Biosocial development model of borderline personality. 5-HT= serotonin; DA= dopamine; HPA= hypothalamic-pituitary -adrenal; RSA= respiratory sinus arrhythmia. Figure adapted from 'The Development of Borderline Personality and Self-Injurious Behaviour' by S.E. Crowell, T.P Beauchaine and M.F. Lenzenweger, 2008, in T.P. Beauchaine and S. Hinshaw (Eds.), Child Psychopathology (p528), Hoboken, NJ: Wiley.

Figure 4.4 Biosocial development model of borderline personality.
Source: Based on figure Crowell et al. (2009: 27).

- Reciprocal reinforcing transactions between biological vulnerabilities and environmental risk processes potentiate emotion dysregulation and more extreme behavioral dyscontrol, and thereby contribute to negative cognitive and social outcomes.
- By mid to late adolescence there is a constellation of identifiable features and maladaptive coping strategies that indicate heightened risk for later borderline personality disorder.
- These traits and behaviors may exacerbate risk for borderline personality disorder across development, due to evocative effects on interpersonal relationships and social functioning and via interference with healthy emotional development.

The cases of Amoli, Hiya and Bhuvan discussed in Chapter 3 show the high possibility of a link between personality disorder and suicidal behavior. Three of them had a dual set of personality traits of introvert, impulsive, aggressive, sensitive, and non-adjusting. Due to poor impulse control, borderline pathology developed in all of them. In case of Hiya, she had developed emotional dysregulation. She became secretive and not really wanting to be answerable to anybody. Bhuvan became so impulsive that he took quick decisions without considering good or bad outcomes. Due to this trait, he developed borderline personality disorder.

Such patients with borderline personality disorder have a range of intense dysphoric affects, sometimes experienced as aversive tension, including rage, sorrow, shame, panic, terror and chronic feelings of emptiness and loneliness. These individuals can be distinguished from other groups by the overall degree of their multifaceted emotional pain.

Hopelessness: catalytic agent

Aaron Beck posited the hopelessness theory of suicide (Beck et al. 1987). He asked what possible force could drive a person to violate and override the 'survival' instinct to kill him or herself. That force turned out to be hopelessness – the 'catalytic agent' that drives the suicidal desire. He found that hopelessness is a stronger indicator of suicidal intent than depression with three hypothesis. First, the theory hypothesizes that suicide ideation results from the combination of pain (usually psychological pain) and hopelessness. Second, among those experiencing both pain and hopelessness, connectedness is a key protective factor against escalating ideation. Third, the theory views the progression from ideation to attempts as facilitated by dispositional, acquired and practical contributors to the capacity to attempt suicide.

Beck proposes that those with depression develop cognitive distortions, a type of cognitive bias sometimes also referred to as faulty or unhelpful thinking patterns. He referred to some of these biases as 'automatic thoughts', suggesting they are not entirely under conscious control. People with depression will tend to quickly overlook their positive attributes and disqualify their accomplishments as being minor or meaningless. They may also misinterpret the care, good will and concern of others as being based on pity or susceptible to being lost easily if those others knew the 'real person' and this fuels further feelings of guilt.

The main cognitive distortions according to Beck are summarized below (Beck et al. 1993: 139ff; Gross 2015: 796ff):

- **Arbitrary inference** – drawing conclusions from insufficient or no evidence
- **Selective abstraction** – drawing conclusions on the basis of just one of the many elements of a situation
- **Overgeneralization** – making sweeping conclusions based on a single event
- **Magnification** – exaggerating the importance of an undesirable event
- **Minimization** – underplaying the significance of a positive event
- **Personalization** – attributing negative feelings of others to oneself

People with the traits of hopelessness view their lives as devoid of pleasure or reward, presenting insuperable obstacles to achieving their important

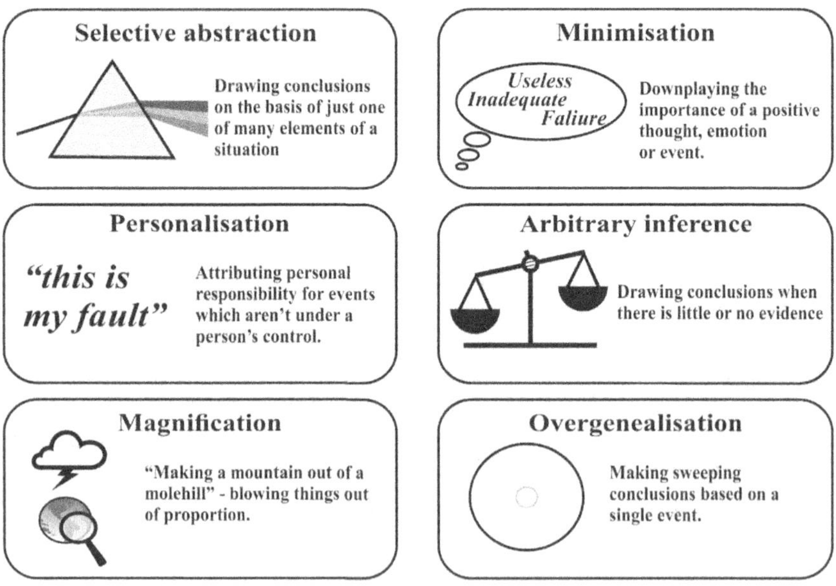

Figure 4.5 Beck's hopelessness model.

goals. This is often manifested as a lack of motivation and leads to the depressed person feeling further withdrawal and isolation as they may be seen as lazy by others. Everything seems to be 'too hard to manage', and other people are seen as punishing. They believe that their troubles will continue indefinitely, and that the future will only bring further hardship, deprivation and frustration. 'Paralysis of the will' results from the depressed patients' pessimism and hopelessness. Expecting their efforts to end in failure, they are reluctant to commit themselves to growth-oriented goals, and their activity level drops. Believing that they cannot affect the outcome of various situations, they experience a desire to avoid such situations (Sadock et al. 2009).

There are number of cases discussed in Chapter 3 stating hopelessness as a trigger to their act of suicide. Take the case of Jay's (p: 82) life: he went into depression and began remaining aloof showing withdrawal symptoms. He started feeling hopelessness and saw life as meaningless. This increased his motivation for self-harm. He even started conversing about ending life with his office colleagues and neighbors. In the case of Krishna, Vijay, Parv and Mohan, financial risk in the form of debt or loss was the prominent reason behind their hopelessness trait. The financial risk built up pressure and stress in them and seeing their inability to repay, they thought to escape from the trauma by ending their life.

In the case of Rajubhai, Meena, Ritesh and Sumanben, hopelessness was coupled with the health issues and feeling of pain and prolonged medications. Illness raised the feeling of their burden to the family along with the sense of purposelessness. Such feelings diminished their hope for life and the meaning to live. Considering themselves as the liability to their dear ones, they thought of setting themselves free by suicide which seemed a plausible choice.

Seven more cases in our study (five completed- and two attempted-suicide) were surrounded and living with the burden of self-blame, rejection or self-failure resulted into complete hopelessness. In Kuljeet's case, the feeling of hopelessness generated due to her infertility. In India, infertility is a stigma socially as well as psychologically particularly on a woman. Societal culture led her for hopelessness and emotional personalization thoughts. In the case of Vidhi and Nehal, their worries were mostly self-imagined surfaced due to feelings of fear and hopelessness. In these cases, it could be stated that emotional state of worry, sorrow or hopelessness were the most intense feelings behind their suicide.

Impact of economic and political turmoil

This study is based on a micro level being specifically oriented to the local findings based on socio-psychological determinants. However, it may have explanatory reasons behind the suicidal acts at the macro level, deducing few general trends and features.

The suicide rate in India is akin to that of Australia and the USA, and the increasing rates during recent decades are consistent with the global trend. As previously mentioned data on suicide in India is available from the National Crime Records Bureau (NCRB; Ministry of Home Affairs). The suicide rates in India rose from 6.3 per 100,000 in 1978 to 8.9 per 100,000 in 1990, an increase of 41.3% during the decade from 1980 to 1990, and a compound growth rate of 4.1% per year. The rate of suicide showed a declining trend from 1999 to 2002 and a mixed trend during 2003–2006, followed by an increasing trend from 2006 to 2010. More recent data, however, reveal a different picture. The rate of suicide showed almost stable trend from 2011 (11.2) to 2016 (12.1).

Do suicide rates have any correlation with economic and political turmoil in India? Table 4.2 shows the suicide rates during the years of economic and political turmoil at Vadodara district, Gujarat State and India level. Table shows an increasing trend during the economic recession years. Indian economy was liberalized during the year 1991. 1996 and 2008–2009 were the years of economic slow-down across the globe. 1990–1998 were the years of political uncertainties in India. 2002 was the year of one of the worst riots in the history of Gujarat. 2016 is the year after the change of guard with change in political ideology in India during 2014. There is no definite correlation established with the data on the rate of suicide in India. There is no definite trend emerging from the data on suicide rate. Hence, the impact of economic and political turmoil is not clearly observed from the data in Table 4.2.

Table 4.2 Suicide rate during economic and political turmoil years

Years	*India*	*Gujarat*	*Vadodara*
	(Rate per 1,00,000 population)		
Economic turmoil years			
1991 (liberalization of Indian economy)	9.2	7.4	9.2
1992 (liberalization of Indian economy)	9.2	8.4	9.7
1996 (economic slow-down)	9.5	8.2	10.1
2008 (economic slow-down)	10.8	10.9	11.5
2009 (economic slow-down)	10.9	10.7	11.9
Political turmoil years			
1990 (political uncertainty)	8.9	7.2	8.9
1991 (political uncertainty)	9.2	7.4	9.2
1997 (political uncertainty)	10.0	8.5	10.2
2002 (Gujarat communal riots)	10.5	8.9	9.6
2016 (change in political ideology)	10.3	12.3	12.1

Source: NCRB data.

One can also examine the relationship of suicide rate with unemployment, GDP per capita growth rate, industrial growth and urbanization. The relationship between suicide rate and unemployment rate is shown in Figure 4.6, which depicts the positive relationship between suicide rate and unemployment rate for all the time points. The correlation coefficient is positive but small in magnitude.

We observe a positive association between suicide rate and GDP per capita growth rate (Figure 4.7), which suggests that in spite of increase in GDP per capita growth rate over a period suicide rate does not reduce at least prima-facie.

Figure 4.8 depicts how the suicide rate and industrial growth moving simultaneously over a period of 1967–2006. It can be seen that, though there is no clear story to tell about their association, both have an increasing trend. It can be noted that industrial growth rate in the year 1979 was 1.6.

Figure 4.9 shows again that over the said period both, the percentage of urban population in total population wherein suicide rate has gone up, though the rate of latter is always higher than that of the former.

The positive and significant coefficients of inflation show that the incidence and rate of suicide increases with increase in inflation rate. This is confirmed by the recent incidence of farmer suicides in India (Pandey and Kaur 2009). Suicide rate increases with the increase in unemployment rate, however, the relationship is weak. Interestingly, GDP per capita growth

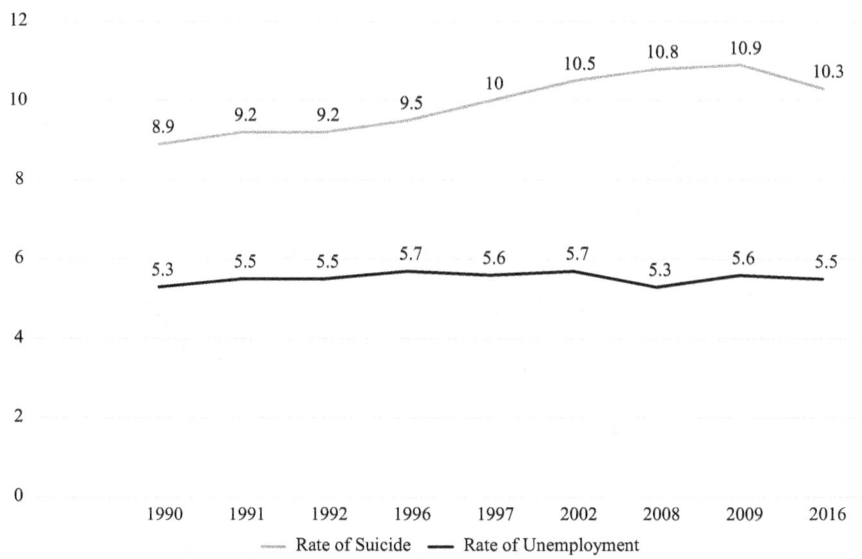

Figure 4.6 Relationship between the suicide rate and unemployment rate.

Source: Based on NCRB Suicide Data, Economic Surveys of Ministry of Finance, Government of India and Annual Reports of Ministry of Housing and Urban Affairs, Government of India.

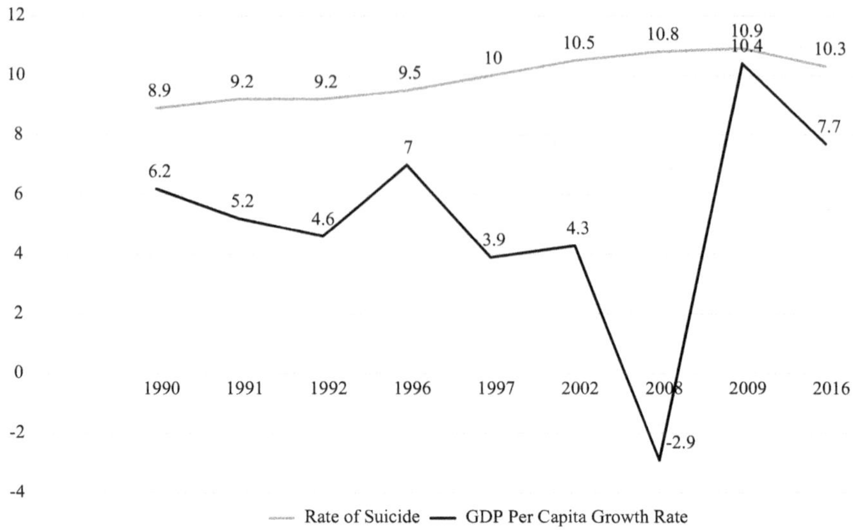

Figure 4.7 Relationship between the suicide rate and GDP per capita growth rate.
Source: Based on NCRB Suicide Data, Economic Surveys of Ministry of Finance, Government of India and Annual Reports of Ministry of Housing and Urban Affairs, Government of India.

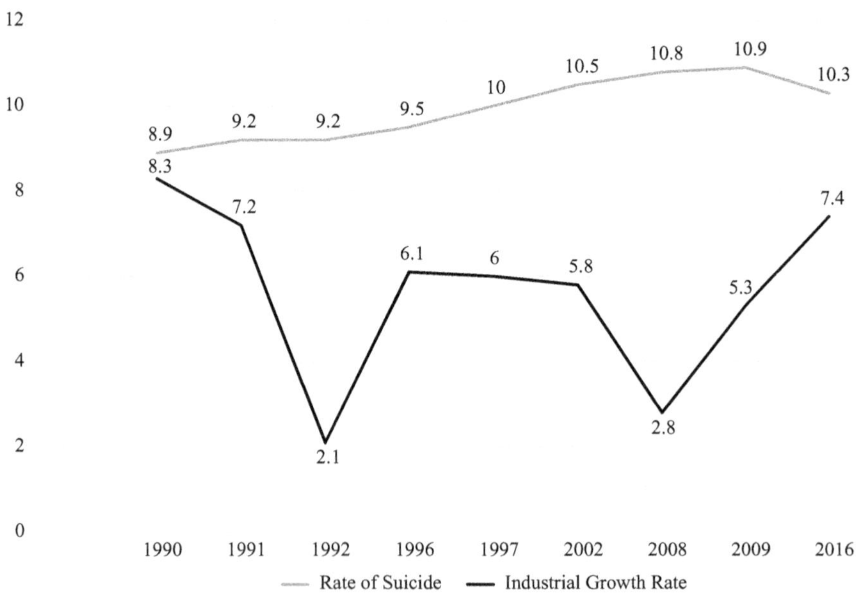

Figure 4.8 Relationship between the suicide rate and industrial growth rate.
Source: Based on NCRB Suicide Data, Economic Surveys of Ministry of Finance, Government of India and Annual Reports of Ministry of Housing and Urban Affairs, Government of India.

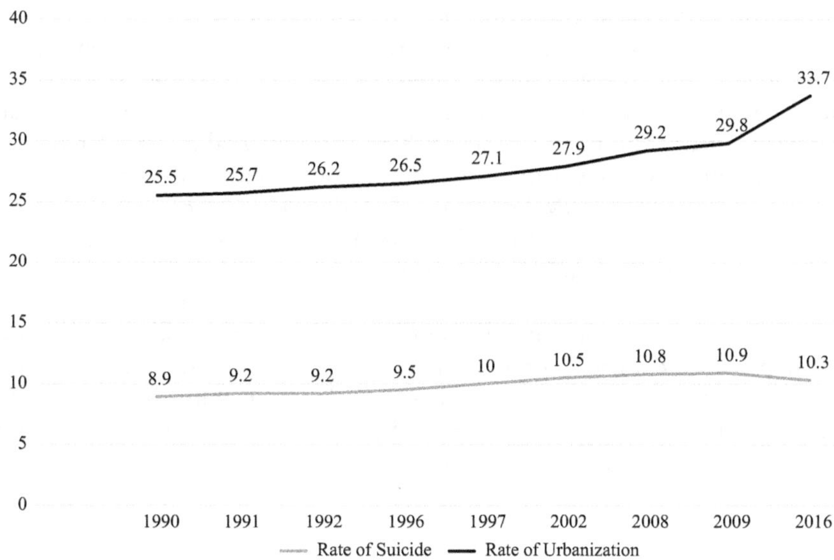

Figure 4.9 Relationship between the suicide rate and urbanization.
Source: Based on NCRB Suicide Data, Economic Surveys of Ministry of Finance, Government of India and Annual Reports of Ministry of Housing and Urban Affairs, Government of India.

rate and suicide rates are almost analogous, except for some periods. Moreover, the positive and significant coefficient of industrial growth rate suggests that industrial growth rate encourages the incidence of suicide. This is probably because industrial growth requires skilled labor, and those who are unskilled and traditional may lose their jobs paving the way for suicide. However, there is no concrete evidence. Again, the positive coefficient of the per capita GDP supports the findings of a few recent studies (Barstad 2008: 87; Viren 1999: 1428ff). This relationship has also been explained by Suzuki (2008: 296ff) using the concept of income uncertainty.

Conclusion

Theoretical links to the case inferences have highlighted certain pathways between intention and act of suicides by individuals. Although selected theories of suicide are discussed here to revisit suicide through the socio-psychological lens, many more might have been left unmentioned. These include theories stemming from research in other disciplines. For example, huge advances have been made in the study of brain in the neurosciences in last 20 years. We have a better understanding of how the brain works and consequently how chemicals in the brain influence how we think and behave. We now have a better idea of how suicidal thoughts are formed, and how these thoughts result in suicidal behaviors.

It is important to note that no single theory can explain the complexities of suicide or suicidal behavior, regardless of whether the theory is rooted in sociology, psychology or even medicine. It is also not feasible to conclude that every theory can be used effectively to treat suicidality. Particular theories may influence newer ones or may fall out of favor altogether. What remains constant is the evolving understanding of why people take their own lives. We get this understanding from the tireless research that goes into formulating theory and its practical application.

As theoretical efforts in suicide prevention continue and our practical treatment of suicidal individuals improves, more people who are suffering will hopefully begin to experience lives that are not quite as painful and intolerable. When this happens, they may no longer feel like Sisyphus, endlessly pushing the rock, rather they can be, as Camus (1991: 212) imagines Sisyphus, content and happy to be alive.

Notes

1 Retrieved March 25, 2020, from https://www.awpnow.com/main/2018/10/31/when-you-run-out-of-willpower/.
2 Theresa Lowry-Lehnen. 2014. Psychache and Suicidal Behaviour – Shneidman. Retrieved March 25, 2020, from https://www.slideshare.net/lehnent/psychache-and-suicidal-behaviour-shneidman.
3 Janet S. McCord. Psychache (n.d.). Retrieved March 25, 2020, from http://www.suicidefindinghope.com/content/psychache.

5 The way forward

Implications for prevention policy and interventions

Suicide as a multidimensional, multi-factorial malaise is a major public health problem in many developing countries. The high suicide mortality has thus led many Western nations in employing national strategies to reduce suicide.

The prevention of suicide has medical, social, psychological, economic and political implications. Notably the development and coordination between the academic and clinical professions, and partnerships between public and private enterprises – the government and NGOs – are central to the success of suicide prevention. Therefore, organizations working in the areas of health, education, social welfare, the police and the judiciary will have to be involved in the planning and organization of such policy and services. It is necessary to develop a sustainable and functional operating structure for partners, with authority, funding, responsibility and accountability for the development and implementation of the national strategy to reduce suicide. Moreover, to develop interdisciplinary support is to evolve a broad-based approach for the suicide prevention and research (Manoranjitham et al 2005).

Suicide: a public health issue

Across world, more than eight lakh people die by suicide every year. Those who attempt suicide and having suicidal tendencies are much higher. Due to non-surveillance, the exact figures are not known. Suicide is taking lives of young and middle age population in India and elsewhere. Social, psychological, cultural and many other factors interact to increase the risk of suicidal behavior. Previous suicide-attempts, mental health problems, harmful use of alcohol, drug use, job or financial loss, relationship breakdown, trauma or abuse, violence, conflict or disaster and chronic pain or illness are some important risk factors (WHO 2014).

Suicide is not an individual problem but also a problem of families, communities and larger society. The individuals' suicide-attempt also affects families and peer groups in terms of emotional turmoil and health hazards. Suicide is also contagious in terms that its exposure leads to risk of subsequent attempts or other persons imitating the same. This implies a likelihood of bereaved family members or peers also contemplating suicide themselves. Further loss of life in many households could also indicate family members being left without assistance to face everyday difficulties. As a tragic incident, many families might also live with adverse coping ways. Such glaring facts are highlighted in our study, and thereby suggest that the menace of suicide can no longer be ignored and need urgent preventive mechanisms.

In view of epidemic of suicide, in 2013, World Health Assembly adopted the WHO Mental Health Action Plan 2013–2020 (WHO 2013). The action plan described suicide prevention as an important priority for achieving the global target of reducing the rate of suicide in countries by 10% by 2020. This action plan highlighted that suicide is a serious public health problem worldwide and that, with appropriate efforts, suicides are preventable.

To achieve preventive action plan, public health or population approach is integral as it can address the issue in many ways. First, such approach would directly focus on improving the health on a large scale. This means a focus on prevention approaches that impact groups and on treatment of individuals. Second, public health focus on preventing suicidal behavior would give attention to the problem before it occurs, and thereby addressing a broad range of risk and protective factors. Third, as a public health issue it would hold a strong commitment to increase our understanding of suicide prevention through new and better scientific solutions. Finally, since public health concern values multi-disciplinary collaboration, it would help bring together many different perspectives and experience to enrich and strengthen the solutions for the many diverse communities.

Suicide prevention: approaches and interventions

To plan effective intervention and prevention strategies, there is a greater need to explore and understand the factors that lead to suicidal behavior while recognizing individuals within their social setting, their interactions, the meanings they derive, their responses and the impact of such interactions. Major models prevalent in the study of suicide prevention can be categorized into biomedical-psychological and socio-cultural.

Biomedical-psychological approach and suicide prevention

People do not end their life all of a sudden, rather there is a suicidal process. Generally, in the beginning, there are negative life events having imperative relationship with social support and help-seeking behaviour. The latter ones play an important role for obstructing the progress of process. In the final stage, mental disturbance associated with the suicidal process gives the final push towards the killing of self. Various studies confirm that in approximately 90% of suicides people suffer from mental disorder in the final stage (Cho 2012). As the process has multiple complex stages, the prevention of the suicide also has several models.

Medical-psychological model of prevention suggests medicalization of suicide. It sees humans as biological organisms and its various illnesses due to pathological conditions. It emphasizes the medical contribution, i.e., doctor's role in treating mental illness through medical and psychiatric services. It also involves improving the medical contribution by way of educational programs about the recognition and treatment of mental illness for general practitioners, especially depressive illness, measures to improve the specialist psychiatric services and associated social services. This approach has two implicit assumptions that treatable mental illnesses are important in a large proportion of suicides and that these potential suicides are in medical contact (Barraclough 1972).

Healthcare reforms and changes in mental health and psychiatric care over recent decades have highlighted the importance of clinical practice for suicide prevention. As psychological-medical approach to treating suicidality, clinical suicidology is an emerging field that covers areas including suicide risk assessment, clinical treatments for suicide risk, professional training in suicide-related practices and issues of ethics and risk management related to suicidal risk. Psychiatric treatment and psychotherapies are part of this field (Jobes et al. 2015).

It is believed that even the mildly depressed person can end life by suicide. Therefore, the suicidal risk for individuals suffering from mental disorders drastically decreases once s/he starts psychiatric treatment. Psychiatric treatment involves assessing the individual's suicidal risk by the psychiatrist, which is very imperative for further diagnosis and progress of the treatment. They do it through the developed systematic suicide risk-assessment strategies. These strategies identify acute, modifiable treatable risk and protective factors essential to informing the psychiatric treatment and safety management to reduce suicidal risk. This is because there are many kinds of risk depending upon the patient's condition.

Further, psychiatrist can verify the nature of suicide risk from acute to chronic level. The term 'acute' describes the intensity (severity) and magnitude (duration) of the symptom based on some observed facts. For example, lack of sleep can vary in severity from early-morning waking to devastating insomnia; duration can range from moments of hopelessness to continuous hopelessness in a depressed suicidal patient. An evidence-based association with suicide supports the high-risk factor. Once a patient is determined to be at acute, high risk for suicide, immediate clinical diagnosis and intervention is required to prevent suicide. Some patients may remain at high risk for hours, days, weeks or a few months, and require inpatient facility (Fawcett 2006). As per the diagnosis of risk-severity, psychiatrist suggests further diagnosis and treatment including psychotherapy such as cognitive behavior therapy (CBT), interpersonal therapy (IPT), dialectical behavior therapy

(DBT), family therapy and psychodynamic therapy (Leenaars 2004). A sub-discipline of psychiatry, drugs or psycho-pharmacotherapy is also used for some suicide risk patients. For instance, a group of psychiatric medications can be used to treat psychiatric disorder of depression. Medicines like clozapine and lithium carbonate showed positive results in decreasing suicides among schizophrenic/schizoaffective disorders and those with mood disorders, respectively (Jogadic et al. 2013). Some evidence however suggest that anti-depressant drug may also increase risk of suicidal ideations and attempts, especially among children and adolescents with depression (Barbui et al. 2009; Juurlink et al. 2006; Nischal et al. 2012).

Notably role of a psychiatrist in prevention strategy is limited in terms that they are professionals who are closely related to hospital or health system, hence, they cannot always prevent suicide, even with the best of available care. Moreover, preventing of suicides counts only those patients who can access psychiatric help and undergo psychotherapy. Many people generally remain out of reach of the psychiatrists, especially in India. Reasons like stigma, infrastructure and money play an important role in the non-approachability. Despite structural voids, psychiatric treatment through psychiatrist is a more desired goal in mental health especially pertaining to suicides. It is so because suicide survivors often find counselling by them as helpful to restore their life back.

Socio-cultural approach and suicide prevention

Socio-cultural approach views suicide problem in holistic way with the concept that any health-related problem is not due to one factor, but it is a combined effect of physical, mental, social, and emotional factors. Social and economic conditions impact the lives of people, but so also the other associated aspects such as cultural and spiritual for individuals. Covering a broad range of problems of social and emotional wellbeing, in individual's life complications can result from unresolved grief and loss, trauma and abuse, domestic violence, removal from family, substance misuse, family breakdown, cultural dislocation, racism and discrimination and social disadvantage (Social Health Reference Group 2004: 9).

The approach was proposed with an argument that cultural dimension associated with suicide is least explored in detail on risk factors and epidemiology of suicide (Colucci et al. 2013; Vijayakumar 2007). It thus suggests attention on understanding the suicide prevention in socio-cultural context in which suicidal behaviour occurs.

As a non-medical model of care for prevention socio-cultural approach advocates about the need for community-based, informal suicide-support centres that are sensitive, pragmatic and congruent with the needs and values of the local context. By promoting broader approach, it highlights that having thoughts of suicide is not necessarily pathological that needs medical intervention and rescuing is possible by counseling, by helping people in dealing with unresolved issues. It acknowledges that care includes an element of being supported to pursue a meaningful, self-determined and contributing life (Davidson 2012). Such model of prevention therefore provides a social angle to care especially in cases where cure of suicidal ideations depends less on drugs/medication but more on personality problems. For instance, curing those suffering from suicidal aspects due to loss of loved ones, repeated suicide-attempters, risk groups showing suicide signs (students/substance abusers, married people, etc.). Rather than medications, direct association of community workers (as trained professionals) with the mentally ill/personality disorders people and their families would affect considerably in reducing the social disabilities and suicides.

Maytree Suicide Respite Centre, London (2002), is an example of such community-based approach that aims to provide support to persons who are suicidal through a 'befriending model'. It serves as an environment that is conducive to open and relaxed conversations, not putting up any barrier to the people about what to speak. Unlike medical and risk-averse models of care, it favours in creating trusting and necessary spaces for persons (called guests) to openly discuss their reasons for suicide. The main aim was to be with the suicidal person rather than having covert agendas to manage or reduce suicidality (Petrov 2013). Evaluation of Maytree indicates positive results with marked transformation points in the recovery from suicidal thoughts and feelings of its users (Briggs et al. 2007, 2012).

Befrienders International is another example of community-based intervention and is perhaps the largest voluntary organization working at the grassroot level providing emotional support to the suicidal. There are 350 crisis centers worldwide with a workforce of about 40,000 volunteers providing care through a non-invasive therapeutic listening service. The service is offered by telephone, face-to-face, letters and email with an element of confidentiality and anonymity of the caller. The volunteers are forbidden to give their opinion let alone advice to caller.

Maithri in Kerala is the first befriending center under the umbrella of Befrienders India started in 1995. Social activists associated with the Rajagiri College of Social Sciences Kalamassery, Kerala, took the initiative of setting up the center. It started in response to the repeated media reports of family suicides in the various parts of state. *Maithri* has been a catalyst in building public opinion in support of suicide prevention initiatives by spreading the message – 'When you are in distress, talk to your friend; when your friend is in distress listen to him. Listening really helps' (Gulvady 2003).

Focus on preventing suicide also requires addressing the social determinants that impact adversely on the social and emotional well-being of individuals, families and community level. It is relevant to provide culturally responsive services for early identification and treatment of mental health issues at the individual level. The intervention in early life conditions, work-related issues, unemployment, social support including both family and peer groups is important as it is assumed that relative deprivations including individual's abilities are implicit causes of illness like mental disorders leading to suicide.

Suicide prevention either through medical-psychological or socio-cultural ways collectively involves various efforts on reducing the incidents of suicide. Preventive efforts in terms of treating psychological symptoms and risks, improving coping strategies of people under suicide risk as in clinical suicidology or reducing the prevalence of conditions known to constitute suicide risk factors like family-conflict, poverty and community factors as in social suicidology are equally significant.

Suicide mortality has become a major challenge but suicide prevention is too often a low priority for governments and policy makers. It needs to be prioritized as a public health concern by using a multidimensional approach that recognizes social, psychological and cultural impacts (WHO 2014). Further one should not stop at formulating prevention mechanisms but more research is required in the prevention field to assess convincingly the effectiveness of such suicide prevention services in reduction of suicides and related behavior in the future. Additionally, to create services that adequately meet the needs of persons who are suicidal, we must also begin to collaborate with those who have lived the experience of suicidality (Fitzpatrick and River 2017).

Way forward: policy implications

Preventive efforts can strategically intervene to reduce the level of risk of suicide if not eradicate suicide incidence or risk totally. It is likely that such efforts are most useful to troubled people. Continuous improvement and their wider availability is also the most anticipated need.

There is a widespread intervention in the areas of public health and diseases especially those related to lifestyle changes, but health policy response to mental health problems is very poor. This could be due to lack of political commitment as strategies remain on paper but not in practice. For reducing suicides and mental health illness in general, commitment from national- and state-level authority is required to ensure that suicide prevention receives the resources it requires to achieve its goal. In the long run it might result in reviewing policies and legislation leading to improvements in approaching self-harm and suicide in terms of better sustained allocation of resources, effective mechanisms of gathering data and introducing curricula on suicide information/prevention for health and social sector professionals.

At the same time, the need to adapt interventions to the local conditions, and assess the feasibility, efficacy and effectiveness of suicide prevention programs and strategies in the Indian setting will require careful planning. Following discussion focuses on the contours of long-term policy implications.

Way forward: researchers and counsellors

Recommendation one: introduce psycho-social autopsy in studying suicide

Predictability of suicidal action is very uncertain and to draw a precise depiction of the suicidal subject in order to intervene is difficult. Nevertheless, prevention of suicide would be effective if one understands the major risk factors that lead to suicide as it could inevitably reduce the suicide incidence. In this regard psycho-social autopsy could be helpful for the stakeholders. It is useful because it aims to reconstruct the social, psychological and medical circumstances, i.e., risk factors of suicide-death through various information resources.

In a number of countries such as the USA, Canada, Great Britain and Finland the method has been used largely for medical and legal reasons. Moreover, various psychological and sociological studies used it to assess and manage suicidal patients, and their findings offered clues for planning suicide prevention strategies. As an outcome, psycho-social autopsies are now being used for suicide prevention, crisis intervention or research both to improve existing knowledge and identify subjects 'at risk' of suicide.

In our country, there is a paucity of studies on suicide and related behavior through psycho-social autopsy. More studies using the method are required for helping in identifying risk and triggering factors specific to our country. This would help in forming prevention strategies, specific to cultural Indian context.

Bearing its usefulness and working toward preventing suicide as a public health priority, we propose that psycho-social autopsy of each and every suicide case, whether attempters or completers, must be made compulsory under the Mental Health Act (IMHA). The approach would also allow a better understanding of the complex interactions involved between the various parameters likely to affect suicide action. Adopting this method should take into account the following aspects for the greater effect (INSERM 2005):

i Ensure better methodological standardization

The psycho-social autopsy procedure has evolved over time as a result of the various studies conducted. The experts emphasize that it would gain from being more rigorous and standardized in its implementation, particularly in the interview process with friends and relatives of the suicidal person, by carrying it out with great caution from an ethical standpoint. In addition, data collected should be evaluated on appropriate and validated psychometric scales if required for scientific evaluation.

ii Recruit appropriate controls

Besides 'case' analysis, to improve performance of this use of method, future studies could be based on comparison with a sufficiently large number of control subjects, suitably matched with suicide subjects according to proper scientific criteria to deal with the objectives of the study under research as well as to get an idea about interventions for suicide prevention. However, this could depend on time and financial viability.

iii Take into account the therapeutic opportunity

Usefulness of this method also opens the possibility of therapeutic aspect to the bereaved members other than that of basic research. Since it involves in-depth interviews and interaction of close kins and others related to the person who died by suicide, their engagement could be an opportunity to unburden themselves. It is recommended that personnel much as experienced psychologist or psychiatrists, who are capable of helping the mourning relatives and friends along with managing their emotions and go through the bereavement process, should be engaged in suicide research. This will also ensure opening of families on the issue of suicide and unraveling the taboo attached to it.

Way forward: knowledge of mental health care through mental health literacy

For scaling down self-harm, the first step is to be aware of its cause, problem and available mechanisms to lessen the risk and thus comes the role of mental health literacy (MHL). It is a construct that has arisen from the domain of health literacy (HL) within the health care environment, focusing on the ability of people to be able to understand and make effective use of medical information, particularly to better understand and better adhere to medication treatments. According to WHO, it refers to "the cognitive and social skills which determine the motivation and ability of individuals to gain access to, understand, and use information in ways which promote and maintain good health" (Nutbeam 1998; Cited in Kanh and Mitic 2009). In view of HL, construct, MHL refers to understanding how to obtain and maintain positive mental health; understanding mental disorders and their treatments, decreasing stigma related to mental disorders and enhancing help-seeking efficacy, i.e., abilities to improve one's mental health care (MHC) and self-management (Jorm 2012; Jorm et al. 1997; Kutcher et al. 2015).

We believe that the basic principles of MHL could help in bringing individuals, family and communities together to aid prevention strategies by breaking stigma and accessing treatment more effectively, thereby assisting in the reduction of self-harm tendencies and suicide and better MHC of people. MHL can be promoted through peer-support interventions (at school and workplace), community interventions, training programs, etc.

Recommendation two: enhancing preventions and interventions

i School/college-based suicide prevention programs

Suicidal behaviors among adolescents and youths are rising. In these groups providing mental health awareness and skills training in the educational setting is an effective preventive strategy to reduce their risk to suicides and related behaviors. Moreover, integrating young people into the design of prevention programs aimed at them could also show better results especially in the design of peer-support programs. Such intervention would enhance in them the skills required to deal with the adverse life situations that could raise suicidal ideations.

ii Training to gatekeepers and Primary Health Care (PHC) professionals

Acknowledging the significant role of gatekeepers and PHC professionals in suicide prevention is necessary. Gatekeepers are those who come into frequent contact with members of the community on a regular basis because of their professional status. Key gatekeepers include primary health care providers, MHC providers, teachers/school staff, community leaders, police officers, counselors, social workers and spiritual/religious leaders (WHO 2012). Trained gatekeepers could recognize risk factors for suicide or in identification of those at risk of suicide as they interact with community members in natural and often in non-medical environments. For instance, family physician/doctors and the professional person of the primary health care unit can contribute to suicide prevention in the variety of ways. They are the one who are first contacted in case of any illness. As a first informative source they have the knowledge about the symptoms of suicidal tendencies or onset of mental illness and of the appropriate treatment (like for depression, schizophrenia). Initial identification is an important contribution in prevention. They can convince the relatives of the patient in seeking help and treatment from medical experts depending on the level of severity, thus averting many suicides.

The Government has to come out with a plan to give specialized training to the gatekeepers and primary health care professionals, considering their responsible role of mediator of self-harm prevention by connecting persons with mental illness or disorders (PMI) to the psychiatrists, counsellors and others. There is also a limitation of psychiatric training currently available for medical and nursing students in India which also needs to be expanded. This could be done by redesigning the curriculum so that issues relevant to primary health care are highlighted. Professional training curriculum could be more effective in reaching out to the goal of preventing suicides.

WHO has published a resource booklet series SUPRE (suicide prevention) addressed to specific social and professional groups, particularly those relevant to the prevention of suicide, as a part of worldwide initiative for the prevention of suicide. There is also a booklet on suicide case registration and one on how to start a survivors' group.[1] These could become the guiding tool in training primary care providers for better outreach of prevention and its outcomes.

iii Helplines and crisis intervention services

There are various helplines and crisis intervention services which should see growth across the country. Most services come from private and voluntary organizations in the form of telephone helplines, counselling centers, rehabilitation and others. For instance, Sneha (Chennai), Aasra (Mumbai), Roshni (Hyderabad), Befrienders-Maithri (Kochi), Samaritans Sahara (Mumbai), Sahai (Bengaluru), Sangath (Goa), Sumaitri (Delhi), Connecting (Pune), Lifeline Foundation (Kolkata), Kashmir Lifeline (Srinagar) and Saath (Ahmedabad). Such services give platform to the people to talk about the issues or sufferings and getting solutions to their problems. It is advocated that people who do not talk about their suicide ideation are generally at greater risk. Not sharing their thoughts with close members means their inability in helping at the time of danger. Helpline and crisis services listen to them and help them to come out from the crisis through proper counselling and guidance by experts. The helplines steer those who use them towards relevant potential resources and positive life outlook or attitude to life.

Setting up helpline number (24X7) or crisis center is not an easy task, as it has to go through its own administrative setup to its final functioning. Public-private association could see more such services at wider level along with retaining their sustainability. Crisis helplines can bridge the gap between public and government in providing prevention support to large people at risk.

iv Involvement of community, caste-council, cultural and faith-based organizations

As individual suffering from self-harm cuts across all faiths and groups, the role of community, faith-based organizations, caste and cultural organization becomes crucial in suicide prevention efforts.

Communities can play a critical role in suicide prevention. To vulnerable individuals they can provide social support and engage in follow-up care besides fighting stigma, helping in coping difficulties and supporting families bereaved by suicide. Being part of the community they can relate to the risk person and can help him/her through a sense of belonging and a feeling of connectedness. Community can be also involved in initiating specific suicide prevention activities relevant to their local conditions or context, a more participatory bottom-up process. In some cases, community members or representatives may take on the so-called gatekeeper role of identifying people at risk of suicidal behavior or noting emerging suicide clusters. Their involvement would channelize the connection between community needs, national policies and evidence-based interventions that are adapted to local circumstances. Adequate implementation of community engagement projects can be advantageous in tackling mental health challenges and also preventing suicide.

Faith-based and caste/cultural organizations are integral part of the community. They represent fellow citizens as well as their engagement with them at grassroots level. For most, they are next to family. Such organizations have features like better outreach, established communication networks and programs for the communities. These organizations partnership can help the discourse of suicide prevention. By reaching out to community they can help in breaking the silence about mental health issues including suicide prevention. It is important to overcome the attached stigma over mental illness and normalizing access to cure. Encouragement by organizations in terms of providing support for families as well as individuals with risk factors could be effective in addition to educating the community about warning signs and available mental health resources. Particular to faith-based organization, religious clergy could be trained for identifying suicide risks and behaviors, the differentiation of mental disorders and faith crises among individuals. With the training, they can reach to more people and can play preventive role in lowering suicide risk and in addressing the needs of suicide survivors. To achieve this, partnership between mental health clinicians and clergy is a first step. It is to note that prevention of suicide is a team effort. It cannot be fulfilled by one person, organization or institution alone, the whole community should come forward and support for the cause.

Recommendation three: increasing awareness through campaigns and social media

Destructive or harmful stereotypes about mental illness often prevent people from speaking or seeking treatment. Hence, the process of developing a suicide prevention strategy offers opportunities for opening up and increasing awareness about suicide prevention. Increased awareness can result in commitment towards the issue and resource allocation to push the process forward and making it to be successful.

The media, both print and visual, can play a vital role by generating wider understanding of suicide and its prevention. The effort can lead in de-stigmatizing mental health problems (a major suicide risk) and openness in conversing about it and seeking professional help for self or helping others. People from different fields like sports, entertainment and social can be made ambassador or representative of awareness campaign. For instance, Indian actress Deepika Padukone who herself had gone through mental illness has been raising awareness on mental health issue including seeking for mental treatment and help. There are other celebrities, national and international, who are talking about the mental issues and its impact in their life. Since celebrities are seen as a role model for many people, involving them in awareness campaigns can bring some positive results. It is believed that when public figures open up about their own struggles with mental health, it aids in breaking down stigma or uneasiness on making a dialogue. The celebrity status dilutes to certain degree in front of shared sufferings between celebrities and commoners. Moreover, conversation about suicide symptoms like stress, depression, anxiety and addiction, when move from private to public sphere it becomes effective as it stimulates important discussions on the problem and encourages people to consider it as a mental health challenge that needs expert treatment and not something that should be concealed.

There is also need to propagate multiple movements and campaigns which are working on suicide prevention through social media. These initiatives are bringing mental health awareness to the forefront. Disseminating information about them is essential.

Recommendation four: role of family in breaking stigma and initiating suicide prevention

Family presents its dual nature in the suicidal phenomenon in the sense that it has both preventive and engendering roles. Social disruption in an individual's life due to factors like negative family environment, over expectations and controls is an important cause behind suicide. Providing healthy environment that balances lively positive atmosphere and largely restricts or stabilizes expectations (over or under) from individual's life would be a step in reducing the incidence of suicide. Individuals and family members should move towards it together.

Suicidal signs are not passing moods but infer calls for help. Being attentive to the signs, communicating and listening out is valuable and a step towards prevention. Communication could offer hope and broaden the view to find different solutions to the problems that are making a person suicidal. An effort has to be made by building it up as a basic unit of emotional bonding, social support and training for resilience.

An individual's life is surrounded around his/her family. The family can act as basic support system for human being. It is they who need to first break the stigma attached to suicide and seek available help and support. Unless family comes forward and accepts suicidal tendencies or ideations of a person as mental sickness that needs medical intervention, any prevention strategies or measures at policy or community level would not work. Therefore, the preventive role of the family must be strengthened through counselling and awareness programs, and through any other possible ways to minimize the suicidal occurrences.

Way forward: policy makers and legal professionals

Recommendation five: revisiting national strategy of suicide prevention

India had took the step to address the huge burden of mental disorders through the Government of India by introducing National Mental Health Programme (NMHP) in the country in 1982. It was launched viewing the burden of mental illness and inadequacy of MHC infrastructure in the country to deal with it. In 1996, District Mental Health Programme (DMHP) was added under which it had covered 232 districts with the aim to provide detection, management and treatment of mental disorders/illness. Specific to suicide, it has restructured to include additional components like suicide prevention services, workplace stress management, life skills training and counselling in schools and colleges.[2] The program was re-strategized in 2003 to include two schemes: first, modernization of state mental hospitals and, second, up gradation of psychiatric wings of medical/colleges/general hospitals. Manpower development scheme (centers of excellence in mental health and training departments of mental health facilities) became part of the program in 2009.[3]

Preventing suicide is not a piecemeal strategy. It is a comprehensive task that encompasses the promotion, coordination and support of activities. Given the magnitude of the public health problems of suicidal behaviours, the need of the hour is to create and follow a comprehensive national strategy for suicide prevention. The strategy should contextualize the problem and an outline of specific actions to be taken at multiple levels. Without such strategy, it would be difficult to address the issue of suicide and mental illness in a determined manner.

The new evidence provided by Dandona et al. (2018) should prompt the additional or development of national- and state-level suicide prevention planning, galvanizing political and community will to address this complex public health tragedy. Special attention is required to address the issue of suicide in the rural community. There is a need for creating awareness among community members, creating village-level mechanism to identify people with potential suicidal behavior and assuring availability and accessibility of counselling and mental health services at primary care level.

It is important to review the national strategy for mental illness and prevention, in order to ensure that it fits with an overall national health development policy. This will enable the identification of any existing gaps with regard to suicide prevention in the other policies/strategies and provide opportunities to propose relevant changes in them. In addition, it could also identify what works and what does not work.

Recommendation six: identifying stakeholders and their role in suicide prevention

Identifying the key stakeholders in suicide prevention is the key element for effective results of preventive strategies. It is significant because the suicide prevention demands a multi-sectoral approach, involving health care professionals as well as representatives from other areas or sectors. For instance, a list of stakeholders should include:

- Members from various government sectors (like health, education, social welfare and agriculture)

- Medical professionals (like public health managers, physicians, nurses, emergency care staff)
- Mental health providers (like service managers, psychiatrists, psychologists, mental health nurses, social workers, bereavement specialists)
- Education professionals (teachers, school counsellors, administrators, other education professionals, student representatives)
- Legal authorities, police personnel and policy makers
- Vulnerable groups (like elderly and youth)
- Survivors and families
- Non-governmental organizations (NGOs), community-based organizations and volunteers
- Media researchers

Identifying stakeholders and their role in prevention strategy could bring positive results besides bringing diverse sectors of society working in the field of suicide and its prevention collectively. For instance, government stakeholders' role is a crucial issue where it is necessary to implement measures to prevent suicides. For instance, if we have to control farmer suicides, control of pesticides (prevalent mode of suicide by farmers) is a must for which important role lies with the Ministry of Agriculture. Similarly, to stop suicides occurring in railway tracks, the role of Ministry of Railways becomes crucial for developing prevention strategies. Likewise, NGOs and other non-profit organizations often continue to work actively in both suicide prevention and advocacy, particularly where the public sector action is weak or absent. NGOs frequently offer counselling services, operate helplines, conduct research, conceptualize and implement public education programs and work with the media. Hence, their role cannot be underestimated.

Such effort could be in line with Mental Health Gap Action Program (mhGAP) of WHO,[4] which identifies the establishment of the collaboration between health and various sectors with special focus on actively involving the community to find locally feasible ways of preventive interventions.

Recommendation seven: enhance mental health infrastructure

i Need of more institutions of mental health

Available literature on suicidology have established that mental illness is becoming an important cause of suicide (like in Gujarat, Punjab, Kerala and other states). This fact brings forth the question of current mental health services in India. There are three centrally run mental health institutes, 40 state-run mental hospitals and 398 Departments of Psychiatry in various medical colleges (183 in government and 215 in private) across the country equipped to treat patients suffering from mental illness.[5]

As of 2019, India constitutes 28 states and 9 union territories. There are 732 districts. In such scenario, the existing mental facilities suggest a shortfall in terms of coverage and number of institutions. The 40 state-run hospitals are divided among 21 states only with major states having one institute. Maximum institutes were in West Bengal (six), followed by Maharashtra and Gujarat (four each). As per 2018 (NCRB), major suicides due to mental illness were high in Punjab (35.4%) and Sikkim (26.6%), followed by Mizoram (17.7%), but in terms of mental facilities, Punjab has one institute while other two have none. The lack of such services highlights the issue of accessibility as going to distant places for the treatment involves constraints of time and finances. In this situation, implementation of IMHA-17 seems important, with its key feature that treats mentally ill people with dignity; gives people the power to make choice in their treatment; and assigns central and state authorities to build range of services, regulate mental health sector and register institutions.

Shortage of medical infrastructure, thus, underscores the need for developing more mental health hospitals or institutes in each state and particularly in each district for easy approachability. At the same time, there is also a need for awareness of such MHC services and centers. Recovery and rehabilitation is also an important part of mental health. However, few mental health hospitals and clinics and few rehabilitation facilities exist in India. The growing mental health disorders among Indian population thus necessitates their numbers to increase.

ii Necessity of adequate medical and trained professionals

Mental illness, just like any other illness, requires treatment from qualified doctors, therapists and counsellors. Unfortunately, as there are limited mental health facilities and so the insufficient medical staff. India's latest National Mental Health Survey 2015–2016 (NIMHANS and GOI 2016) carried out across 12 states suggested the overall prevalence for current mental health morbidity of 10.6%. It also pointed that an estimated 150 million people across India are in need of MHC interventions, both short and long term. However, the lack of inadequate numbers of trained MHC professionals as well as shortfall of available services lead to a massive treatment gap ranging from 70% to 90%. There are just 0.3 psychiatrists, 0.07 psychologists and 0.07 social workers per 100,000 people in India. To compare, the ratio of psychiatrists in developed countries is 6.6 per 100,000 and the average number of mental hospitals globally is 0.04 per 100,000 while it is only 0.004 in India. Hence, efforts are required to fill the gap by bringing in medical professionals trained in treating mental illness and those with the expertise in treating suicidal risk and other factors. Apart from doctors, other employees and staff of hospitals/centers must also be adequate as well as the centers being equipped with improved technologies and equipment. Notably, shortage of human resources trained in the treatment and care of mental health would act as hurdle in the goal of suicide prevention in India.

Medical schools should have specific curriculam on suicide risks and prevention training along with medical eduation training programs for physicians or other medical professionals from time to time. Such intervention would help in detecting and managing the suicidal behavior of risk groups in much better way.

In terms of better outreach, Primary Healthcare Centres (PHCC), which have extensions at the remotest part of the country, could be utilized to support and respond to the mental health and social and emotional well-being needs of individuals, families and communities. This could be done by training the medical practitioners at these centers with restructured equipment and an update of the latest techniques, knowledge and treatments in the area of mental illness and suicidology. The IMHA 2017 also points out the role of PHCC as tertiary care in the mental illness. Emphasis should also be on ensuring necessary arrangements so that the people, who cannot themselves pay for care, can receive it. It is to be addressed considering that medical care of such kinds is expensive and many who suffer are kept out of this network due to cost of treatment.

iii National network for suicide research and data

In our country, various suicide prevention programs exist addressing to various vulnerable populations like youth, senior citizens, students and women, particularly at grassroots or at community level. Some of these are self-oriented and some might be in collaboration with national and international organizations. Such research and data is relevant to understand the suicide issues and their mitigation. Though such studies are location specific, yet they can generate a larger body of evidence on suicide research. There is a need to come up with a national network for suicide research and data. This would help in locating the diverse issues, works and evaluative interventions at the particular space or setting, and could help in being an integral component in the development of a suicide prevention strategy at a national level.

Recommendation eight: enhancing the database on suicide

Due to the stigma involved in suicide, suicidal behaviors remain unreported or underreported in India. This is also true in many other countries. National Crime Records Bureau (under Ministry of Home Affairs, GOI) collects national data on suicide. Its data is gathered from the reported cases of suicides in police stations across the country. It releases the statistics in its annual publication – 'Accidents and Suicides in India'. This source of information has its own shortcomings as it presents only those suicide-deaths recorded by the police. It is believed that suicide-deaths are much more prevalent than what official data reports. Moreover, there is no database for recording suicide-attempts and those with suicidal tendencies. Hospitals (private and government) and practicing psychiatrists might have information about them but it could be limited. Further, the ethical code in cases of suicidal behavior additionally impedes the overall information on suicide-related data.

Hence, there is a need to enhance the database on suicide not only on deaths but also on attempters and people with suicidal ideations. Since hospitals and psychiatrists/counsellors would deal with attempters/suicidal ideation patients, they can bring out publications or a report in line with NCRB detailing under Medical Council of India (MCI) or National Psychiatric Association (NPA). Additionally, it would be better to have a quarterly or half-yearly publication from these data sources. Simultaneously, research on suicidal behaviors should be encouraged, so as to facilitate systematic review and analysis of this data. Identifying and triangulating multiple sources of data could be a useful approach towards data collection and validation.

Mental health legislations

Mental health is an important element of well-being. It infers a state of mind in which the individual can experience sustained joy of life, while working productively, interacting with others meaningfully and facing adversity without losing capacity to function physically, psychologically and socially. Occurrence of suicides, however, negates the same inferences as suicide ideation and behavior disturb inner harmony. Moreover, while solving internal conflicts and problems, their overall well-being gets disturbed with its repercussion on social and physical health. Historical expression of mental health and illness in India explains it as an inherited idiosyncrasy, a family curse or a lifelong affliction with near supernatural origin. This creates a challenge in breaking people's false belief and myth related to mental health as well as a major hurdle in achieving success in the field of mental health (Kumar 2002). Nevertheless, legal aspects related to mental health at different phases have been useful at least in terms of raising significance of mental health and recognizing the role of treatment and care to the mentally ill persons. Following section details out the development of mental health legislations in India, with a particular focus on recently passed Mental Health Act, 2017.

Mental health legislation in India

Attempted-suicide under Section 309 of Indian Penal Code, 1860 was considered a punishable offence and allowed the person liable to be arrested, prosecuted and imprisoned for one year. Due to this, all hospitals are legally bound to inform the police whenever a survivor of attempted-suicide is brought in, sometimes also motions harassment of the patient and the family. The outcome is gross under-reporting of attempted-suicide cases as well as non-seeking of psychiatric help. The subject of punishable offence and arrest of the person is no more applicable as per the Indian Mental Health Act, 2017 (IMHA-2017).

Much of the contemporary Indian Laws are largely based on English Common Law, a system of law based on recorded judicial precedents and shows substantial European and American influence, and many of the legislations introduced by the British are still operative. Therefore, the roots of most of the legislations in respect of PMI can be traced to the British periods (Narayan and Shikha 2013). After the takeover of the administration of India by the British Crown in 1858, a large number of laws were enacted in quick succession for controlling the care and treatment of mentally ill persons in British India (Banerjee 2001). These laws were:

- The Lunacy (Supreme Courts) Act, 1858
- The Lunacy (District Courts) Act, 1858
- The Indian Lunatic Asylum Act, 1858 (with amendments passed in 1886 and 1889)
- The Military Lunatic Acts, 1877

These Acts gave guidelines for the establishment of mental asylums and procedure to admit mental patients. The British in the middle of the nineteenth century served as the background of lunacy legislations in that period in India. The various Acts of 1858 naturally reflected the legalistic frame for the management of the mentally ill (Somasundaram 1987).

During the first decade of the twentieth century, public awareness about the pitiable conditions of mental hospitals accentuated as a part of the growing political awareness and nationalistic views spearheaded by the Indian intelligentsia. As a result, the Indian Lunacy Act, 1912 (ILA-1912), was enacted, which also guided the destiny of Psychiatry in India (Banerjee 2001).

Due to the ILA-1912, central authority took hold the supervision and regulation of lunatic asylums, and also renamed them as mental hospitals in 1922. This clearly defined the procedure of admission and certification. Voluntary admission was introduced, and preventing the society from danger of mentally ill and taking care that no sane person is admitted in these asylums was under check. Psychiatrists were appointed as full-time officers in these hospitals. Act also had the provisions of judicial inquisitions for mentally ill persons (Narayan and Shikha 2013).

After World War II, the UN General Assembly adopted Universal Declaration of Human Rights. This lead Indian Psychiatric Society submitting a draft of Mental Health Bill in 1950 to replace the outmoded ILA-1912. Mental Health Act (MHA) was finally enacted in 1987 (MHA-1987) after a long and protracted course (ibid.). Main features of the Act are as follows:

- Definition of mental illness in a progressive way and introducing modern concept of their treatment with stress on care and treatment rather than on custody

- Establishment of Central/State Mental Health Authority to regulate and supervise the psychiatric hospitals/nursing homes and to advise Central/State Governments on Mental Health matters
- Admission in special circumstances in psychiatric hospital/nursing homes. Provisions of voluntary admission and admission on the reception orders were retained
- Role of Police and Magistrate to deal with cases of wandering PMI and PMI cruelly treated
- Protection of human rights of PMI
- Guardianship and Management of properties of PMI
- Provisions of penalties in case of breach of provisions of the Act

Despite having positive features, the MHA-87 received criticism since its inception. It was seen as a drawback due to involved legal procedure of licensing, regulating admissions and guardianship issues. There was no appropriate address of human rights issues and MHC delivery of PMI (Narayan et al. 2011). Large number of complicated procedures, defects and absurdities as well as rules made under the act further worried its proper implementation (Dutta 2001). Human right activists also questioned the constitutional validity of the MHA-1987 because it involved curbing of the personal liberty without the provision of proper review by any judicial body (Dhandha 2010). However, legislations drafted after 1980s tend to give some stress on the rights of PMI also.

United Nations Convention for Rights of Persons with Disabilities (UNCRPD) was published in 2006 and came into force in 2008. It attempts to emphasize and address the attitudinal and environmental barriers that individuals with impairments face. UNCRPD included those with long-term mental or intellectual impairment also as person with disabilities.[6] This has been perceived as a progressive and irreversible step away from a 'medical model' of disability and towards a social model: a move from a 'charity based' to a 'rights based' approach to disability (Kelly 2016; Rao et al. 2016b). Since its inception, 160 countries have signed; India consented to it in May, 2008, that implies the countries to revise their laws in concurrence with the convention. In response to it, the process of amendment in MHA-87 was set in motion and a draft of Mental Health Care Bill-2011 (MHCB-2011) has been prepared. The most salient feature of MHCB is that it enshrines duties on the government to establish and provide mental health services to all citizens and act appropriately with apt measures. There is a provision for the replacement of licensing of mental health establishments to registration and establishment of Mental Health Review Commission with its state panels. The bill also states elaborate provisions in respect of human rights of the PMI as a separate chapter. The MHCB-11 finally enacted into the Mental Healthcare Act-2017 (IMHA-2017). Another important legislation in consonance with UN-CRPD was the Rights of Persons with Disability Act-2016 (RPDA-2016) (Narayan and Shikha 2013; Rao et al. 2016b).

Main features of IMHA-2017 include:

- New definitions of 'mental illness' and 'mental health establishment'
- Revised consideration of 'capacity' in relation to MHC
- Advance directives to permit persons with mental illness to direct future care
- Nominated representatives, who need not be family members
- The right to MHC and broad social rights for the mentally ill
- Establishment of governmental authorities to oversee services
- Mental Health Review Boards to review admissions and other matters
- Revised procedures for 'independent admission' (voluntary admission), 'supported admission' (admission and treatment without patient consent) and 'admission of minor'
- Revised rules for governing treatment, restraint and research
- De facto decriminalization of suicide
- Public health programs to reduce suicides and attempted-suicides

With respect to suicidal tendencies, the Section 115 of IMHA-2017 presumes "suicide attempters to be living with severe stress and not to be punished". The government is duty bound to provide care, treatment and rehabilitation to reduce the risk of suicide-attempt recurrence. Decriminalization aspect of IMHA is significant because this might lead to openly seeking help, improvement in epidemiological data, better planning and resource allocation for suicide-prone individual (Ranjan et al. 2014). As per Section 115 (2) under the IMHA-2017, a mental health service has a "duty to provide care, treatment and rehabilitation to a person, having severe stress and who attempted to commit suicide". However, it implies its own caution and challenges. High suicide risk was identified in 0.9% individuals in India, so this requirement of Act could put an unmanageable burden of MHC services. Considering that certain personality disorders are associated with high rates of suicidality such feature can make up a significant proportion of the workload of psychiatric services (Chesney et al. 2014). Under Section 115 of IMHA-2017, government's role in providing care and treatment to anyone who attempts suicide would inevitably mean many individuals with personality disorders will come in contact with the mental health services. As a result, inappropriate supported admissions and treatment are bound to happen due to failures in making direct reference to severe mental disability and kind of required need and support.

A detailed description on 'Rights of person with mental illness' also makes the Act patient-centric, especially because it mentions about the right and acceptance of PMI (also their family members and caregivers) to access MHC services and its treatment of good quality at affordable cost. It is stated that 'every person with mental health illness will have right to protection from cruel, inhuman, and degrading treatment'. This feature brings in the role of government to address the human resource needs (training of medical officers and other persons) and bring up range of services like half-way homes; sheltered/supported accommodation; rehabilitation centers (hospital and community-based); free medicines; specialized mental health services of child, adolescent and aged.

The Act also specifies about the government ensuring the necessary budgetary provisions for effective implementation along with integration of mental health services into general health care at all levels of health as well as the responsibility to plan, design and implement programs for mental health. Mental health insurance has remained a neglected area for long. This feature of the IMHA-2017 will have huge and significant impact for the persons with mental illness, family and caregivers.

Revision in the Mental Health Care Act, 2017

The IMHA-2017[7] is a welcome step which it incorporates various stakeholders in dealing the issue of mental illness at various levels and clearly depicts that the Act is to protect, promote and fulfill the rights of persons with mental illness during delivery of MHC and services. As mentioned earlier, its key features make it progressive and rights based in nature, but such rights of PMI largely limit itself till treatment in the hospital and is silent about their care in the community. Invisible growth of mental problems such as suicidal attempts, aggression and violence, prevalent use of substances, increasing incidences of marital discord and divorce rates emphasizes the need to prioritize and make a paradigm shift in the strategies to promote and provide appropriate mental health services in the community. Transferal move of MHC from psychotic disorders to common mental disorders and from mental hospitals to primary health centers is needed (Antony 2014).

We propose the following changes in the IMHA:

iv Revision in the Definition of Mental Health Establishment under Section 2 (p)

The IMHA mandates all the mental health establishments to take license for treating patients. Those private hospitals and nursing homes without license may refuse to treat patients with mental illness. Similarly, in order to keep persons with mental illness, various institutions, like hostels; prisons; jails; juvenile home; child protection centers; reception centers; centers for destitute; beggars' home; religious places such as temples, churches, dargahs and faith healers, need to take license (Gundugurti et al. 2016; Narayan and Shikha 2013).

In order to protect and promote human rights of PMI, by mandating licensing of the mental health establishments, IMHA will defeat its purpose and will invite 'license raj' of harassing the MHC providers. By doing so, it goes against the NMHP and the implementation of the policy that advocates integration of mental health into general and primary health care. To encourage treatment and community rehabilitation of PMI and integrate mental health into general health, it would be practical to keep medical and other care centers out of the purview of licensing.

v Capacity to make MHC and treatment decisions (Chapter II of IMHA)

This by default considers that everyone has capacity and one has to prove that person with mental illness lacks capacity before initiating involuntary treatment. One has to approach the mental health board to take permission to initiate involuntary treatment. There is no scope to take guardians' consent to initiate involuntary treatment under the IMHA. This issue of capacity to make MHC and treatment decisions is inadequate and may have risky consequences. Person with mental illness may refuse treatment owing to mood disorder and absent of insight, or because of illness symptoms, affecting his/her decision-making. Even family members find difficulty in caring individuals with serious mental illnesses and may also refuse admission and treatment.

This aspect of act will add an enormous burden to family members and MHC providers in treating involuntary patients with severe mental disorders. Hence, it is recommended that this clause be revised by either deleting it or considering informed consent from the parents and family members, or two doctors (preferably family physician and a psychiatrist) opinion be taken to initiate involuntary treatment. This can help the patient and also the family members in providing timely care. Hence, the IMHA needs to make provision for treatment (involuntary) in all supported (involuntary) admissions through informed consent from the parents and/or by family members to restore liberty by treatment. It has been stated very rightly that in the regulation of involuntary treatment, a balance must be found between duties of care and protection and the right to self-determination (Antony 2014; Rao et al. 2016a; Rao et al. 2016b).

vi Revision in Advance Directives (Chapter III of IMHA)

Person with mental illness may revoke, amend or cancel advanced directives many times in a day, and family members will be finding difficult to handle such situations. Only the mental health board has powers to amend or overrule the advance directive. This needs to be done in very short time to enable the treatment (24–48 hours). If the patient has been prescribed costly treatment or private/corporate hospital (which family cannot afford) in advance directives, then who will bear the cost of costly treatment. Considering the available human resources (medical and judicial), economic constraint and our collective community efforts in treating patients with mental illness, our country is not ready for such advanced directives.

Above all these, research studies data does not support the use of advance directives in person with mental illness (Cochrane[8] review) (Sarin et al. 2012). It would be prudent to do more research in this area in our population before introducing this advance directive clause in IMHA. This advance directive operates on the basic premise that 'if a person develops mental illness' – Which mental illness? If multiple illnesses occur, then?

If it becomes comorbid with physical illness, then? What severity? Under what circumstances? – These issues are wide open and threaten each individual. If an MHC provider writes an advance directive, he/she needs to write for each disorder “if I develop mania”, “If I develop schizophrenia”, like a textbook, how he/she should be cared or not be cared?

This advance directive will welcome more litigious and heavy burden on family members. It is advisable that advance directive needs to be kept out of the purview of the IMHA. The Cochrane database of systematic review on advance treatment directives for people with severe mental illness reported that there are too few data available to make definitive recommendations to introduce it (Campbell and Kisely 2009). Even in the West, this has certainly not had its intended benefit. For the Indian reality, to be rushing in with legislation on this count is rather hasty and ill-conceived (Sarin 2012).

vii Revision in Nominated Representative (Chapter IV of IMHA)

A person with mental illness may revoke his/her decision of nomination of a representative as he/she suffers by reason of severe mental illness coloring his/her perception, alters many times in a day. (1) Only mental health board has powers to overrule the nominated representative. (2) This needs to be done in a very short time to enable the treatment. (3) If nominated representative is requesting for costly treatment (which family cannot afford), then who will bear the cost of costly treatment: is it family or nominated representative or the State? (4) Considering the available human resources (medical and judicial), economic constraint and our collective community efforts in treating patients with mental illness, our country is not ready for such a departure from family as a caregiver to a patient-chosen nominated representative. (5) This nominated representative breaks the Indian family system who cares and bears the brunt of patients’ unpleasant behavior and still willing to support his/her treatment (Avasthi 2010). Ultimately, family may disown the patient and which may have serious consequences in the form of abandoning the patient and wandering mentally ill at large, which defeats the very purpose of the IMHA in protecting the patient.

Family members are the true value and assets in the Indian context to provide community care for persons with mental illness. Hence, family members are the natural guardians until proven otherwise. This “Nominated Representative” breaks the very backbone and fabric of our society “the family” (Antony 2016). In most of the cases, family members are the caregivers and this need to be fostered and enhanced. This clause on Nominated Representative needs to be removed from the IMHA.

viii Revision in Mental Health Review Boards (Chapter XI of IMHA)

The district-level mental health review boards, which are quasi-judicial bodies overseeing the effective implementation of the MHC delivery system, could introduce new hurdles for treatment delivery and unnecessary delay. This could be simply because of non-availability of judicial workforce and other resources to operate at every district level. If these issues are not addressed, this may cause a delay in initiating treatment, which may cause enormous amount of stress on the care providers. Delay in addressing the issue can defeat the purpose of the IMHA. If these boards do not operate on day-to-day basis at each hospital level, then this can cause serious adversarial impact on the MHC of the person. Unfortunately, MHC can take an ugly turn similar to Western countries where involuntary MHC is argued in the court of law. These mental health review boards need to have time limit (within 72 hours) to take a decision, especially with regard to capacity to consent for treatment issues. The mainstream judicial system is incapable of handling such complaints because of lack of sensitivity and also being clogged with a huge quantum of pending mainstream cases (Kala 2013).

These boards need to move away from tardy judicial processes/procedures. Alternatively, the first level of review could be independent hospital review board, which can address those contentious issues in a cost-effective and timely manner at the patient's doorsteps/hospital. Hence, it would be prudent to create consumer-friendly (independent) MHC hospital boards at every hospital using local resources. This MHC hospital board could be comprised of independent psychiatrist/mental health professionals, family caregivers and recovered patient. Another alternative is to create a board of visitors at each hospital (along the lines of old Mental Health Act, 1987) to perform similar functioning (Rao et al. 2016a).

ix Right to Confidentiality (Section 22 and 23 of IMHA)

The IMHA Bill also gives power to nominated representative to unlimited access to the records of the persons with mental illness. Mental health professionals have expressed reservations over sharing of information, describing it as "breach of confidentiality", as per the Medical Council Ethics, 2002.[9] However, according to the Section 22 and 23 of IMHA, information regarding MHC needs to be shared with the nominated representative. This issue impinges on the fundamental right, "Right to Privacy". Hence, there is a need to introduce a clause that information shared will be only with family members and will be in verbal form only. Written documents or medical records will be shared only with patients/legal authorities on obtaining a written request (ibid.).

x Revision in Discharge Planning (Section 98 of IMHA)

The psychiatrist is expected to be responsible for patient care and treatment in the future after discharge. This clause is idealistic but may not be possible in custodial care (involuntary patients), destitute patients and voluntary admissions, wherein only the patient can be briefed or counseled regarding the future treatment. The ultimate decision of continuing treatment or not is the choice of the patient. Discharge planning should not be considered as negligence as it is not possible without active cooperation of the patient and family members.

If the law makers are very serious about this issue of 'the continuity of care', then they should enable the MHC providers and family members by introducing the Compulsory Community Treatment Order. Unfortunately, the IMHA is silent on the much-needed community treatment order. Inclusion of compulsory community treatment orders may play a significant role in providing care for the chronically ill patients and also better the lives of the family members and caregivers. Availability of community treatment order to the family members and caregivers enables them to provide continuous care. The community treatment order brings relief to families of persons with mental illness, encourages use of less restrictive forms of inpatient treatment, reduces violence, prevents unnecessary criminalization and brings greater stability to the lives of the seriously mentally ill (ibid.).

Hence, there is a need to have a community treatment order in place. The New York's Compulsory Community Treatment Order (Ritz et al. 2016) is comprehensive and can be adopted with minor modification suiting our society and resources. Implementation of such a law can bring in continuity of care after discharge.

xi Role of family members during admission and treatment

The IMHA undermines the role of family members played in providing care in hospital environment. The Bill needs to make provisions that at least one family member needs to be present with the patient during inpatient treatment. There is a high need that family members be involved in the provision of the care. This process not only protects patient's rights but also protects family members getting involved in active treatment processes such as psycho-education, supervised medication and family therapy to be co-therapist, and also in rehabilitation process which makes a huge difference in continuity and outcome of the treatment (Avasthi 2010).

If there are no family members, the medical board (comprising of two mental health professionals) will waive the requirement of family member. Not involving family members will drive the mental hospital to the nineteenth century of overcrowding and institutionalization syndrome. Many institutions such as NIMHANS (Bengaluru), DIMHANS (Dharwad) and many other centers of excellence across India have popularized the concept of family participation during inpatient care (ibid.).

A clause needs to be introduced wherever involuntary inpatient treatment is required, by default one family member needs to accompany and be with the persons with mental illness during inpatient treatment. The duration for inpatient criteria for supported admission need not apply when family members are physically present in the ward and participate in treatment and decision-making process. A separate category for admission with family members needs to be introduced and promoted. Promote family support system to provide solace to the ailing minds that have been proved beyond doubt in Indian scientific research across the country.

Management of properties of persons with severe mental illness is completely absent. Rehabilitation and integration of homeless mentally ill into the community and management of their assets and properties are completely absent. There is a need to have this issue of management of properties of persons with severe mental illness to be addressed in the IMHA (Rao et al. 2016a).

As increasing population in India succumbing to mental tribulations, IMHA-17 is an important and timely effort; however, in view of specified roles for various stakeholders it seems to look ambitious and may pose huge responsibility to all that might affect its effective implementation. Nevertheless, if implemented cautiously with proper groundwork, the promotion, prevention and reduction of mental health stigma and suicide could be attained.

In conclusion

The human and economic cost of suicidal behavior to individuals, families, communities and society makes suicide a serious public health problem around the world with far-reaching socio-economic, political and emotional consequences. Suicide is a complex problem, with myriad factors leading to it. Interventions cannot be as straightforward as it is for the polio or TB, for example, through countrywide immunization programs or medicine course and widespread awareness. Nor is it something that state or society can afford to wash its hands of, on the grounds of it being a 'personal issue'. Diverse approaches and means will have to be implemented simultaneously in order to produce any major reduction in suicide incidents and its rates. A national strategy encompassing diverse inputs and efforts needs to be in place to achieve any degree of success in suicide prevention.

In India, suicide prevention is more of a social and public health objective than a traditional exercise in the mental health sector. Mental health programs, IMHA Act, decriminalizing the attempt to suicide are welcome steps; yet India will need to do a lot more, if it wants to reduce it as a highest cause of death among its youth and the ninth biggest cause of death in the general population.

Suicide is a voluntary end of one's life, triggered by both internal and external pressures, and depends on the contexts, level of vulnerability and endurance to pressures. Reducing and preventing suicide is first about identifying barriers of which acceptance of mental illness, information and resource insufficiency and distribution are prime. Collaboration, coordination, cooperation and commitment are needed at different level, i.e., from state to community to family and to individual to overcome these barriers. A stringent inclusive national plan with a check on barriers, which is cost-effective, appropriate and relevant to the needs of the community, is need of the hour. The time is ripe for society in the role of community gatekeepers, mental health professionals and, most importantly, family to adopt proactive leadership roles in suicide prevention and save the lives of thousands of suicide-prone persons.

Notes

1 Retrieved April 6, 2019, from https://www.who.int/mental_health/resources/preventingsuicide/en/.
2 Retrieved April 6, 2019, from https://www.nhp.gov.in/national-mental-health-programme_pg.
3 Retrieved April 6, 2019, from https://dghs.gov.in/content/1350_3_NationalMentalHealthProgramme.aspx.
4 The WHO Mental Health Gap Action Programme (mhGAP) aims at scaling up services for mental, neurological and substance use (MNS) disorders for countries especially with low- and middle-income. The program asserts that with proper care, psychosocial assistance and medication, tens of millions could be treated for depression, schizophrenia and epilepsy, prevented from suicide and begun to lead normal lives – even where resources are scarce. mhGAP objective is to reinforce the commitment of governments, international organizations and other stakeholders to increase the allocation of financial and human resources for care of MNS disorders (WHO 2008; Retrieved March 3, 2019, from https://www.who.int/mental_health/mhgap/en/).
5 Retrieved March 9, 2019, from http://pib.nic.in/newsite/PrintRelease.aspx?relid=112890.
6 United Nations. 2006. *Convention on the Rights of Persons with Disabilities*. Geneva: United Nations Publications.
7 For more details see: Retrieved August 7, 2017, from http://www.prsindia.org/uploads/media/Mental%20Health/Mental%20Healthcare%20Act,%202017.pdf.
8 Cochrane reviews are systematic of primary research in human health care and health policy, and are internationally recognized as the highest standard in evidence-based health care. They investigate the effects of interventions for prevention, treatment and rehabilitation. They also assess the accuracy of a diagnostic test for a given condition in a specific patient group and setting. They are published online in *The Cochrane Library*.
9 Medical Council of India. Code of Ethics Regulations. Retrieved April 5, 2019 from http://www.mciindia.org/RulesandRegulations/CodeofMedicalEthicsRegulations2002.aspx.

Annexure 1

Checklist-cum-interview schedule

This schedule comprises the information covering various domains of suicide-attempters' and -completers' life: personal, family, medical, socio-psycho details and events at the time of death/attempt.

I. Personal description

   i Age
   ii Gender
   iii Living arrangement: alone/family/others
   iv Family type

      - Nuclear: No. of members/relationship
      - Joint: No. of members/relationship

   v Marital status

      - Unmarried/married/divorcee/separated/widowed

   vi Education
   vii Job status: Employed/unemployed/searching/studying

II Person vs. family description

   i Families economic status

      - Earning members
      - Kind of job

   ii Interpersonal relationships: level of intimacy – close/normal/conflict

      - vs. Parents/in-laws
      - vs. Siblings
      - vs. Friends
      - vs. Spouse/children
      - vs. Relatives/neighbors/others

   iii Feeling towards family

      - Neglect/mistreatment
      - Less love/attention

- Control (parents/others)
- Ignoring demands/wishes
- More expectations

III Person vs. psycho-social description (different life-stages) (trauma-difficulties)

i Early development: growing up years

- Physical abuse
- Neglect, etc.

ii At school

- Bullying/harassment
- Academic performance

iii Job

- Interest
- Pressure
- Working environment
- Colleagues relationships
- Loss/conflict/harassment

iv Fears

v Personal relationships (spouses/partner)

- Sustainability (long/short)
- Conflicts/differences
- Supportive/non-supportive
- Abusive-reasons
- Demanding
- Forbidden relations

vi Communication and interaction with family members: quality/quantity

vii Person been/being part of

- Dysfunctional family
  - Divorced/separated/deserted member
  - Witness to family violence
  - Witness to family disputes

IV Medical-psychiatric description

i Medical treatment

ii Illness

- Current/past
- Type

iii Taking of sleeping pills

V Dreams/desires

  i Interests/hobbies
  ii Life aspirations/life goals

VI Personality and lifestyle

  i Nature

    - Jovial/quiet
    - Social/unsocial
    - Introvert/extrovert

  ii Addictions

    - Drinking/smoking/drugs/others
      - No/occasionally/daily

  iii Response to bad events

    - Anger/violent/quiet/withdrawal

  iv Behavior

    - Adjustment issues
    - Aggressive behavior
    - Low self-esteem
    - Depressive behavior
    - Negativity (with self/others)

VII Account of suicidal behavior

  i Act of suicide: where/when/method/timing
  ii Previous attempts

    - History of previous suicide-attempt: when/why/what kind
    - History of previous suicide threat: when/why
    - Family history of suicide: heard/witnessed

  iii Talk of suicide/death in talk

    - Normal conversation: with whom/frequency
    - To threaten: why/when/outcome

  iv People's reaction over person's attempt/death: expected/never expected/shock

VIII Recent events (prior to attempt/death)

  i Failures/loss/stress due to job/school/family/others
  ii Personal difficulties: recent fights/breakup
  iii Deaths in the family/known person
  iv Mood swings

    - Over food habits

- Appetite loss/weight loss
- Sleep disturbances
- Over friendly/indulgent vs. quiet/withdrawal
- Frequency of anger

IX Post-effect of suicide (attempt/death)

i Attempted: on self/on family
ii Completed: on family

Annexure 2

Socio-demographic profile and inherent aspects of suicide act

Case narratives

Table A.1 Gender distribution by marital status and age, case narratives (in numbers)

Gender	*Married*				*Unmarried*				*Divorcee/separated*			
	15–29 years	*30–44 years*	*45–59 years*	*60 years and above*	*15–29 years*	*30–44 years*	*45–59 years*	*60 years and above*	*15–29 years*	*30–44 years*	*45–59 years*	*60 years and above*
Males	1	9	5	3	8	3	–	–	–	1	–	–
Females	2	2	6	–	8	–	–	–	1	–	–	–
Total	3	11	11	3	16	3	–	–	1	1	–	–

Source: Compiled by authors based on case-interviews.

Table A.2 Educational distribution by gender, marital status and age, case narratives (in numbers)

Educational status	*Gender*		*Marital status*			*Age group*			
	Males	*Females*	*Married*	*Unmarried*	*Divorcee/ separated*	*17–29 years*	*30–44 years*	*45–59 years*	*60 years and above*
No-education	3	3	6	–	–	–	–	4	2
Primary	2	1	2	1	–	1	1	1	–
Middle	2	3	4	–	1	2	3	–	–
Secondary	7	2	5	3	1	2	6	1	–
Higher-Secondary	2	2	3	1	–	2	1	1	–
Diploma	6	–	1	5	–	4	2	–	–
Graduation	6	6	3	9	–	9	1	2	–
Unknown	2	2	4	–	–	–	1	2	1
Total	30	19	28	19	2	20	15	11	3

Source: Compiled by authors based on case-interviews.

Table A.3 Occupational distribution by gender and age, case narratives (in numbers)

		Salaried job (pvt./govt.)	*Student*	*Self-employed*[a]	*Un-employed*	*Housewife*	*Daily-wage earner*	*House-maid*	*Skilled worker*[b]	*Retired*	*Total*
Gender	Male	11	2	6	5	–	2	–	3	1	30
	Female	3	3	1	1	5	–	4	2	–	19
Age group	15–29 years	6	5	3	3	3	–	–	–	–	20
	30–44 years	6	–	1	3	–	1	2	2	–	15
	45–59 years	2	–	1	–	2	1	2	3	–	11
	60 years and above	–	–	2	–	–	–	–	–	1	3

Source: Compiled by authors based on case-interviews.

a Involves doing own business or family business.
b Involves occupation of a driver/tailor/cook.

Table A.4 Causal distribution of suicide by gender, marital status and age, case narratives (in numbers)

Causes	*Gender*		*Marital status*			*Age group*			
	Male	*Female*	*Married*	*Unmarried*	*Divorcee/ separated*	*15–29 years*	*30–44 years*	*45–59 years*	*60 years and above*
Family problems/issues	4	5	6	2	1	4	5	–	–
Long-term disease	4	2	5	1	–	1	–	3	2
Due to love-affair	1	3	–	4	–	4	–	–	–
Overprotected/pampered upbringing	2	1	–	3	–	3	–	–	–
Emotional blackmailing	1	–	1	–	–	1	–	–	–
Indebtedness	1	–	–	1	–	1	–	–	–
Expected aspirations and fear of failure	1	2	1	2	–	2	1	–	–
Unemployment	1	–	–	1	–	1	–	–	–
Not having children	–	1	1	–	–	1	–	–	–
Mental illness/depression	4	2	3	2	1	1	2	3	–
Alcoholism	6	–	6	–	–	–	4	1	1
Criminal act and fear	1	–	–	1	–	–	1	–	–
Extra marital affair	1	–	1	–	–	–	–	1	–
Financial loss	2	–	1	1	–	–	1	1	–
Unknown	1	3	3	1	–	1	1	2	–
Total	30	19	28	19	2	20	15	11	3

Source: Compiled by authors based on case-interviews.

Table A.5 Distribution of adopted suicide methods by suicide status, gender and marital status, case narratives (in numbers)

		Hanging	*Consuming poison*	*Drowning/ jumping in lake*	*Consuming pills*	*Self-injury*	*Self-immolation*	*Total*
Suicide status	Attempted	–	8	1	2	2	–	13
	Completed	23	7	1	–	–	5	36
Gender	Male	14	9	1	2	2	2	30
	Female	9	6	1	–	–	3	19
Marital status	Married	10	8	1	2	2	5	28
	Unmarried	11	7	1	–	–	–	19
	Divorcee/separated	2	–	–	–	–	–	2

Source: Compiled by authors based on case-interviews.

Table A.6a Distribution of various inherent aspects of suicidal act, case narratives (in numbers)

Inherent aspects			*Attempted*	*Completed*
1 Family dynamics	Family type	Nuclear family	9	20
		Extended family	4	16
	Income group	Lower class	3	9
		Middle class	8	24
		Upper class	2	3
	Level of integration	Person pampered by the family/person over-dependent on the family	2	3
		Person's over-indulgent in the family	1	–
2 Intervening social factors		Person indulged or facing family conflicts/person's abusive behavior towards others	3	7
		Person thinking of not doing enough for the family/ person unable to do something for the family due to no job	4	4
		Person disturbed because of kin's death	1	2
		Person's addiction to alcohol and its impact on household	2	3
		Person's non-responsible behavior (due to wrongdoings)	2	–
3 Personality traits/aspects		Person's personality of being		
		Introvert/non-sharing/ non-adjustment	1	11
		Overbearing/non-adjustment	1	–
		Stubborn/impulsive/ aggressive	–	2
		Introvert/non-adjustment/ short-tempered	1	1
		Extrovert/jovial/friendly	2	15
		Anger/non-patience/ non-adjustment	1	4
		Restricted socialization to close kins/group	–	1
		Shy/introvert/submissive/ sensitive	5	4

(*Continued*)

Inherent aspects		Attempted	Completed
4 Social and community constraints	Person loaded with sense of responsibility: expected and inability	2	3
	Person feeling shame/guilt for self-failures	1	2
	Person living with guilt/ shame – over the suicide act/over their actions or behavior bringing insult to self and family	1	3
	Person's atmosphere – growing up in religious-cultural family environment/religious person	1	3
5 Sense of deprivation	Sense of burden or/and fear in person – due to health issues	–	12
	Sense of burden in person – due to blaming (self/ others)/rejection/failure	2	5
	Person having feeling of hopelessness/person occupied with self-imagined worries	2	–
	Others	–	3
6 Aspirations/achievements/ expectations	Person's struggle with his/her aspirations/ expectations from life and the reality	1	6

Source: Compiled by authors based on case-interviews.

Table A.6b Distribution of various inherent aspects of suicidal act, case narratives (in numbers)

Inherent aspects		*Attempted*	*Completed*
7 Mental illness	Person showing: sudden change in behavior/sign of mental disturbances/abnormal actions	1	3
	Signs of depression/loneliness in person	1	–
8 Debt/financial loss	Person taken debt	1	3
	Person faced financial loss	–	2

(*Continued*)

Inherent aspects		Attempted	Completed
9 Suicidal tendency and exposure to suicide	Person was exposed to the suicide incidences at neighborhood/of friends/peers	1	2
	Person heard/witnessed suicides of the family/relatives	1	3
	Person has the history of suicide-attempts	3	3
	Person conversing about suicide/ death/dying with the family/ friends/neighbors	–	7

Table A.7 Responses over suicidal act of the family/self of suicide-attempters and the family of suicide-completers (in numbers)

S.no	Responses	Suicide-attempters	Suicide-completers
1	Feeling of shock/unbelievable feeling of family towards the act	–	22
2	Families yet to cope with the person's loss	–	13
3	Families acceptance to the loss as they witnessed person's sufferings/pain/behavior	1	4
4	Families/self-feeling regret/guilty towards attempt or death. Considering act to be an impulsive	10	3
5	Person considering it a rageful act with no regret feeling	1	–
6	Families acceptance of ignoring person's suicide symptoms	1	3
7	Person's death resulted in loss of financial support	–	3
8	Person's death resulted in loss of social and emotional support	–	5
9	Person's death resulted in loss of both: financial and social/ emotional support	–	4
10	Family facing financial constraints due to person's death-repaying debt/financial issues	1	5
11	Family considering suicidal death as fate (due to their behavior)	–	6
12	No emotions/reactions by family over suicidal act	1	1
13	Family feeling that suicide could be avoided		
	i If acted timely	–	4
	ii If given assurance of well-being/removing insecurity of the person	–	4
14	Shift of household responsibility on others due to person's death	–	5
15	Family condemning/regretting suicidal act of the person	6	9

Source: Compiled by authors based on case-interviews.

References

Agnew, R. 1992. 'Foundation for a General Strain Theory of Crime and Delinquency', *Criminology*, 30 (1), pp. 47–88.

American Association of Suicidology (AAS). 1989. *Postvention Guidelines: School Suicide Prevention Programs Committee*, Denver, CO: American Association of Suicidology.

Andriessen, K. 2009. 'Can Postvention be Prevention?', *Crisis*, 30, pp. 43–47.

Antony, J.T. 2014. 'The Mental Health Care Bill 2013: A Disaster in the Offing?', *Indian Journal of Psychiatry*, 56, pp. 3–7.

———. 2016. 'Mental Health Legislation: A Journey Back to "Madhouses Era?"', *Indian Journal of Psychiatry*, 58, pp. 1148.

Appleby, L., Cooper, J., Amos, T., and Faragher, B. 1999. 'Psychological Autopsy Study of Suicides by People Aged under 35', *British Journal of Psychiatry*, 175 (8), pp. 168–174.

Avasthi, A. 2010. 'Preserve and Strengthen Family to Promote Mental Health', *Indian Journal of Psychiatry*, 52, pp. 113126.

Baechler, J. 1979. *Suicides*, New York City: Basic Books.

Bailley, S.E., Dunham K., and Kral, M.J. 2000. 'Factor Structure of the Grief Experience Questionnaire', *Death Studies*, 24, pp. 721–738.

Bailley, S.E., Kral, M.J., and Dunham, K. 1999. 'Survivors of Suicide Do Grieve Differently: Empirical Support for a Common Sense Position', *Suicide and Life Threatening Behavior*, 29 (3), pp. 256–270.

Baldwin, R., and Jolley, D. 1986. 'The Prognosis of Depression in Old Age', *British Journal of Psychiatry*, 149, pp. 574–583.

Bancroft, J., Skrimshire, A., and Simkins, S. 1976. 'The Reasons People Give for Taking Overdoses', *British Journal of Psychiatry*, 128, pp. 538–548.

Banerjee, G. 2001. 'The Law and Mental Health: An Indian Perspective', Retrieved from http://www.psyplexus.com/excl/lmhi.html.

Bantjes, J., Lemmi, V., Coast, E., Channer, K., Leone, T., McDaid, D., Palfreyman, A., Stephens, B. and Lund, C. 2016. 'Poverty and Suicide Research in Low and Middle Income Countries: Systematic Mapping of Literature Published in English and Proposed Research Agenda', *Global Mental Health*, 3, e32, pp. 1–18.

Barbui, C., Esposito E., and Cipriani, A. 2009. 'Selective Serotonin Reuptake Inhibitors and Risk of Suicide: A Systematic Review of Observational Studies', *Canadian Medical Association Journal*, 180 (3), pp. 291–297.

Barett, T.W., and Scott, T.B. 1990. 'Suicide Bereavement and Recovery Patterns Compared with Non-suicide Bereavement Patterns', *Suicide and Life-Threatening Behavior*, 20 (1), pp. 1–15.

Barraclough, B. 1972. 'A Medical Approach to Suicide Prevention', *Social Science and Medicine*, 6, pp. 661–671.

Barraclough, B., Bunch, J., Nelson, B., and Sainsbury, P. 1974. 'A Hundred Cases of Suicide: Clinical Aspects', *British Journal of Psychiatry*, 125 (587), pp. 355–373. doi:10.1192/bjp.125.4.355.

Barstad, A. 2008. 'Explaining Changing Suicide Rates in Norway 1948–2004: The Role of Social Integration', *Social Indicators Research*, 87, pp. 47–64.

Baumeister, R.F. 1990. 'Suicide as Escape from Self', *Psychological Review*, 99, pp. 90–113.

Baumeister, R.F., Ellen, B., Mark, M., and Tice, D.M. 1998. 'Ego Depletion: Is the Active Self a Limited Resource?', *Journal of Personality and Social Psychology*, 74 (5), pp. 1252–1265.

Beautrias, A.L. 1994. 'Risk Factors for Suicide and Attempted Suicide among Young People', *Australian and New Zealand Journal of Psychiatry*, 34 (3), pp. 420–436.

Beck, A.T. 1967. *Depression*, New York: Harper and Row.

Beck, A.T., Kovacs, M., and Weissman, A. 1975. 'Hopelessness and Suicidal Behaviour: An Overview', *The Journal of the American Medical Association*, 234, pp. 1146–1149.

Beck, A.T., Rush, A.J., Shaw, Brian. F., and Emery, G. 1987. *Cognitive Therapy of Depression*, New York: Guilford Press.

Beck, A.T., Steer, R.A., Beck, J.S., and Newman, C.F. 1993. 'Hopelessness, Depression, Suicidal Ideation, and Clinical Diagnosis of Depression', *Suicide and Life-Threatening Behaviour*, 23 (2), pp. 139–145.

Begley, M., and Quayle E. 2008. 'The Lived Experience of Adults Bereaved by Suicide: A Phenomenological Study', *Crisis*, 28, pp. 26–34.

Behere, P.B., and Behere, A.P. 2008. ''Farmers' Suicide in Vidarbha Region in Maharashtra State: A Myth or Reality?', *Indian Journal of Psychiatry*, 50, pp. 124–127.

Benton, S., Foster, P., and Maple, M. 2014. 'Suicide and Language: Why we Should not Use the 'C' Word', *InPsych*, 35 (1),pp. 30–31.

Berman, A.L. 2000. *Comprehensive Textbook of Suicidology*, New York: Guilford, pp. 268–270, 319–320.

Berman, A.L., and Jobes, D.A. 1991. *Adolescent Suicide: Assessment and Intervention*, Washington, DC: American Psychological Association.

Beskow, J. 1979. 'Suicide in Mental Disorder in Swedish Men', *Acta Psychiatrica Scandinavica*, 277, pp. 1–138.

Beskow, J., Runeson, B., and Asgard, U. 1990. 'Psychological Autopsies: Methods and Ethics', *Suicide Life-Threatening Behaviour*, 20, pp. 307–323.

Bhagat, V. 1994. 'Unnatural Deaths of Women in Gujarat', *Resources for Feminist Research*, 23 (3), p. 43.

Bhatia, S.C., Khan, M.H., Mediratta, R.P., and Sharma, A. 1987. 'High Risk Suicide Factors across Cultures', *International Journal of Social Psychiatry*, 33, pp. 226–236.

Bhugra, D. 2002. 'Suicidal Behavior in South Asians in the UK', *Crisis*, 23 (3), pp. 108–113.

Birtchnell, J., and Alarcon, J. 1971. 'The Motivational and Emotional State of 91 Cases of Attempted Suicide', *British Journal of Medical Psychology*, 44, pp. 42–52.

Bonner, R.L., and Rich, A.R. 1987. 'Toward a Predictive Model of Suicidal Ideation and Behavior: Some Preliminary Data in College Students', *Suicide and Life-Threatening Behavior*, 17, pp. 50–63.

Borges, G., Nock, M.K., Haro Abad, J.M., Hwang, I., Sampson, N.A., Alonso, J., Andrade, L.H., et al. 2010. 'Twelve-month Prevalence of and Risk Factors for Suicide Attempts in the World Health Organization World Mental Health Surveys,' *Journal of Clinical Psychiatry*, 71 (12), pp. 1617–1628.

Borges, G., and Rosovsky, H. 1996. 'Suicide Attempts and Alcohol Consumption in an Emergency Room Sample', *Journal of Studies on Alcohol and Drug*, 57, pp. 543–548.

Bowlby, J. 1969. *Attachment and Loss: Volume I. Attachment*, New York: Basic Books.

———. 1980. *Attachment and Loss: Volume III. Loss*, New York: Basic Books.

———. 1988. *A Secure Base: Parent–Child Attachment and Healthy Human Development*, New York: Basic Books.

Brennan, K.A., Clark, C.L., and Shaver, P.R. 1998. 'Self-Report Measurement of Adult Attachment: An Integrative Overview', in J.A. Simpson and W.S. Rholes (eds.), *Attachment Theory and Close Relationships*, New York: The Guilford Press, pp. 46–76.

Brent, D.A., and Mann, J.J. 2005. 'Family Genetic Studies, Suicide, and Suicidal Behaviour', *American Journal of Medical Genetics Part C*, 133C, pp. 13–24.

Brent, D.A., and Perper, J.A. 1995. 'Research in Adolescent Suicide: Implications for Training, Service Delivery, and Public Policy', *Suicide Life Threat Behavior*, 25, pp. 222–230.

Brezo, J., Paris, J., and Turecki, G. 2006. 'Personality Traits as Correlates of Suicidal Ideation, Suicide Attempts, and Suicide Completions: A Systematic Review', *Acta Psychiatrica Scandinavaca*, 113 (3), pp. 180–206.

Briere, J., and Zaidi, L.Y. 1989. 'Sexual Abuse Histories and Sequelae in Female Psychiatric Emergency Room Patients', *American Journal of Psychiatry*, 146, pp. 1602–1606.

Briggs, S., Linford, H., and Harvey, A. 2012. *Guests Experience of Maytree during and after Their Stay*, London: University of East London and Tavistock Clinic. http://www.maytree.org.uk/download/CSWR-2012.pdf.

Briggs, S., Webb, L., Buhagiar J., and Braun, G. 2007. 'Maytree: A Respite Center for the Suicidal', *Crisis*, 28 (3), pp. 140–147.

Broidy, L., and Agnew, R. 1997. 'Gender and Crime: A General Strain Theory Perspective', *Journal of Research in Crime and Delinquency*, 34, pp. 275–306.

Brown, G.K., Beck, A.T., Steer, R., and Grisham, J. 2000. 'Risk Factors for Suicide in Psychiatric Outpatients: A 20-Year Prospective Study', *Journal of Consulting and Clinical Psychology*, 68, pp. 371–377.

Brown, G.K., Jeglic, E., Henriques, G.R., and Beck, A.T. 2006. 'Cognitive Therapy, Cognition, and Suicidal Behaviour', in T.E. Ellis (ed.), *Cognition and Suicide: Theory, Research and Therapy*, Washington, DC: American Psychological Association, pp. 53–74.

Bryan, H., Brophy, K., Cunningham, A., and Schwarz, R. 2012. *Now What Do We Do? The Emotional Impact of a Suicide Attempt on Families*. Heidi Bryan Consulting, LLC. https://www.starsinc.com/wp-content/uploads/2016/02/Now-What-Do-We-Do.pdf

Burge, V., Felts M., Chenier, T., and Parillo, A.V. 1995. 'Drug Use, Sexual Activity and Suicidal Behavior in US High School Students', *The Journal of School Health*, 65, pp. 222–227.

Campbell, L.A., and Kisely, S.R. 2009. 'Advance Treatment Directives for People with Severe Mental Illness', *Cochrane Database Systematic Reviews*, CD005963.

Camus, A. 1991. *The Myth of Sisyphus and Other Essays*, New York: Vintage Books, p. 212. (Original Published in 1955.)

Canetto, S.S. 1991. 'Gender Roles, Suicide Attempts, and Substance Abuse', *Journal of Psychology*, 125, pp. 605–620.

———. 1992. 'Gender and Suicide in the Elderly', *Suicide Life Threatening Behaviour*, 22, pp. 80–97.

Canetto, S.S., and Sakinofsky, I. 1998. 'The Gender Paradox in Suicide', *Suicide and Life-threatening Behavior*, 28 (1), pp. 1–23.

Canter, D.V. 2000. 'Psychological Autopsies', in Jay, Siegal and Pekka, Saukko (eds.), *Encyclopedia of Forensic Sciences*, London: Elsevier, pp. 1281–1290.

Carroll, O.P.W., and Potter, L.B. 1994. 'Suicide Contagion and the Reporting of Suicide: Recommendations from a National Workshop. United States Department of Health and Human Services', *Morbidity and Mortality Weekly Report*, 43 (RR-6), pp. 9–17.

Cerel, J., Jordan, J.R., and Duberstein, R.P. 2008. 'The Impact of Suicide on the Family', *Crisis*, 29 (1), pp. 38–44.

Chan, C.H., Caine, E.D., You, S., Fu, K.W., Chang, S.S., and Yip, P.S.F. 2014. 'Suicide Rates among Working-age Adults in South Korea before and after the 2008 Economic Crisis', *Journal of Epidemiology and Community Health*, 68, pp. 246–252.

Chang, S.S., Stuckler, D., Yip, P., and Gunnell, D. 2013. 'Impact of 2008 Global Economic Crisis on Suicide: Time Trend Study in 54 Countries', *British Medical Journal*, 347, f5239.

Chapple, A., Ziebland, S., and Hawton, K. 2015. 'Taboo and the Different Death? Perceptions of Those Bereaved by Suicide or Other Traumatic Death', *Sociology of Health and Illness*, 37 (4), pp. 610–625.

Chatterjee, I., and Basu, J. 2010. 'Perceived Causes of Suicide, Reasons for Living and Suicidal Ideation among Students', *Journal of the Indian Academy of Applied Psychology*, 36 (2), pp. 311–316.

Chatterjee, P., and Bailey, D. 1993. 'False Empowerment: Lessons from Three Sociological Autopsies of Community Action', *Case Analysis*, 3 (2), pp. 113–131.

Chavan, B.S., Singh, G.P., and Kaur, J. 2008. 'Psychological Autopsy of 101 Suicide Cases from Northwest Region of India', *Indian Journal of Psychiatry*, 50, pp. 34–38.

Chemin, M., Joost, D.L, and Johannes, H. 2013. 'Negative Rainfall Shocks Increase Levels of the Stress Hormone Cortisol among Poor Farmers in Kenya'. Available at SSRN 2294171.

Chen, Y.Y., Wu, K.C., Yousuf, S., and Yip, P.S. 2012. 'Suicide in Asia: Opportunities and Challenges', *Epidemiological Review*, 34 (1), pp. 129–144. doi:10.1093/epirev/mxr025.

Cheng, A.T.A. 1995. 'Mental Illness and Suicide', *British Journal of Psychiatry*, 170, pp. 441–446.

Cheng, A.T.A, Chen, T.H., Chen, C.C., and Jenkins, R. 2000. 'Psychosocial and Psychiatric Risk Factors for Suicide: Case-control Psychological Autopsy Study', *British Journal of Psychiatry*, 177, pp. 360–365.

Cheng, Y.Y., Shein, P.P., and Chiou, W.B. 2012. 'Escaping the Impulse to Immediate Gratification: The Prospect Concept Promotes a Future-oriented mind Set, Prompting an Inclination towards Delayed Gratification', *British Journal of Psychology*, 103 (1), pp. 129–141.

Chesney, E., Goodwin, G.M., and Fazel, S. 2014. 'Risks of All-Cause and Suicide Mortality in Mental Disorders: A Meta-Review', *World Psychiatry*, 13, pp. 153–160.

Cho, Y. 2012. 'Clinical Psychiatry and Suicide Prevention', *Seishin Shinkeigaku Zasshi*, 114 (5), pp. 553–558. Retrieved from https://www.ncbi.nlm.nih.gov/pubmed/22746046.

Clarck, D.C., and Horton-Deutsch, S.L.1992. 'Assessment in Absentia: The Value of the Psychological Autopsy Method for Studying Antecedents of Suicide and Predicting Future Suicides', in R.W. Maris, A.L. Berman, J.T. Maltsberger, and R. Yufit (eds.), *Assessment and Prediction of Suicides*, New York: The Guilford Press, pp. 144–182.

Clark, L.P. 1922. 'A Study of the Unconscious Motivations in Suicides', *New York Medical Journal*, 116, pp. 254–263.

Cluver, L., Orkin, M., Boyes, M.E., and Sherr, L. 2015. 'Child and Adolescent Suicide Attempts, Suicidal Behavior, and Adverse Childhood Experiences in South Africa: A Prospective Study', *Journal of Adolescent Health*, 57 (1), pp. 52–59. doi:10.1016/j.jadohealth.2015.03.001; PMID:25936843.

Colucci, E., Lester, D., Hjelmeland, H., and Ben Park, B.C. (eds.). 2013. *Suicide and Culture: Understanding the Context*, Ashland: Hogrefe Publishing.

Conner, K.R., and Duberstein, P.R. 2004. 'Predisposing and Precipitating Factors for Suicide among Alcoholics: Empirical Review and Conceptual Integration', *Alcoholism, Clinical and Experimental Research*, 28 (5 Suppl.), pp. 6S–17S.

Conwell, Y., Duberstein, P., and Cox, C. 1996. 'Relationships of Age and Axis I Diagnoses in Victims of Completed Suicide: A Psychological Autopsy Study, *American Journal of Psychiatry*, 153, pp. 1001–1008.

Cooper, J. 1999. 'Ethical Issues and Their Practical Application in a Psychological Autopsy Study of Suicide', *Journal of Clinical Nursing*, 8 (4), pp. 467–475.

Crammer, J. 1984. 'The Special Characteristics of Suicide in Hospital In-Patients', *British Journal of Psychiatry*, 145 (5), pp. 460–463. doi:10.1192/bjp.145.5.460.

Crichton-Miller, H. 1931. 'The Psychology of Suicide', *British Medical Journal*, 2, pp. 239–241.

Cronin, C. 2009. *Forensic Psychology* (Second Edition), Dubuque, IA: Kendall Hunt Pub Co.

Crosby, A.E., and Sacks, J.J. 2002. 'Exposure to Suicide: Incidence and Association with Suicidal Ideation and Behavior: United States', *Suicide and Life Threatening Behaviour*, 32 (3), pp. 321–328.

Crowell, S.E., Theodore, B., and Linehan, M.M. 2009. 'A Biosocial Developmental Model of Borderline Personality: Elaborating and Extending Linehan's Theory', *Psychological Bulletin*, May, 135 (3), pp. 495–510.

Cvinar, J.G. 2005. 'Do Suicide Survivors Suffer Social Stigma: A Review of the Literature', *Perspective of Psychiatric Care*, 41, pp. 14–21.

Dandona, R., Kumar, A., and Dhaliwal, R.S. 2018. 'Gender Differentials and State Variations in Suicide Deaths in India: The Global Burden of Disease Study 1990–2016', *Lancet Public Health*, 3, e478–e489.

Dang, J. 2018. 'An Updated Meta-analysis of the Ego Depletion Effect', *Psychological Research*, 82 (4), pp. 645–651.

Das, P.P., Grover, S., Avasthi, A., Chakrabarthi, S., Malhotra, S., and Kumar, S. 2008. 'Intentional Self Harm Seen in Psychiatric Referrals in a Tertiary Care Hospital', *Indian Journal of Psychiatry*, 50, pp. 187–191.

Das, S. 2017. 'Suicide among the Elderly: A Psychological Perspective, *International Journal of Social Work and Human Services*, 5 (1), pp. 35–42.

Davidson, L. 2012. 'Living Recovery', *Epidemiological Psychiatric Science*, 21 (4), pp. 365–366.

Devi, R.W., and Prakash, J. 2015. 'Personality Profile and Suicidal Behaviour among College Students', *International Journal of Recent Research in Social Sciences and Humanities*, 2 (3), pp. 29–35.

De Wilde, E., Kienhorst, I.C., Diekstra, R.F., and Wolters, W.H. 1991. 'The Relationship between Adolescent Suicidal Behavior and Life Events in Childhood and Adolescence', *American Journal of Psychiatry*, 149 (1), pp. 45–51.

Dhandha, A. 2010. *Status Paper on Rights of Persons Living with Mental Illness in Light of the UNCRPD, in Harmonizing Laws with UNCRPD*, Report Prepared by the Centre of Disability Studies. Human Right Law Network.

Dikshit, P.C. 2010. 'Autopsy Procedures and Exhumation', *Textbook of Forensic Medicine and Toxicology*, New Delhi: Peepee Publishers, pp. 112–113.

Douglas, J., and Klein-Benheim, M. 1995. 'The Psychological Autopsy: A Useful Tool for Determining Proximate Causation in Suicide Cases', *Bulletin of American Academy of Psychiatry and Law*, 23 (2), pp. 165–182.

Douglas, J.D. 1967. *The Social Meanings of Suicide*, Princeton, NJ: Princeton University Press.

Draper, B. 1996. 'Attempted Suicide in Old Age', *International Journal of Geriatric Psychiatry*, 11, pp. 577–588.

Dumbrava, D.P., Anipan S., Siserman, C., Fulga, I., and Opincaru, I. 2010. 'Virtopsy-An Alternative to the Conventional Autopsy', *Roman Journal of Legal Medicine*, 1, pp. 75–78.

Duneier, M. 2006. 'Ethnography, the Ecological Fallacy, and the 1995 Chicago Heat Wave', *American Sociological Review*, 71, pp. 679–688.

Durkheim, E. 1951(original 1897). '*Suicide: A Study in Sociology*', Trans. Spaulding, John A and Simpson, George, New York: The Free Press.

Dutta, A.B. 2001. 'The Long March of Mental Health Legislation in Independent India', Dr. L.P.Shah Oration delivered at IPS-WZ Conference at Goa. Published by Goa Psychiatry Society.

Ebert, B.W. 1987. 'Guide to Conducting a Psychological Autopsy', *Professional Psychology: Research and Practice*, 18 (1), pp. 52–56.

Egeland, J.A., and Sussex, J.N. 1985. 'Suicide and Family Loading for Affective Disorders', *JAMA*, 254, pp. 915–918, 938.

Ehnvall, A., Parker, G., Hadzi-Pavlovic, D., and Malhi, G. 2008. 'Perception of Rejecting and Neglectful Parenting in Childhood Relates to Lifetime Suicide Attempts for Females – But Not for Males', *Acta Psychiatrica Scandinavaca*, 117 (1), pp. 50–56.

Evans, D.R., Boggero, I.A., and Segerstrom, S.C. 2016. 'The Nature of Self-Regulatory Fatigue and "Ego Depletion": Lessons from Physical Fatigue', *Personality and Social Psychology Review*, 20 (4), pp. 291–310.

Fawcett, J. 2006. 'Depressive Disorders', in R.I. Simon and R.E. Hales (eds.), *The American Psychiatric Publishing Textbook of Suicide Assessment and Management*, Washington, DC: American Psychiatric Pub, pp. 255–275.

Fielden, J.M. 2003. 'Grief as a Transformative Experience: Weaving through Different Life Worlds after a Loved One has Completed Suicide, *International Journal of Mental Health Nursing*, 12, pp. 74–85.

Fincham, B., Langer, S., Scourfield, J., and Michael, S. 2011. *Understanding Suicide: A Sociological Autopsy*, Basingstoke: Palgrave Macmillan.

Fitzpatrick, Scott, and River, Jo. 2017. 'Beyond the Medical Model: Future Directions for Suicide Intervention Services', *International Journal of Health Services*, June 26, Online, pp. 1–15.

Freud, S. 1953. 'Three Essays on the Theory of Sexuality' (1905 orig.), in Standard Edition of the complete works of Sigmund Freud, Vol. 7, translated by James Strachey et al. London: The Hogarth Press, pp. 125–243.

———. 1923. *The Ego and the Id*, Standard Edition, London: Hogarth Press, 19, pp. 1–66.

Fuse, T. 1997. *Suicide, Individual and Society*, Toronto, ON: Canadian Scholars Press.

Gajalakshmi, V., and Peto, R. 2007. 'Suicide Rates in Rural Tamil Nadu, South India: Verbal Autopsy of 39,000 Deaths in 1997–1998', *International Journal of Epidemiology*, 36 (1), pp. 203–207.

George, A.L., and Bennet, A. 2005. *Case Studies and Theory Development in the Social Sciences*, Cambridge, MA: The MIT Press.

Giddens, A. 1971. 'Durkheim and His Contemporaries', in A. Giddens (ed.), *The Sociology of Suicide: A Selection of Readings*, London: Frank Cass and Company, pp. 3–4.

Gill, S.S. 2005. 'Economic Distress and Suicides in Rural Punjab', *Journal of Punjab Studies*, 12, pp. 219–237.

Gillebaart, M. 2018. 'The 'Operational' Definition of Self-Control', *Frontiers in Psychology*, 9, p. 1231.

Gomes, M., Begum, R., Prabha, S., Dikshit, R., Gupta, P.C., Kumar, R., Sheth, J., Habib, A., and Jha, P. 2017. 'Nationwide Mortality Studies to Quantify Causes of Death: Relevant Lessons from India's Million Death Study', *Health Affairs*, 36 (11), pp. 1887–1895. doi:10.1377/hlthaff.2017.0635.

Gordon, R.G. 1922. 'Certain Personality Problems in Relation to Mental Illness with Special Reference to Suicide and Homicide', *British Journal of Medical Psychology*, 9, pp. 60–66. doi:10.1080/13811118.2017.1334610.

Gross, R. 2015. *Psychology: The Science of Mind and Behaviour*, Seventh Edition, London: Hodder Education, pp. 796–797.

Gulvady, M. 2003. 'Befriending in Developing Countries', in Lakshmi Vijayakumar (ed.), *Suicide Prevention: Meeting the Challenge Together*, Chennai: Orient Longman Limited, pp. 191–197.

Gupta, S.C., Singh, H., and Trivedi, J.K. 1992. 'Evaluation of Suicidal Risk in Depressives and Schizophrenics: A Two Year Follow Up Study', *Indian Journal of Psychiatry*, 34, pp. 298–310.

Gururaj, G., and Issac, M.K. 2004. 'Psychiatric Epidemiology in India: Moving beyond Numbers', in S.P. Agarwal, D.S. Goel, et al. (eds.), *Mental Health in Indian Perspective 1946–2003*, Delhi: Ministry of Health and Family Welfare, Elsevier, pp. 37–61.

Gururaj, G., Isaac, M.K., Subbakrishna, D.K., and Ranjani, R. 2004. 'Risk Factors for Completed Suicides: A Case-control Study from Bangalore-India', *Injury Control and Safety Promotion*, 11 (3), pp. 183–191.

Gutierrez, P.M., Osman, A., Kopper, B.A., and Barrios, F.X. 2000. 'Why Young People Do Not Kill Themselves: The Reasons for Living Inventory for Adolescents', *Journal of Clinical Child Psychology*, 29 (2), pp. 177–187.

Hamdi, E., Price S., Qassem, T., Amin, Y., and Jones, D. 2008. 'Suicides Not in Contact with Mental Health Services: Risk Indicators and Determinations of Referral', *Journal of Mental Health*, 17, pp. 398–409.

Hamermesh, D.S., and Soss, N.M. 1974. 'An Economic Theory of Suicide', *Journal of Political Economy*, 82, pp. 83–98.

Harris, E.D., and Barraclough, B. 1977. 'Suicide as an Outcome of Mental Disorders', *British Journal of Psychiatry*, 170, pp. 205–228.

Harvard Women's Health Watch. 2009. 'Left Behind After Suicide'. Harvard Health Publishing. Retrieved from https://www.health.harvard.edu/mind-and-mood/left-behind-after-suicide.

Hastings, M.E., Northman L.M., and Tangney J.P. 2002. 'Shame, Guilt, and Suicide', *Suicide Science*. Boston, MA: Springer, MAP, pp. 67–79.

Hawton, K., and Heeringen, K.V. 2001. *The International Handbook of Suicide and Attempted Suicide*, New York: Wiley.

Hegde, R.S. 1980. 'Suicide in a Rural Community of North Karnataka', *Indian Journal of Psychiatry*, 22, pp. 368–370.

Heidi, H., Gudrun, D., Dyregrov, K., Knizek, B.L., and Leenaars, A.A. 2012. 'Psychological Autopsy Studies as Diagnostic Tools: Are They Methodologically Flawed?', *Death Studies*, 36 (7), 605–626. doi:10.1080/07481187.2011.584015.

Heikkinen, M., Aro, H., and Lonngvist, J. 1993. 'Life Events and Social Support in Suicide', *Suicide and Life Threatening Behaviour*, 23 (4), pp. 343–358.

Hendin, H.1964. *Suicide and Scandinavia*, Oxford: Grune & Stratton.

———. 1982. *Suicide in America*, New York: Norton.

———. 2008. 'Introduction', in H. Hendin, M.R. Phillips, et al. (eds.), *Suicide and Suicide Prevention in Asia*, Geneva: WHO, pp. 1–5.

Hendin, H., Phillips, M., Vijayakumar, L., Pirkis, J., Wang, H., Yip, P., Wasserman, D., Bertolote, J., and Fleischmann, A. 2008. *Suicide and Suicide Prevention in Asia,* Geneva: World Health Organization. Retrieved from: http://www.who.int/mental_health/resources/suicide_prevention_asia.pdf.

Hershatter, G. 1991. 'Prostitution and the Market in Women in Early 20th Century Shanghai', in R.S. Watson and P.B. Ebrey (eds.), *Marriage and Inequality in Chinese Society*, Berkeley: University of California Press.

Higgins, E.T. 1987. 'Self-Discrepancy: A Theory Relating Self and Affect', *Psychological Review*, 94, pp. 319–340.

Higgins, E.T., Klein, R., and Strauman, T. 1985. 'Self-Concept Discrepancy Theory: A Psychological Model for Distinguishing among Different Aspects of Depression and Anxiety', *Social Cognition*, 3, pp. 51–76.

Hong, J., Knapp M., and McGuire, A. 2011. 'Income-Related Inequalities in the Prevalence of Depression and Suicidal Behaviour: A 10-year Trend Following Economic Crisis', *World Psychiatry*, 10, pp. 40–44.

Houston, K., Hawton, K., and Shepperd, R. 2001. 'Suicide in Young People Aged 15–24: A Psychological Autopsy Study', *Journal of Affective Disorders*, 63, pp. 159–170.

INSERM Collective Expertise Centre. 2005. *Suicide: Psychological Autopsy, A Research Tool for Prevention*, Paris: Institut national de la santé et de la recherche médicale (National Institute for Health and Medical Research). Retrieved from https://www.ncbi.nlm.nih.gov/books/NBK7126/

Interian, A., Chesin, M., and Kline, Anna., Miller, R., St Hill, L., Latorre, M., Shcherbakov, A., King, A., and Stanley, B. 2018. 'Use of the Columbia-Suicide

Severity Rating Scale (C-SSRS) to Classify Suicidal Behaviors', *Archives of Suicide Research*, 22 (2), pp. 278–294.

Isometsa, E. 2001. 'Psychological Autopsy Studies: A Review', *European Psychiatry*, 16, pp. 379–385.

Jacobs, D., and Klein, M.E. 1993. 'The Expanding Role of Psychological Autopsies', in A.A. Leenaars (ed.), *Suicidology Essays in Honor of Edwin S. Shneidman*, Northvale, NJ: Jason Aronson, pp. 209–247.

Jacobs, Jerry. 1967. 'A Phenomenological Study of Suicide Notes', *Social Problems*, 15 (2), pp. 60–72.

Jain, M., Bhatia, R., and Mathur, T.N. 2012. 'Work Place Stress and Suicide: A Study with Reference to Public Sector Organisation', *International Journal of Multidisciplinary Research*, 2 (7), pp. 186–197.

Jain, V., Singh, H., Gupta, S.C., and Kumar, S. 1999. 'A Study of Hopelessness, Suicidal Intent and Depression in Cases of Attempted Suicide', *Indian Journal of Psychiatry*, 41, pp. 122–130.

James, L. Knoll. 2008. 'The Psychological Autopsy, Part I: Applications and Methods', *Journal of Psychiatric Practice*, 14 (6), pp. 393–397.

Ji, J., Kleinman, A., and Becker, A.E. 2001. 'Suicide in Contemporary China: A Review of China's Distinctive Suicide Demographics in their Sociocultural Context', *Harvard Review of Psychiatry*, 9, pp. 1–12.

Jobes, D.A. 2006. *Managing Suicidal Risk: A Collaborative Approach*, New York: The Guilford Press.

Jobes, D.A., Au, S.J., and Siegelman, A. 2015. 'Approaches to Suicide Treatment and Prevention', *Current Treatment Options in Psychiatry*, 2, pp. 363–370.

Jobes, D.A., Casey, J., Berman, A., and Wright, D.G. 1991. 'Empirical Criteria for the Determination of Suicide Manner of Death', *Journal of Forensic Science*, 36, pp. 244–256.

Jogadic, H.K., Agius M., and Pregali, P. 2013. 'Psychopharmacotherapy Prescription and Suicidal Behaviour', *Psychhiatria Danubina*, 25 (2), pp. S324–S328.

Joiner, T.E., Conwell, Y., Fitzpatrick, K.K., Witte, T.K., Schmidt, N.B., Berlim, M.T., Fleck, Marcelo P.A. and Rudd, D.M. 2005. 'Four Studies on How Past and Current Suicidality Relate Even When "Everything but the Kitchen Sink" Is Covaried', *Journal of Abnormal Psychology*, 114(2), pp. 291–303.

Jordan, J.R. 2001. 'Is Suicide Bereavement Different? A Reassessment of the Literature', *Suicide and Life-Threatening Behavior*, 31, pp. 91–102.

Jorm, A. 2012. 'Mental Health Literacy: Empowering the Community to take Action for Better Mental Health', *American Psychologist*, 67 (3), pp. 231–243.

Jorm, AF., Korten, A., Jacomb, P., Christensen, H., Rodgers, B., and Pollitt, P. 1997. 'Mental Health Literacy: A Survey of the Public's Ability to Recognize Mental Disorders and their Beliefs about the Effectiveness of Treatment', *Medical Journal of Australia*, 166 (4), pp. 182–186.

Juurlink, D.N., Mamdani, M.M., Kopp, A., and Redelmeier, D.A. 2006. 'The Risk of Suicide with Selective Serotonin Reuptake Inhibitors in the Elderly', *American Journal of Psychiatry*, 163 (5), pp. 813–821.

Kaila, H.L. 2005. 'Democratizing Schools across the World to Stop Killing Creativity in Children: An Indian Perspective', *Counselling Psychology Quarterly*, 18 (1), pp. 1–6.

Kala, A. 2013. 'Time to Face New Realities; Mental Health Care Bill-2013', *Indian Journal of Psychiatry*, 55 (3), pp. 216–219.

Kar, N. 2010. 'Profile of Risk Factors Associated with Suicide Attempts: A Study from Orissa, India', *Indian Journal of Psychiatry*, 52 (1), pp. 48–56.

Kaushal, N. 2019. 'India's Youth Suicide Binge', *The Times of India*, Baroda, February 7.

Kazdin, A.E. 1982. *Single Case Research Designs*, Oxford: Oxford University Press.

Kelly, B.D. 2016. *Mental Illness, Human Rights and the Law*, London: RC Psych Publications.

Kessler, R.C., Crum, R.M., Warner, L.A., Nelson, C.B., Schulenberg, J., and Anthony, J.C. 1997. 'Lifetime and Co-Occurrence of DSM-III-TR Alcohol Abuse and Dependence with Other Psychiatric Disorders in the National Comorbidity Survey', *Archives of General Psychiatry*, 54, pp. 313–321.

Kety, S.1986. 'Genetic Factors in Suicide', in A. Roy (ed.), *Suicide*. Baltimore, MD: Williams & Wilkins, pp. 41–45.

Khan, F.A., Anand, B., Devi, M.G., and Murthy, K.K. 2005. 'Psychological Autopsy of Suicide – A Cross-sectional Study', *Indian Journal of Psychiatry*, 47, pp. 73–78.

King, R.A., Schwab-Stone, M., Flisher, A.J., Greenwald, S., Kramer, R.A., Goodman, S.H., Lahey, B.B., Shaffer, D. and Gould, M.S. 2001. 'Psychosocial and Risk Behavior Correlates of Youth Suicide Attempts and Suicidal Ideation', *Journal of the American Academy of Child and Adolescent Psychiatry*, 40(7), pp. 837–846.

Klinenberg, E. 2002. *Heat Wave: A Social Autopsy of Disaster in Chicago*, Chicago, IL: Chicago University Press.

———. 2006. 'Blaming the Victims: Hearsay, Labeling, and the Hazards of Quick-hit Disaster Ethnography', *American Sociological Review*, 71, pp. 689–698.

Kposowa, A.J. 2001. 'Unemployment and Suicide: A Cohort Analysis of Social Factors Predicting Suicide in the US National Longitudinal Mortality Study', *Psychological Medicine*, 31 (1), pp. 127–138.

Kraiskopf, C.J., and Saunders, D.R. 1994. *Personality and Ability-The Personality Assessment System*, Lanham, MD: University Press of America.

Krueger, R.F., Caspi, A., and Moffitt, T.E. 2000. 'Epidemiological Personology: The Unifying Role of Personality in Population-based Research on Problem Behaviors', *Journal of Personality*, 68, pp. 967–998.

Krysinska, K.E. 2003. 'Loss by Suicide: A Risk Factor for Suicidal Behavior', *Journal of Psychosocial Nursing and Mental Health Services*, 41 (7), pp. 34–41.

Kuhlberg, J.A., Pena, J.B., and Zayas, L.H.C. 2010. 'Familism, Parent-Adolescent Conflict, Self-Esteem, Internalizing Behaviors and Suicide Attempts among Adolescent Latina', *Child Psychiatry and Human Development*, 41 (4), pp. 425–440. doi:10.1007/s10578-010-0179-0.

Kumar, A. 2002. 'Mental Health in India: Issues and Concerns', *Journal of Mental Health and Aging*, 8 (3), pp. 255–260.

Kumar, S., Pathak, A., and Mangal, H.M. 2011. 'Trends of Fatal Poisoning in Saurashtra Region of Gujarat (A Prospective Study)', *Journal of Indian Academy of Forensic Medicine*, 33 (3), pp. 197–199.

Kumar, S.P.N. 2004. 'An Analysis of Suicide Attempters versus Completers in Kerala', *Indian Journal of Psychiatry*, 46 (2), pp. 144–149.

Kutcher, S., Bagnell, A., and Wei, Y. 2015. 'Mental Health Literacy in Secondary Schools: A Canadian Approach', *Child and Adolescent Psychiatric Clinics of North America*, 24 (2), pp. 233–244.

Lakshmi, A.R., and Arora, M. 2006. 'Perceived Parental Behaviour as Related to Student's Academic School Success and Competence', *Journal of the Indian Academy of Applied Psychology*, 32 (1), pp. 47–52.

Latha, K.S., Bhat, S.M., and D'Souza, P. 1996. 'Suicide Attempters in a General Hospital Unit in India: Their Socio-Demographic and Clinical Profile-Emphasis on Cross-Cultural Aspects', *Acta Psychiatrica Scandinavaca*, 94, pp. 26–30.

Law, S., and Liu, O. 2008. 'Suicide in China: Unique Demographic Patterns and Relationship to Depressive Disorder', *Current Psychiatry Reports*, 10 (1), pp. 80–86.

Leenaars, A.A. 2004. *Psychotherapy with Suicidal People: A Person-Centred Approach*, San Francisco, CA: John Wiley.

Lester, D. 1987. 'National Distribution of Blood Groups, Personal Violence (Suicide and Homicide), and National Character', *Personality and Individual Differences*, 8, pp. 575–576.

———. 1989. *Suicide from a Sociological Perspective*, Springfield, MI: Charles C Thomas Pub. Ltd.

———. 1994. 'An Empirical Examination of Thomas Masarykís Theory of Suicide', *Archives of Suicide Research*, 3, pp. 125–31.

———. 2000. *Why People Kill Themselves: A 2000 Summary of Research on Suicide*, Springfield, MI: CC Thomas.

Leonard, B.E. 2005. 'The Biochemistry of Suicide', *Crisis: The Journal of Crisis Intervention and Suicide Prevention*, 26 (4), pp. 153–155. doi:10.1027/0227-5910.26.4.153.

Lewinsohn, P.M., Rohde, P., and Seeley, J.R. 1996. 'Adolescent Suicidal Ideation and Attempts: Prevalence, Risk factors, and Clinical Implications', *Clinical Psychology Science Practice*, 3, pp. 25–46.

Litman, R.E. 1980. 'Psychological Aspects of Suicide'. In W.J. Curran, A.L. McGarry, and Petty CModern (eds.), *Legal Medicine, Psychiatry, and Forensic Science*. Philadelphia, PA: FA Davis.

Lizardi, D., Grunebaum, M.F., Burke A., Stanley B., Mann J.J., Harkavy-Friedman J., and Oquendo, M. 2011. 'The Effect of Social Adjustment and Attachment Style on Suicidal Behavior', *Acta Psychiatrica Scandinavaca*, 124 (4), pp. 295–300.

Lobo, L., and Bharati, K. 2018. 'Suicidal Trends and Tendencies with their Socio-economic and Psychological Determinants in Gujarat: A Pilot Study of Vadodara District', Vadodara: Centre for Culture and Development.

Ludman, E., Katon, W., Robinson, P., Von Korff, M., Lin, E., Bush, T., Simon, G., and Walker, E. 1996. 'A Multifaceted Intervention to Improve Treatment of Depression in Primary Care', *Archives of General Psychiatry*, 53, pp. 924–932.

Lukes, S. 1973. *Emile Durkheim: His Life and Work*. Stanford, CA: Stanford University Press, p. 192.

Mahla, V.P., Bhargava, S.C., Dogra, R., and Shome, S. 1992. 'The Psychology of Self-immolation in India', *Indian Journal of Psychiatry*, 34, pp. 108–113.

Majid, A., Suhaff, A.A., and Khan, A.W. 2017. 'Psychological Autopsy: Reconstructing the Mystery of Suicide', *Indian Journal of Private Psychiatry*, 11 (2), pp. 24–25.

Mann, J.J., Waternaux, C., et al. 1999. 'Toward a Clinical Model of Suicidal Behavior in Psychiatric Patients', *American Journal of Psychiatry*, 156 (2), pp. 181–189.

Manoranjitham, S.D., Rajkumar, A.P., Thangadurai, P., Prasad, J., Jayakaran, R., and Jacob, K.S. 2010. 'Risk Factors for Suicide in Rural South India', *British Journal of Psychiatry*, 196 (1), pp. 26–30.

Manoranjitham, S., Abraham, S., and Jacob, K.S. 2005. 'Towards a National Strategy to Reduce Suicide in India', *The National Medical Journal of India*, Vol.18 (3), pp. 118–122.

Marangell, L.B., Bauer, M.S., Dennehy, E.B., Wisniewski, S.R., Allen, H.M., Miklowitz, D.J., Oquendo, M.A., Frank, E., Perlis, R.H., Martinez, J.M., Fagiolini, A., Otto, M.W., et al. 2006. 'Prospective Predictors of Suicide and Suicide Attempts in 1556 Patients with Bipolar Disorders Followed for up to 2 Years', *Bipolar Disorders*, 8, pp. 566–575.

Maris, R.W. 1981. *Pathways to Suicide: A Survey of Self-Destructive Behaviors*, Baltimore, MD: Johns Hopkins University Press.

Maris, R.W., Berman, A.L., and Silverman, M.M. 2000. *Comprehensive Textbook of Suicidology*, New York: Guilford.

Marshall, B.C., and Meier, R.F. 2011. *Sociology of Deviant Behavior*, Wadsworth, OH: Cengage Learning.

Maskill, C., Hodges, I., McClellan, V., and Collings, S. 2005. *Explaining Patterns of Suicide: A Selective Review of Studies Examining Social, Economic, Cultural and Other Population-Level Influences*, Wellington, New Zealand: Ministry of Health, p. 8.

Mason, J. 2006. 'Mixing Methods in a Qualitatively-driven Way', *Qualitative Research*, 6 (1), 9–25.

Mayer, P. 2016. 'Thinking Clearly about Suicide in India: Desperate Housewives, Despairing Farmers', *Economic and Political Weekly*, 51 (14), pp. 44–54.

Mayer, P., and Tahereh, Z. 2002. 'Suicide, Gender, and Age variations in India: Are Women in Indian Society Protected from Suicide?', *The Journal of Crisis Intervention and Suicide Prevention*, 23 (3), pp. 98–103. doi:10.1027// 0227-5910.23.3.98.

McGirr, A., Renaud, J., Séguin M., Alda, M., and Turecki, G. 2008. 'Course of Major Depressive Disorder and Suicide Outcome: A Psychological Autopsy Study', *Journal of Clinical Psychiatry*, 69, pp. 966–970.

McIntosh, J. 1993. 'Control Group Studies of Suicide Survivors: A Review and Critique', *Suicide Life Threatening Behaviour*, 23, pp. 146–161.

Meehan, P.J., Saltzman, L.E., and Sattin, R.W. 1991. 'Suicides among Older United States Residents: Epidemiologic Characteristics and Trends', *American Journal of Public Health*, 81, pp. 1198–1200.

Meltzer, H., Bebbington, P., Brugha, T., Jenkins, R., McManus, S., and Dennis, M.S. 2011. 'Personal Debt and Suicidal Ideation', *Psychological Medicine*, 41 (4), pp. 771–778.

Menninger, K.A. 1938. *Man against Himself*, New York: Harcourt, Brace.

Mental Health Care Act (MHCA). 2017. Government of India, New Delhi.

Merton, R.K. 1938. 'Social Structure and Anomie', *American Sociological Review*, 3 (5), pp. 672–682.

———. 1957. *Social Theory and Social Structure,* Revised Edition, New York: Free Press.

Miller, A.L., Muehlenkamp, J.J., and Jacobson, C.M. 2008. 'Fact or Fiction: Diagnosing Borderline Personality Disorder in Adolescents', *Clinical Psychology Review*, 28, pp. 969–981.

Miller, F., and Chabrier, L.A. 1987. 'The Relation of Delusional Content in Psychotic Depression to Life-threatening Behavior,' *Suicide and Life-Threatening Behavior*, 17, pp. 13–17.

Milner, A., Morrell, S., and LaMontagne, A.D. 2014. 'Economically Inactive, Unemployed and Employed Suicides in Australia by Age and Sex Over a 10-year Period: What Was the Impact of the 2007 Economic Recession?', *International Journal of Epidemiology*, 43, pp. 1500–1507.

Minayo, M., Cecília, C., Fátima, G., and Souza, E.R. 2006. 'Methodological Proposal for Studying Suicide as a Complex Phenomenon', *Cadernos de Saúde Pública*, 22 (8), pp. 1587–1596. doi:10.1590/S0102-311X2006000800007.

Mishara, B.L. 2008. 'Suicide and the Economic Depression: Reflections on Suicide during the Great Depression', IASP, *News Bulletin*, December.

Mishra, R., Ansari, S., and Mishra, S. 2012. 'A Comparative Study of Changing Family Composition, Structure and Practices in Urban Area of Kanpur City (U.P.)', *International Journal of Scientific and Research Publications*, 2 (10), pp. 1–5.

Missouri Department of Mental Health (MDMH). 2011. *Understanding Mental Illness: A Guide to Brain Disorders, Medication, and Therapy*. Jefferson City, MO. https://dmh.mo.gov/docs/mentalillness/understandingmentalillness.pdf.

Mitchell, A.M., Kim, Y., Prigerson, H.G., and Mortimer-Stephens, M. 2004. 'Complicated Grief in Survivors of Suicide', *Crisis*, 25, pp. 12–18.

Moeller, F.G., Barratt, E.S., Dougherty, D.M., Schmitz, J.M., and Swann, A.C. 2001. 'Psychiatric Aspects of Impulsivity', *American Journal of Psychiatry*, 158 (11), pp. 1783–1793.

Monk, M. 1987. 'Epidemiology of Suicide', *Epidemiological Review*, 9, pp. 51–69.

Moscicki, E.K. 1995. 'Suicide in Children and Adolescents', in F.C. Verhulst and H.M. Koot (eds.), *The Epidemiology of Child and Adolescent Psychopathology*, New York: Oxford University Press, pp. 291–308.

———. 1997. 'Identification of Suicide Risk Factors Using Epidemiologic Studies', *Psychiatric Clinics of North America*, 20, pp. 499–517.

———. 2001. 'Epidemiology of Completed and Attempted Suicide: Toward a Framework for Prevention', *Clinical Neuroscience Research*, 1, pp. 310–323.

Mukherjee, S., and Kumar, U. 2017. 'Theorizing Suicide – Multiple Perspectives and Implications for Prevention', in Updesh Kumar (ed.), *Handbook of Suicidal Behaviour*, Singapore: Springer, pp. 11–12.

Muller, E.D., and Thompson, C.L. 2003. 'The Experience of Grief after Bereavement: A Phenomenological Study with Implications for Mental Health Counseling', *Journal of Mental Health Counseling*, 25 (3), pp. 183–204.

Muraven, M., Tice, D., and Baumeister, R. 2000. 'Self-Regulation and Depletion of Limited Resources: Does Self-Control Resemble a Muscle', *Psychological Bulletin*, 126, pp. 247–259.

Murphy, G.E., and Wetzel, R.D. 1999. 'The Lifetime Risk of Suicide in Alcoholism', *Archives of General Psychiatry*, 47, pp. 383–392.

Murphy, E. 1983. 'The Prognosis of Depression in Old Age', *British Journal of Psychiatry*, 142, pp. 111–119.

Murthy, V.C.R. 2010. 'Psychological Autopsy-A Review', *Al Ameen Journal of Medical Sciences*, 3 (3), pp. 177–181.

Nagathan, S., Poddar, R.A., Kunnal, L.B., et al. 2011. 'A Probe into Socio-economic and Psychological Profile of Farmers' Suicide in Karnataka', *Karnataka Journal of Agricultural Sciences*, 24 (2), pp. 157–160.

Narang, R.L., Mishra, B.P., and Nitesh, M. 2000. 'Attempted Suicide in Ludhiana', *Indian Journal of Psychiatry*, 42, pp. 83–87.

Narayan, C.L., Narayan, M., and Shikha, D. 2011. 'The Ongoing Process of Amendments in MHA-87 and PWD Act-95 and their Implications on Mental Health Care', *Indian Journal of Psychiatry*, 53, pp. 343–350.

Narayan, C.L., and Shikha, D. 2013. 'Indian Legal System and Mental Health', *Indian Journal of Psychiatry*, 55 (2), pp. S177–S181.

National Crime Records Bureau (NCRB). 2008. *Accidental Deaths and Suicides in India,* New Delhi: New Ministry of Home Affairs, Government of India.

———. 2014. *Accidental Deaths and Suicides in India*, New Delhi: New Ministry of Home Affairs, Government of India.

———. 2015. *Accidental Deaths and Suicides in India*, New Delhi: New Ministry of Home Affairs, Government of India.

———. 2016. *Accidental Deaths and Suicides in India*, New Delhi: New Ministry of Home Affairs, Government of India.

———. 2017. *Accidental Deaths and Suicides in India*, New Delhi: New Ministry of Home Affairs, Government of India.

———. 2018. *Accidental Deaths and Suicides in India*, New Delhi: New Ministry of Home Affairs, Government of India.

———. 2019. *Accidental Deaths and Suicides in India*, New Delhi: New Ministry of Home Affairs, Government of India.

National Injury Mortality Surveillance System (NIMSS). 2004. *A Profile of Fatal Injuries in South Africa* (6th Annual Report). http://www.sahealthinfo.org/violence/national 2004.

National Institute of Mental Health (NIMH). 2004. 'Care Managers', Help Depressed Elderly Reduce Suicidal Thoughts, Press Release Bethesda, MD: National Institute of Mental Health.

National Institute of Mental Health and Neuro Sciences (NIMHANS) and Government of India (GOI). 2016. *Mental Health Survey of India, 2015–2016: Prevalence, Pattern and Outcomes*, Bangaluru: NIMHANS.

Nischal, A., Tripathi, A., Nishal, A., and Trivedi, J.K. 2012. 'Suicide and Antidepressants: What Current Evidence Indicates', *Mens Sana Monographs*, Jan–Dec, 10 (1), pp. 33–44.

Njie, B., and Asimiran, S. 2014. 'Case Study as a Choice in Qualitative Methodology', *IOSR Journal of Research and Method in Education*, 4 (3, Ver. I), pp. 35–40.

Nock, M.K., and Mendes, W.B. 2008. 'Physiological Arousal, Distress Tolerance, and Social Problem Solving Deficits among Adolescent Self-injurers', *Journal of Consulting and Clinical Psychology,* 76, pp. 28–38.

Nock, M.K., Green, J.G., Hwang, I., Mclaughlin, Katie A., Sampson, Nancy A., Zaslaysky, Alan, M. and Kessler, Ronald C. 2013. 'Prevalence, Correlates, and Treatment of Lifetime Suicidal Behavior among Adolescents: Results from the National Comorbidity Survey Replication Adolescent Supplement', *JAMA Psychiatry*, 70(3), pp. 300–310.

Nutbeam, D. 1998. Health Promotion Glossary, *Health Promotion International*, 13, pp. 349–364.

Ocko, J.K. 1991. 'Women, Property and the Law in Peoples Republic of China', in R.S. Watson and P.B. Ebrey (eds.), *Marriage and Inequality in Chinese Society*, Berkeley: University of California Press, pp. 313–346.

O'Connor, R.C. 2011. 'Towards an Integrated Motivational-Violional Model of Suicidal Behaviour', in R.C. O'Connor, S. Platt, and J. Gordon (eds.), *International Handbook of Suicide Prevention: Research, Policy and Practice*, Chichester: Wiley, pp. 98–181.

Oliver, P., Horspool, M., Rowse, G., Parry, M., Keen, J., and Mathers, N. 2007. 'A Psychological Autopsy Study of Non-deliberate Fatal Opiate-related Overdose', *Research Briefing: 24*, The National Treatment Agency for Substance Misuse (NTA), England.

Overholser, J.C., Miller, I.W., and Norman, W.H. 1987. 'The Course of Depressive Symptoms in Suicidal vs. Non-suicidal Depressed Patients', *Journal of Nervous and Mental Disease*, 175, pp. 450–456.

Owens, C., Booth N., Briscoe, M., Lawrence, C., and Lloyd, K. 2003. 'Suicide Outside the Care of Mental Health Services: A Case-controlled Psychological Autopsy Study', *Crisis*, 24, pp. 13–21.

Owens, C., Lambert H., Lloyd, K., and Donovan, J. 2008. 'Tales of Biographical Disintegration: How Parents Make Sense of Their Sons' Suicides', *Sociology of Health and Illness*, 30 (2), pp. 237–254.

Pagee, R.M., and West, J.H. 2011. 'Suicide Ideation and Psychosocial Distress in Sub-Saharan African Youth', *American Journal of Health Behaviour*, Mar–Apr, 352, pp. 129–141. doi:10.5993/AJHB.35.2.1; PMID: 21204676.

Pandey, M., and Kaur, C. 2009. 'Investigating Suicidal Trend and Its Economic Determinants: Evidence from India', *Munich Personal RePEc Archive (MPRA)*, 15732, University Library of Munich, Germany.

Patel, V., Ramasundarahettige C., Vijayakumar L., Thakur J.S., Gajalakshmi V., Gururaj, G., Suraweera, W., and Jha, Prabhat. 2012. 'Suicide Mortality in India: A Nationally Representative Survey', *Lancet*, 379 (9834), pp. 2343–2351. doi:10.1016/S0140-6736(12)60606-0.

Pathak, A., and Sharma, S. 2010. 'The Study of Un-Natural Female Deaths in Vadodara City', *Journal of Indian Academy of Forensic Medicine*, 32 (3), pp. 220–223.

Pearson, V. 1995. 'Goods on Which One Loses: Women and Mental Health in China', *Social Science and Medicine*, 41 (8), pp. 1159–1173.

Peenikaparambil, J. 2018. 'Why Students Commit Suicide', *Indian Currents*, XXX (21), 21–27 May, pp. 21–23.

Perlman, C., Neufeld, E., Martin, L., Goy, M., and Hirdes, J.P. 2011. *Suicide Risk Assessment Inventory: A Resource Guide for Canadian Health Care Organizations*, Toronto, ON: Ontario Hospital Association and Canadian Patient Safety Institute.

Petrov, K. 2013. 'The Art of Dying as an Art of Living: Historical Contemplations on the Paradoxes of Suicide and the Possibilities of Reflexive Suicide Prevention', *Journal of Medical Humanities*, 34 (3), pp. 347–368.

Phillips, M.R., Liu, H., and Zhang, Y. 1999. 'Suicide and Social Change in China', *Culture, Medicine and Psychiatry*, 23 (1), pp. 25–50.

Pillai, A., Andrews, T., and Patel, V. 2009. 'Violence, Psychological Distress and the Risk of Suicidal Behavior in Young People in India', *International Journal of Epidemiology*, 38, pp. 459–469.

Pirkola, S., Isometsa, E., Heikkinen, M., Henriksson, M.M., Marttunen, M.J., and Lönnqvist, J.K. 1999. 'Female Psychoactive Substance-dependent Suicide

Victims Differ from Male-Results from a Nationwide Psychological Autopsy Study', *Comprehensive Psychiatry*, 40 (2), pp. 101–107.

Pitman, A., Osborn, D., King, M., and Erlangsen, A. 2014, 'Effects of Suicide Bereavement on Mental Health and Suicide Risk', *The Lancet, Suicide 3 Series*, 1 (1), pp. 86–94.

Pitman, A., Rantell, K., Marston, L., King, M., and Osborn, D. 2017. 'Perceived Stigma of Sudden Bereavement as a Risk Factor for Suicidal Thoughts and Suicide Attempt: Analysis of British Cross-sectional Survey Data on 3,387 Young Bereaved Adults', *International Journal of Environmental Health Research*, 14 (3), p. 286.

Platt, S. 1992. 'Suicide and Unemployment in Italy', *Social Science and Medicine*, 34, pp. 1191–1201.

Pompili, M., Serafini, G., Innamorati, M., Dominici, G., Ferracuti, S., Kotzalidis, G.D., Serra, G., Girardi, P., et al. 2010. 'Suicidal Behavior and Alcohol Abuse', *International Journal of Environmental Research and Public Health*, 7, pp. 1392–1431. doi:10.3390/ijerph7041392.

Ponnudurai, R., Jeyakar, J., and Saraswathy, M. 1986. 'Attempted Suicides in Madras', *Indian Journal of Psychiatry*, 28, pp. 59–62.

Prajapati, K.B., Dipali, S., Prajapati, T.B., and Merchant, S.P. 2013. 'Trends of Suicidal Poisoning Deaths in Females of Ahmedabad (Gujarat Region)', *Gujarat Medical Journal*, 68 (2), pp. 58–63.

Praveenlal, K. (n.d.). *Family Suicide in Kerala: An Explorative Study into Pattern, Determinants and Consequences*, Centre for Development Studies (CDS), pp. 1–21. Retrieved from http://www.cds.ac.in/krpcds/report/praveenlal.pdf.

Radhakrishnan, R., and Andrade, C. 2012. 'Suicide: An Indian Perspective', *Indian Journal of Psychiatry*, 54 (4), pp. 304–319.

Ram, B., and Singh, S.P. 2017. 'Agrarian Crisis in India-Its Causes and Effects', *International Journal of Advance Research and Innovative Ideas in Education*, 3 (1), pp. 1821–1828.

Rane, A., and Nadkarni, A. 2014. 'Suicide in India: A Systematic Review', *Shanghai Archives of Psychiatry*, 26 (2), pp. 69–80.

Ranjan, R., Kumar, S., Pattanayak, R.D., Dhawan, A., and Sagar, R. 2014. '(De-) Criminalization of Attempted Suicide in India: A Review', *Indian Psychiatry Journal*, 23 (1), pp. 4–9.

Rao, A.V. 1972. 'Attempted Suicide and Suicide among Students in Madurai', *Indian Journal of Psychiatry*, 14 (4), pp. 389–397.

Rao, A.V., and Madhavan, T. 1983. 'Depression and Suicide Behaviour in the Aged', *Indian Journal of Psychiatry*, 25 (4), pp. 251–259.

Rao, A.V., Mahendran, N., Gopalakrishnan, C., et al. 1989. 'One Hundred Female Burns Cases: A Study in Suicidology', *Indian Journal of Psychiatry*, 31 (1), pp. 43–50.

Rao, G.P., Math, S.B., Raju, M.S.V., Saha, G., Jagiwala, M., Sagar, R., and Rao, T.S. 2016a. 'Mental Health Care Bill, 2016: A Boon or Bane', *Indian Journal of Psychiatry*, 58 (3), pp. 244–249.

Rao, G.P., Ramya, V.S., and Math, S.B. 2016b. 'The Rights of Persons with Disability Bill, 2014: How "Enabling" Is it for Persons with Mental Illness?', *Indian Journal of Psychiatry*, 58, pp. 121–128.

Rehkopf, D.H., and Buka, S.L. 2006. 'The Association between Suicide and the Socio-Economic Characteristics of Geographical Areas: A Systematic Review'. *Psychological Medicine*, 36 (2), pp. 145–157.

Registrar General. 2014. *Report on Causes of Death in India-2010–2013*, New Delhi: Office of the Registrar General, India, Vital Statistics Division.

Reiss, S.N., and Mark, D(n.d.). 'Becoming Suicidal: Biological Contributions', *Mentalhelp.net*, American Addiction Centers, Inc. (AAC), https://www.mentalhelp.net/articles/becoming-suicidal-biological-contributions/.

Rich, C.L., and Runeson, B.S. 1992. 'Similarities in Diagnostic Comorbidity between Suicide among Young People in Sweden and the United States', *Acta Psychiatrica Scandinavica*, 86, pp. 335–339.

Rich, C.L., Young, D., and Fowler, R.C. 1986. 'San Diego Suicide Study: I. Young vs old Subjects', *Archieve of General Psychiatry*, 43 (6), pp. 577–582.

Ritz, D., Andrew, M., Catherine, M., Pearse, M., and Jorun Rugkasa. 2016. 'Community Treatment Orders in the UK 5 Years On: A Repeat National Survey of Psychiatrists', *BJPsych Bulletin*, 40 (3), pp. 119–123.

Robins, E. 1986. 'Psychosis and Suicide', *Biological Psychiatry*, 21 (7), pp. 665–672.

Rosenberg, M.L., Davidson, L.E., Smith, J.C., Berman, A.L., Buzbee, H., Gantner, G., Gay, G.A., Moore-Lewis, B., D H Mills., et al. 1988. 'Operational Criteria for the Determination of Suicide', *Journal of Forensic Sciences*, 33 (6), pp. 1445–1456.

Rothman, K.J. 1986. *Modern Epidemiology*, Boston, MA: Little, Brown & Co.

Roy, A. 1989. 'Suicide', in H.I. Kaplan and B.M. Sadock (eds.), *Comprehensive Textbook of Psychiatry*, vol.2, 5th ed. Baltimore, MD: Williams & Wilkins, pp. 1414–1427.

Roy, A. 1995. 'Suicide', in H.I. Kaplan and B.M. Sadock (eds.), *Comprehensive Textbook of Psychiatry*, vol.2, 6th ed. Baltimore, MD: Williams & Wilkins, pp. 1739–1751.

Roy, A., Segal, N.L., Centerwall, B.S., and Robinette, C.D. 1991. 'Suicide in Twins', *Archive of General Psychiatry*, 48, pp. 29–32.

Runeson, B., and Åsberg, M. 2003. 'Family History of Suicide among Suicide Victims', *American Journal of Psychiatry*, 160 (8), pp. 1525–1526.

Runeson, B.S. 1989. 'Mental Disorder in Youth Suicide: DSM-III-R Axes I and II', *Acta Psychiatrica Scandinavica*, 79, pp. 490–497.

Sabrina, F. 2018. 'Autopsies: When Are They Done?', *WebMD Medical Reference*, November 5.

Sahoo, S., Prasad, M.N., and Saxena, M.K. 2010. 'Attempted Suicides in India: A Comprehensive Look', *Archives of Suicide Research*, 14(1), pp. 56–65.

Sadock, B.J., Virginia, A.S., and Pedro, R. 2009. *Kaplan and Sadock's Comprehensive Textbook of Psychiatry*, Philadelphia, PA: Lippincott Williams and Wilkins.

Salvatore, T. 2010. *Suicide Loss Research*. Springfield, PA. Retrieved from http://lifegard.tripod.com/research.html.

Samithamby, S., and Kanthasamy, S. 2015. 'Suicide-is it a Killing by a Society?', *International Journal of Innovative Research and Practices*, 3 (5), pp. 7–13. Retrieved September 23, 2017, from https://www.researchgate.net/publication/282355936_SUICIDE_-IS_IT_A_KILLING_BY_A_SOCIETY.

Sarin, A. 2012. 'On Psychiatric Wills and the Ulysses Clause: The Advance Directive in Psychiatry', *Indian Journal of Psychiatry*, 54 (3), p. 2067.

Sarin, A., Murthy, P., and Chatterjee, S. 2012. 'Psychiatric Advance Directives: Potential Challenges in India', *Indian Journal of Medical Ethics*, 9 (2), pp. 104–107.

Schmidt, W., and Lint, De J. 1972. 'Causes of Death of Alcoholics', *Quarterly Journal of Studies on Alcohol*, 33 (1), pp. 171–185.

Schramm, W. 1971. *Notes on Case Studies of Instructional Media Projects*, Stanford University: California, Institute for Communication Research.

Schwartz, M. 1997. 'The Use of Psychological Autopsy'. Paper Presented to the 3rd Bi-Regional Adolescent Suicide Prevention Conference, DHHS, Breckenridge, CO. September 21.

Scott, L.C., Swartz, E., and Warbuton, K. 2006. 'The Psychological Autopsy: Solving the Mysteries of Death', *Psychiatric Clinics of North America*, 29 (3), pp. 805–822.

Scottish Association for Mental Health (SAMH). 2012. *'After a Suicide'*, Booklet for Scotland's Mental Health, Glasgow: SAMH.

Scourfield, J. 2005. 'Suicidal Masculinities', *Sociological Research Online*, 10 (2). Retrieved November 1, 2018, from http://www.socresonline.org.uk/10/2/scourfield.html.

Scourfield, J., Fencham, B., Langer, S., and Shiner, M. 2012. 'Sociological Autopsy: An Integrated Approach to the Study of Suicide in Men', *Social Science and Medicine*, 74 (4), pp. 466–473.

Seguin, M., Lesage, A., Turecki, G., Bouchard,M., Chawky, N., Tremblay, N., Daigle, F., and Guy, A. 2007. 'Life Trajectories and Burden of Adversity: Mapping the Developmental Profiles of Suicide Mortality', *Psychological Medicine*, 37 (11), pp. 1575–1583.

Selby, E., Joiner, T., and Ribeiro, J. 2014. 'Comprehensive Theories of Suicidal Behaviours, in Nock (ed.) *The Oxford Handbook of Suicide and Self-Injury*, New York: Oxford University Press, p. 290.

Shaffer, D. 1988. 'The Epidemiology of Teen Suicide: An Examination of Risk Factors'. *Journal of Clinical Psychiatry*, 4Y (suppl. 9), pp. 36–41.

Shaffer, D., Gould M.S., Fisher P., Trautman, P., Moreau, D., Kleinman, M., and Flory, M. 1996. 'Psychiatric Diagnosis in Child and Adolescent Suicide', *Archive of General Psychiatry*, 53 (4), pp. 339–348.

Shafii, M., Carrigan S., Whittinghill, J.R., and Derrick, A. 1985. 'Psychological Autopsy of Completed Suicide in Children and Adolescents', *American Journal of Psychiatry*, 142 (9), pp. 1061–1064.

Shah, A.M. 1973. *The Household Dimension of the Family in India: A Field Study in a Gujarat Village and a Review of Other Studies*, New Delhi: Orient Longman.

Shani, C., Yelena, S., Reut, B.K., Adrian, S., and Sami, H. 2016. 'Suicidal Risk among Infertile Women Undergoing in-vitro Fertilization: Incidence and Risk Factors', *Psychiatry Research*, 240, pp. 53–59.

Sharma, R., Grover, V.L., and Chaturvedi, S. 2008. 'Suicidal Behavior amongst Adolescent Students in South Delhi', *Indian Journal of Psychiatry*, 50 (1), pp. 30–33.

Sharma, R.C. 1998. 'Attempted Suicide in Himachal Pradesh', *Indian Journal of Psychiatry*, 40 (1), pp. 50–54.

Sheftall, A.H., Mathias, C.W., Furr, M.R., and Dougherty, D.M. 2013. 'Adolescent Attachment Security, Family Functioning, and Suicide Attempts', *Attachment and Human Development*, 15 (4), pp. 368–383. https://www.ncbi.nlm.nih.gov/pmc/articles/PMC3713165/#R78.

Sher, L. 2006. 'Alcoholism and Suicidal Behaviour: A Clinical Overview', *Acta Psychiatria Scandinavica*, 113 (1), pp. 13–22.

Shiva, V., and Jalees, K. (n.d.). *Farmers Suicides in India*, New Delhi: Research Foundation for Science, Technology and Ecology (RFSTE). Retrieved from https://www.navdanya.org/attachments/Organic_Farming10.pdf

Shneidman, E.S. 1976. *Suicidology: Contemporary Developments*, New York: Grune and Stratton.

———. 1981. 'Orientations toward Death: Sub-intentioned Death and Indirect Suicide', *Suicide and Life-Threatening Behaviour*, 11 (4), pp. 232–253.

———. 1985. *Definition of Suicide*, New York: Wiley Press.

———. 1993. 'Suicide as Psychache,' *The Journal of Nervous and Mental Disease*, 181, pp. 145–147.

———. 1995. *Suicide as Psychache: A Clinical Approach to Suicidal Behaviour*, Lanham, MD: Rowman & Littlefield Inc.

———. 1996. *The Suicidal Mind*, New York: Oxford University Press.

———. 1999. 'The Psychological Pain Assessment Scale', *Suicide and Life-Threatening Behavior*, 29, pp. 287–294.

Shukla, G.D., Verma, B.L., and Mishra, D.N. 1990. 'Suicide in Jhansi City', *Indian Journal of Psychiatry*, 32 (1), pp. 44–51.

Shuttleworth, M. 2008. 'Case Study Research Design'. Retrieved February 21, 2019, from Explorable.com: https://explorable.com/case-study-research-design.

Siddamsetty, A.K., Aggarwal, N.K., and Bhatia, M.S. 2014. 'Concept of Psychological Autopsy', *Delhi Psychiatry Journal*, 17 (2), pp. 458–461.

Simon, R. 2002. 'Murder, Suicide, Accident, or Natural Death? Assessment of Suicide Risk Factors at the Time of Death', in R. Simon and D. Shuman (eds.), *Retrospective Assessment of Mental States in Litigation,* Washington, DC: American Psychiatric Press, pp. 135–153.

———. 2004. *Assessing and Managing Suicide Risk: Guidelines for Clinically based Risk Management*, Washington, DC: American Psychiatric Press.

Singh, S. 2018. 'Death in the Midst of Plenty: Farmer Suicides in Punjab', *Economic and Political Weekly*, LIII (19), pp. 15–17.

Slater, Y.G. 2005. *Firearm Suicide among Older Adults: A Sociological Autopsy.* Thesis. School of Social Work, Indiana University.

Smith, J.C., Mercy, J.A., and Conn, J.M. 1988. 'Marital Status and the Risk of Suicide', *American Journal of Public Health*, 78, pp. 78–80.

Social Health Reference Group. 2004. *National Strategic Framework for Aboriginal and Torres Strait Islander People's Mental Health and Social and Emotional Well Being 2004–2009*, National Aboriginal and Torres Strait Islander Health Council and National Mental Health Working Group.

Sofair, J.B. 2011. 'Feeling Socially Safe', *Psychiatric Times*, 28 (6), p. 65.

Somasundaram, O. 1987. 'The Indian Lunacy Act, 1912: The Historic Background', *Indian Journal of Psychiatry*, 29, pp. 3–14.

Sonja, A.S., and Colman, I. 2013. 'Association between Exposure to Suicide and Suicidality Outcomes in Youth', *Canadian Medical Association Journal*, 185 (10), pp. 870–877.

Soy, S.K. 1997. *The Case Study as a Research Method* (Unpublished paper), University of Texas, Austin.

Spaulding, A.J., and Simpson, G. 1951. *Suicide: A Study in Sociology (by Emile Durkheim)*, Glencoe, IL: Free Press, Translated Version.

Srivastava, M.K., Sahoo, R.N., Ghotekar, L.H., Dutta, S., Danabalan, M., Dutta, T.K., and Das, A.K. 2004. 'Risk Factors Associated with Attempted Suicide: A Case Control Study', *Indian Journal of Psychiatry*, 46, pp. 33–38.

Stack, S. 2000a. 'Media Impacts on Suicide: A Quantitative Review of 293 Findings', *Social Science Quarterly*, 81 (4), pp. 957–971.

Stack, S. 2000b. ‘Suicide: A 15-year Review of the Sociological Literature Part I: Cultural and Economic Factors’, *Suicide and Life-Threatening Behavior*, 30 (2), pp. 145–162.

Stake, R.E. 1994. ‘Case Studies’, in N.K. Denzin and Y. Lincoln (eds.), *Handbook of Qualitative Research*, Thousand Oaks, CA: Sage Publications, pp. 236–247.

———. 1995. *The Art of Case Study Research*, Thousand Oaks, CA: Sage.

Staples, J., State Crime Record Bureau (SCRB). 2014, 2015. Gujarat.

Stillion, J.M., and McDowell, E.E. 1996. *Suicide across the Life Span*, Washington, DC: Taylor and Francis.

Street, S., and Kromrey, J. 1994. ‘Relationships between Suicidal Behavior and Personality Types’, *Suicide and Life Threatening Behaviour*, 24 (3), pp. 282–292.

Stroebe, M., and Schut, H. 2001. ‘Models of Coping with Bereavement: A Review’, in M. Stroebe, R.O. Hansson, W. Stroebe, and H. Schut (eds.), *Handbook of Bereavement Research: Consequences, Coping, and Care*, Washington, DC: American Psychological Association, pp. 375–404.

Substance Abuse and Mental Health Services Administration (SAMHSA). 2015. *A Journey Toward Health and Hope: Your Handbook for Recovery after a Suicide Attempt*. Rockville, MD: SAMHSA, HHS Publication No. SMA-15-4419.

Suzuki, T. 2008. ‘Economic Modelling of Suicide under Income Uncertainty: For Better Understanding of Middle-Aged Suicide’, *Australian Economic Papers*, 47 (3), pp. 296–310.

Takahashi, Y., and Berger, D. 1996. ‘Cultural Dynamics and the Unconscious in Suicide in Japan’, in A.A. Leenaars and D. Lester (eds.), *Suicide and the Unconscious*, Northvale, NJ: Jason Aronson, pp. 248–258.

Tanna, K.J., Goyal, A., and Rana, N.M. 2015. ‘Psychological Autopsy of Suicide Cases in Vadodara Region of Gujarat’, *International Research and Publications in Medical Sciences*, 1 (1), pp. 25–29.

Taylor, S. 1988. *The Sociology of Suicide*, London: Longman.

Thali, M.J., Jackowski, C., Oesterhelweg, L., Ross, S.G., and Dirnhofer, R. 2007. ‘Virtopsy-the Swiss virtual Autopsy Approach’, *Legal Medicine*, 9, pp. 100–104.

Tishler, C.L., McKenry, P.C., and Morgan, K.C. 1981. ‘Adolescent Suicide Attempts: Some Significant Factors’, *Suicide and Life-Threatening Behavior*, 11, pp. 86–92.

Totten, J. 2008. *Coping after a Suicide*, Families for Depression Awareness (NGO), Waltham (www.familyaware.org).

Tousignant, M., Seshadri, S., and Anthony, R. 1998. ‘Gender and Suicide in India: A Multi Perspective Approach’, *Suicide and Life Threating Behaviour*, 28 (1), pp. 50–61.

Traskman-Bendz, L., Alling, C., Oreland, L., Regnell, G., Vinge, E., and Ohman, R. 1992. ‘Prediction of Suicidal Behaviour from Biologic Tests’, *Journal of Clinical Psycho-pharmacology*, 12 (2 Suppl), pp. 21s–26s.

Traskman-Bendz, L., and Mann, J.J. 2000. ‘Biological Aspects of Suicidal Behaviour’, in K. Hawton and K. Van Heeringen (eds.), *The International Handbook of Suicide and Attempted Suicide*, Chichester: John Wiley and Sons Ltd., pp. 65–77.

Turecki, G. 2005. ‘The Biological and Genetic Dimensions of Suicide Risk’, *Visions-BC’s Mental Health and Addictions Journal*, 2 (7), pp. 13–14. Retrieved from http://www.heretohelp.bc.ca/sites/default/files/visions_suicide.pdf.

Turnbull, A.J., Osborn, M., and Nicholas, N. 2015. ‘Hospital Autopsy: Endangered or Extinct?’, *Journal of Clinical Pathology*, 68 (8), pp. 601–604.

Van der W.J. 1989. 'The Aftermath of Suicide: A Review of Empirical Evidence', *Omega*-Journal of Death and Dying, 20 (2), pp. 149–171.

Van Orden, K.A. 2011. 'Suicides in Late Life', *Current Psychiatry Reports*, 13 (3), pp. 234–241.

Van Orden, K.A., and Conwell, Y. 2016. 'Issues in Research on Aging and Suicide', *Aging Mental Health*, 20 (2), pp. 240–251. doi:10.1080/13607863.2015.1065791.

Van Orden, K.A., Lynam M.E., Hollar, D., and Joiner, T.E. Jr. 2006. 'Perceived Burdensomeness as an Indicator of Suicidal Symptoms', *Cognitive Therapy and Research*, 30 (4), pp. 457–467.

Van Orden, K.A., Wiktorsson, S., Duberstein P., Berg, A.I., Fassberg, M.M., and Waern, M. 2015. 'Reasons for Attempted Suicide in Later Life', *American Journal of Geriatric Psychiatry*, 23, pp. 536–544.

Van Orden, K.A., Witte, T.K., Cukrowicz, K.C., Braithwaite, S.R., Selby, E.A., and Joiner, T.E. 2010. 'The Interpersonal Theory of Suicide', *Journal of Psychological Review*, 117 (2), pp. 575–600.

Varnik, P. 2012. 'Suicide in the World', *International Journal of Environmental Research and Public Health*, 9, pp. 760–771. doi:10.3390/ijerph9030760.

Vasudeva, V. 2017. 'Alarming Rise in Farm Suicides in Seven Punjab Districts', *The Hindu*, 16 June, Chandigarh. https://www.thehindu.com/news/national/alarming-rise-in-farm-suicides-in-seven-punjab-districts/article19090202.ece.

Vijayakumar, L. 2003. 'Psychosocial Risk Factors for Suicide in India', in Lakshmi Vijayakumar (ed.), *Suicide Prevention: Meeting the Challenge Together*, Chennai: Orient Longman, pp. 149–162.

———. 2006. 'Suicide and Mental Disorders – A Maze?', *Indian Journal of Medical Research*, 124 (4), pp. 371–374. (Editorial published on the occasion of the World Mental Health Day – October 10.)

———. 2007. 'Suicide and Its Prevention: The Urgent Need in India', *Indian Journal of Psychiatry*, 49 (2), pp. 81–84.

Vijayakumar, L., and Thilothammal, N. 1993. 'Suicide Pacts', *Crisis-The Journal of Crisis Intervention and Suicide Prevention*, 14 (1), pp. 43–46.

Vijayakumar, L. and Rajkumar, S. 1999. 'Are Risk Factors For Suicide Universal? A Case-Control Study in India', *Acta Psychiatrica Scandivanica*, 99 (6), pp. 407–411.

Viren, M. 1999. 'Testing the 'Natural Rate of Suicide' Hypothesis', *International Journal of Social Economics*, 26 (12), pp. 1428–1440.

Wagner, B.M. 1997. 'Family Risk Factors for Child and Adolescent Suicidal Behavior', *Psychological Bulletin*, 121 (2), pp. 246–298.

Ward, J.T. 2013. 'What is Forensic Psychology?', *Psychology Student Network, American Psychological Association*, September 23, https://www.apa.org/ed/precollege/psn/2013/09/forensic-psychology.

Weisman, A.D. 1967. 'The Psychological Autopsy and the Potential Suicide', *Bulletin of Suicidology*, 2, p. 15–24.

Weiss, J.M.A., and Scott, K.F. 1974. 'Suicide Attempters Ten Years Later', *Comprehensive Psychiatry,* 15 (2), pp. 165–171.

Werlang, G.B., and Botega, N.J. 2003. 'A Semi-Structured Interview for Psychological Autopsy in Suicide Cases', *Revista Brasileira de Psiquiatria*, 25 (4), pp. 212–219.

Williams, E.Y. 1936. 'Some Observations on the Psychological Aspects of Suicide', *Journal of Abnormal and Social Psychology*, 31 (3), pp. 260–265.

Williams, J.M.G. 1997. *Cry of Pain: Understanding Suicide and Self-harm*, London: Penguin.

Williams, J.M.G., and Pollock, L.R. 2000. 'The Psychology of Suicidal Behaviour', in K. Hawton and K. van Heeringen (eds.), *The International Handbook of Suicide and Attempted Suicide*, Chichester: John Wiley and Sons Ltd., pp. 79–93.

Winnie, J.F., and Gittinger, J.W. 1973. 'An Introduction to the Personality Assessment System', *Journal of Clinical Psychology, Monograph Supplement*, 38, pp. 1–68.

Wong, P.W.C., Chan, W.S.C., and Beh, P.S.L. 2007. 'What Can We Do to Help and Understand Survivors of Suicide in Hong Kong?', *Crisis: The Journal of Crisis Intervention and Suicide Prevention*, 28 (4), pp. 183–189.

Worden, W.J. 1991. *Grief Counseling and Grief Therapy: A Handbook for the Mental Health Professional*, New York: Routledge.

World Health Organization (WHO). 1968. *Prevention of Suicide*, Public Health Paper, No.35, Geneva.

———. 2001. *The World Health Report 2001-Mental Health: New Understanding, New Hope*, Geneva: World Health Organization.

———. 2003. *Investing in Mental Health*, Geneva: World Health Organization.

———. 2008. Preventing Suicide- A Resource for Media Professionals, Geneva: World Health Organization.

———. 2012. Public Health Action for the Prevention of Suicide – A Framework, Geneva: World Health Organization.

———. 2013. *Mental Health Action Plan 2013–2020*, Geneva: World Health Organization.

———. 2014. *Preventing Suicide: A Global Imperative*, Geneva: World Health Organization.

———. 2018a. *National Suicide Prevention Strategies: Progress, Examples and Indicators*, Geneva: World Health Organization.

———. 2018b. *Mental Health Atlas*, 2017, Geneva: World Health Organization.

———. 2018c. *Suicide-Key Facts*, Geneva: World Health Organization.

Wu, K., Chen, Y., and Yip, P. 2012. 'Suicide Methods in Asia: Implications in Suicide Prevention', *International Journal of Environmental Research and Public Health*, 9 (4), pp. 1135–1158. doi:10.3390/ijerph9041135.

Yin, R.K. 2003. *Case Study Research: Design and Methods*, Thousand Oaks, CA: Sage.

———. 2009. *Doing Case Study Research,* Fourth Edition, Thousand Oaks, CA: Sage.

Yip, P.S., and Liu, K. 2006. 'The Ecological Fallacy and the Gender Ratio of Suicide in China', *The British Journal of Psychiatry*, 189, pp. 465–466. doi:10.1192/bjp.bp.106.021816.

Yip, P.S., Yang, K.C.T., Ip, B.Y.T., Law, Y.W., and Watson, R. 2007. 'Financial Debt and Suicide in Hong Kong SAR1', *Journal of Applied Social Psychology*, 37 (12), pp. 2788–2799.

Yohn, C.N., Gergues, M.M., and Samuels, B.A. 2017. 'The Role of 5-HT Receptors in Depression', *Molecular Brain*, 10 (1): 28. doi:10.1186/s13041-017-0306-y.

Yong-hwan, N. 2009. 'Does Unemployment Increase Suicide Rates? The OECD Panel Evidence', *Journal of Economic Psychology*, 30 (4), pp. 575–582.

Young, I.T., Iglewicz, A., Glorioso, D., Lanouette, N., Seay, K., Ilapakurti, M., and Zisook, S. 2012. 'Suicide Bereavement and Complicated Grief', *Dialogues in Clinical Neuroscience*, 14 (2), pp. 177–186.

Young, T.J. 1992. 'Procedures and Problems in Conducting a Psychological Autopsy', *International Journal of Offender Therapy and Comparative Criminology*, 36 (1), pp. 43–52.

Zhang, J., Jiang,C., Jia,S., and Wieczorek, W.F. 2002. 'An Overview of Suicide Research in China', *Archives of Suicide Research*, 6 (2), pp. 167–184. doi:10.1080/13811110208951174.

Zhang, J. 2019. 'The Strain Theory of Suicide', *Journal of Pacific Rim Psychology*, 13 (e27), pp. 1–15.

Zilboorg, G. 1937. 'Considerations on Suicide, with Particular Reference to that of the Young'. *American Journal of Orthopsychiatry*, 7 (1), pp. 15–31.

Index

abnormal behaviour 12, 53, 64, 81, 84, 27
abusive behaviour 68, 84, 183
acceptance 7, 67, 78, 93, 110, 116, 135, 166, 172, 185
adolescent/s 4, 10, 16, 27, 47, 70, 81, 137, 150, 167
alcohol 22, 25, 40, 46, 68, 70, 86, 115, 120, 133, 147, 183
alcoholism 17, 22, 68, 70, 127, 181
alienation 8, 68
anger 6, 24, 28, 63, 67, 76, 113, 115, 122, 126, 135, 138
anomie 6, 10, 35, 135
Antony, J. T. 167, 168, 169
anxiety 1, 7, 10, 17, 82, 100, 104, 115, 133, 157
apprehensions 58, 106, 107, 114
arranged marriage 20, 66, 100
ashamed 15, 92, 110, 114
aspirations 1, 6, 15, 52, 78, 79, 81, 135, 177, 181
attachment 7, 47, 65, 67, 83, 68
attitudes 24, 75
autopsy 2, 21, 23, 29, 33, 35, 37–39, 41, 46, 49, 60, 135, 153
Avasthi, Ajit 169, 171
awareness 81, 100, 154, 157–159, 161, 164, 172

Baechler, Jean 6
Bailley, Steven E. 111, 119
Banerjee, G. 164
bankruptcy 25, 86, 90
Barraclough, Brian 22, 82, 149
Baumeister, Roy F. 81, 132
Beautrias, Annette 75
Beck, Aaron T. 8, 139, 140
Behere, Prakash 17, 68, 86
beliefs 3, 8, 35, 43, 85, 124, 130
bereavement 2, 28, 62, 111, 114, 119, 121–124, 129, 148, 154, 160
Bhagat, Varsha 29, 32
Bhugra, Dineish 20
Bowlby, John 65
Brent, David A. 10, 27
burden 5, 11, 18, 31, 59, 70, 78, 87, 90, 95–97, 100, 115, 119, 125, 135, 158, 166, 184

Canetto, Silvia 14, 15
Carroll, O. P.W. 108
case study 33, 48, 50, 62, 64, 121
caste 36, 69, 156
Chen, Ying Y. 2, 14, 20
Cheng, Andrew T. 22, 44, 132
clinical assessment 38, 43
cognitive 7, 8, 34, 38, 121, 132, 137–140, 149, 154; theory 8
Colucci, Erminia 90, 150
communication 16, 38, 49, 69, 89, 156, 176
community 4, 5, 26, 30, 31, 52, 62, 69, 74, 86, 90, 93–95, 101, 114, 151, 154–160, 162, 167–169, 171, 184
community conscience 30, 90
confidentiality 49, 55, 57–60, 151, 170
conflicts 20, 31, 36, 41, 66, 68–70, 72, 77, 105, 108, 163, 176, 183
consent 49, 56, 57, 83, 100, 166, 170
contagious 108, 127, 147
coping 1, 17, 28, 65, 72, 104, 111, 114–116, 121, 129, 134, 139, 148, 152, 156
counsellors 150, 153, 155, 158–160, 163
crime 6, 15, 35, 45–47, 54, 73, 127, 133, 142, 162

crisis 11, 15, 19, 24, 30, 44, 53, 63, 65, 86, 91, 121, 126, 135, 151
Cronin, Christopher 38
cultural factors 3; norms 3
culture 27, 46, 90, 131, 141
customs 90

daily wage earner/labourer 70, 92, 98, 180
Dandona, Rakhi 14, 159
death 2, 5–9, 13, 18, 26, 28, 33–35, 37–41, 43–45, 51, 59–61, 64, 65, 71, 78, 85, 89, 97, 99, 101, 103, 107–112, 114–119, 121–125, 172, 175, 183, 185
debt 11, 18, 47, 59, 74, 86–91, 95, 118–120, 128, 133, 141, 184
deceased 28, 30, 39–44, 46, 50, 122
decriminalizing suicide 58
delinquency 6
denial 7, 104, 112, 120–122, 126
depression 1, 8, 10, 13, 17, 19, 20, 22, 25, 31, 41, 46, 53, 63, 68, 81, 82, 86, 100, 104, 110, 115, 121, 127, 134, 139–141, 150, 157, 173, 181, 184
deprivation 6, 46, 52, 63, 96, 141, 184
deviant behaviour 2, 6, 31
distress 3, 14, 20, 24, 28, 31, 47, 81, 120, 132, 151
domestic violence 14, 150
Douglas, Jacobs 4, 5, 6, 42, 44–46
dowry 20, 27
Draper, Brian 23
drug abuse 25, 68
Durkheim, Emile xi, 3, 4, 6, 10, 35, 42, 135, 136

elderly suicides 14
embarrassment 16, 34, 81, 93, 119, 122
emotions 5, 10, 28, 41, 67, 75, 104, 113–116, 121, 136, 154, 185
ethics 31, 48, 58, 149, 170, 173
expectations 4, 15, 17, 26, 35, 45, 52, 63, 75, 78, 91, 102, 127, 158, 176, 184
exposure 9, 12, 52, 108, 127, 147, 185
extended household 64
extrovert 76–78, 177, 183

failures 15, 31, 47, 78, 80, 109, 127, 135, 166, 177
faith based organization/s 156
family 1–3, 10–12, 14, 17, 19–21, 23–28, 30, 36, 39, 41, 44–47, 49–53, 55–60, 62–73, 75–77, 82, 83–123, 125–129, 131, 137, 141, 148, 150, 154–156, 163, 166–172, 175–178, 180, 183–185; conflicts 31, 68, 72, 183; support 20, 66, 171
farmer suicide/s 18, 143, 160
fate 117, 121, 185
fears 7, 40, 78, 91, 105, 176
financial constraint/s 71, 119, 133, 185
financial loss 21, 52, 86, 95, 119, 128, 147, 181, 184
Fincham, Langer 42, 47
forensic autopsy 37; psychology 37, 38
Freud, Sigmund 7, 8, 75, 76
Fuse, Toyomasa 90

gatekeepers 155, 172
gender 3, 11, 14, 19, 29, 32, 39, 46, 82, 127, 175, 179–182
globalization 1, 18, 25
grief 28, 96, 111, 115, 118, 122–124, 126, 133, 150
guilt 5, 25, 28, 30, 34, 45, 63, 76, 92, 96, 100, 104, 111, 113, 115, 117–119, 122
Gururaj, G. 20, 26, 82

hallucinations 85
hanging 32, 66, 70, 76, 79, 84, 89, 94, 99, 101, 108, 112, 115, 120, 128, 182
harassment 16, 91, 108, 118, 163, 176
healing 28, 110, 116
helplines 155, 156, 160
Hendin, Herbert 1, 2, 21, 25, 104
Higgins, Tory E. 100
honour 47
hopelessness 8, 13, 20, 22, 26, 35, 41, 63, 68, 86, 100, 107, 110, 121, 138, 139–141, 149, 184
hostility 63, 68, 126, 135
household 11, 28, 33, 52, 57–59, 62, 64, 69–74, 84, 87, 92, 94, 95, 103, 111, 114, 118–120, 122, 126, 133, 148, 183, 185
household responsibilities 119–121, 74, 103, 126
housewives 18, 21
humiliation 7, 18, 96, 114, 136

ill-health, illness 2, 6, 19, 22–24, 27, 45, 50, 58–60, 70, 82, 85, 91, 98,

97–101, 111, 116, 122, 127, 128, 131, 141, 147, 152, 157–164, 166–172, 176, 184
impulsive 8, 10, 12, 22, 31, 63, 67, 75–77, 93, 105, 114, 138, 139, 183, 185
income-group 3, 52, 64, 88, 98, 183
indebtedness 17, 181
infertility 103, 113, 141
insecticide 71, 88, 105, 128
insecurity/insecurities 66, 85, 90, 118
institution/s 30, 35, 38, 62, 66, 81, 135, 157, 160, 167, 171
insult 92, 184
interference 72, 133, 139
interpretive approach 4–6
interviews 33–35, 41–43, 48, 50, 55–57, 106, 154, 179–182, 184, 185
introvert 76–78, 106, 117, 139, 177, 183
irresponsible behaviour 69, 72, 74

James, Knoll 39, 42, 44, 45, 50
Jobes, David A. 8, 40, 56, 61, 134, 149
Joiner, Thomas 8, 67, 110, 130
joint family 24
Jordan, John R. 28, 111

Klinenberg, Eric 46
Kumar, Suresh 4, 7, 8, 26, 27, 29, 163

Lester, David 14, 26, 35, 75, 90
lethality 8, 26, 40, 44, 134
life crisis 31, 53, 63, 90
Litman, R. E. 39, 45
loneliness 15, 53, 74, 82, 107, 115, 119, 131, 139, 184
love affair/s 16, 57, 92, 96, 127, 128, 181

Mann, John J. 9, 10, 50, 78
Maris, Ronald W. 12, 107
marital bond 31; conflicts 66, 108; status 3, 18, 20, 29, 33, 39, 175, 179, 181, 182
Mason, Jennifer 42
Mayer, Peter 13–15, 18
medico-legal autopsies 29
mental dilemma/s 30, 63; action plan 148; health 2, 17, 21, 35, 45–47, 81, 116, 123, 124, 147, 149–154, 156–163, 165–172; Health Act 2017 163; healthcare 46, 154, 165, 167; illness 6, 22, 27, 45, 52, 58–60, 82, 85, 123, 127, 149, 155, 157–162, 164, 166–172, 181; institute/s 160; legislations 35, 163; services 159, 165–167; literacy 154 ; sickness 81, 127, 158; disorder/s 14, 27, 35, 41, 68, 81, 85, 123, 148, 149, 152, 157–159, 161, 167, 168; stress 19, 30, 53, 117; trauma/s 21, 31
Merton, Robert 6, 78
methodological challenges 34, 49, 52
middle-class 64, 79, 87, 107, 119, 183
migration 1, 125
modernization/s 1, 25, 35, 159
mood disorder/s 9, 27, 39, 44, 82, 150, 168
Moscicki, Eve K. 12, 23 28
Murphy, Elaine 22
Murphy, G.E. 100

Narayan, C.L. 164, 165, 167
narratives 15, 34, 57, 59, 62, 65, 68, 77, 107, 111, 123, 179–184
National Crime Records Bureau (NCRB) 142, 162
neighbourhood 93
neurological 9, 173
Nock, Matthew K. 13, 14

O'Connor, Rory C. 9
OCDS 40
Owens, Christabel 45, 46

pain 7–9, 24, 27, 30, 71, 81, 97, 99, 100, 109, 115–117, 121, 133–135, 137, 141, 147, 185
participation 49, 56, 57, 171
Peenikaparambil, Jacob 15
peer group 17, 47, 81, 108, 147, 151
personality 7, 10, 16, 17, 22, 27, 31, 39, 49–53, 56, 62, 71, 75–79, 86, 106, 117, 122, 131, 137–139, 151, 166 177, 183
pesticide/s 15, 18, 19, 25, 98, 103, 106, 160
Pitman, Alexandra 108, 123
poison 19, 32, 67, 71, 82, 91, 109, 114, 128, 182
poverty 1, 10, 18, 21, 152
prevention 27, 35, 39, 43, 44, 61, 108, 115, 122, 146–162, 172; approach 35, 148; programs 152, 154, 162
primary kin/s 51, 74, 129
psychache 8, 133, 134, 146
psychiatric disorder 12, 22–24, 150

psychiatrist/s 48, 55, 84, 123, 149, 150, 154, 160–164, 168
psychoanalytic theory 7
psychological autopsy 23, 27, 33, 37–39, 61, 131
psychological determinants 2, 141
psychopathology 2, 10, 24, 137, 138
psycho-social autopsy 30, 34, 37, 47, 153
public health 35, 46, 147, 152, 159, 166, 172; issue 35, 148; problem 159, 172

Rao, G.P. 165, 168, 170, 172
Rao, Venkoba A. 14, 23, 27
reality 7, 47, 73, 78, 85, 96, 102, 112, 115, 169, 184
regret 30, 70, 77, 113, 115, 122, 185
rejection 24, 28, 67, 75, 81, 100–102, 104, 112, 141, 184
reliability 45, 52, 59
religion 2, 35, 60
risk factors 6, 11, 18, 21, 26, 30, 35, 39, 44–46, 59, 62, 68, 86, 110, 125, 131, 137, 147, 150, 152, 157
risk group/s 12, 17, 29, 52, 55, 151, 162
Roy, Alec 22, 26
Runeson, B.S. 23, 123

Saddichha, Sahoo 2
Sarin, Alok 168, 169
schizophrenia 82, 85, 155, 169, 173
Schramm, Wilbur 48
Scourfield, Jonathan 43, 47
self-blame 28, 100, 103, 119, 141; destruction 7, 17; esteem 13, 16, 81, 104, 177; harm 6, 23, 26, 31, 37, 46, 55, 59, 62, 66, 82, 90, 91, 114, 124, 127, 141, 152, 154–156; injury 9, 32, 137, 138
sensitive 30, 49, 51, 58–60, 75–77, 105, 109, 139, 150, 183
sexual abuse 14, 19, 27
Shaffer, David 12, 45
Shah, A.M. 64
shame 16, 25, 47, 63, 92, 100, 111, 114, 123, 133, 138, 184
shock 11, 28, 94, 112, 121, 126, 177, 185
short-tempered 76, 117, 183
Simon, Robert 44–46
Slater, Greeta 42, 46
social change/s 25, 35, 135; conditions 3, 53; context 1, 39, 47, 53, 62, 126; deprivation 46; environment 3, 6, 62, 82, 90, 130; factors 3, 135, 183; forces 30, 53; image 78, 92–96, 106, 117, 136; imbalance 30; institutions 30, 62, 135; integration 3, 10, 65, 130, 135; isolation 2, 23, 125, 131, 138; issue 90; media 106, 157; norms 12, 78; order 30, 63; prestige 94; problem 2, 30, 42; responsibility 90; risks 24; settings 30, 64, 65; solidarity 4; status 14, 74, 114, 123; support 22, 24, 68, 131, 138, 148, 151, 156, 158
socialization 15, 31, 62, 183
society 1, 2, 6, 11, 16, 19, 23, 30, 35, 62, 74, 90, 96, 106, 114, 147, 160, 169, 171, 172
suicidal tendency/tendencies 1, 6, 19, 28, 35, 52, 62, 72, 104, 127, 147, 155, 162, 166, 185
sociological approach 30, 42; autopsy 34, 37, 42, 47; theory/ies 3
Somasundaram, O. 164
Stack, Steven 11, 14
Stake, Robert E. 33
State Crime Records Bureau (SCRB) 29, 31, 54, 65, 68
stigma 28, 45, 59, 60, 96, 111, 123, 127, 150, 154, 156–158, 162, 172
strain theory 6, 130
strained relationship 66, 69
stress 1, 6, 11, 16–22, 28, 30, 34, 38–40, 46, 47, 50, 63, 66, 72, 75, 78, 81, 86–92, 94–96, 99, 102, 117, 120, 123–125, 136, 136, 141, 157, 159, 164–166, 170, 177
subconscious 68
substance abuse 6, 82, 86, 133, 152
suicidal behaviour 1, 4, 8–10, 12–14, 16, 17, 22–25, 27, 31, 43, 75, 82, 86, 108, 110, 125, 139, 146–148, 154, 159, 162, 172, 177
suicidal death/s 2, 18, 28, 39, 44, 54, 64, 67, 70, 85, 93, 104, 108, 185
suicidality 9, 25, 108, 110, 134, 146, 149, 166
suicide attempt/s 1–3, 9, 14, 18, 20, 26–28, 30–32, 37–39, 48, 49, 56, 58, 64, 65, 67–70, 74, 78, 86, 91, 97, 103, 107–110, 112–114, 120, 133, 136, 141, 157, 164–166, 170
suicide ideation/s 13, 17, 19, 62, 74, 78, 122, 126, 139, 156, 163; pacts 25; patterns 14; prevention 35, 39, 43, 55, 61, 108, 115, 122, 126, 146–162, 172; rate/s 1, 2, 11, 13–15, 19, 24, 29, 35, 40, 46, 142–145; survivors 28, 111, 129, 150, 157; symptoms

118, 157, 185; suicide-attempter/s 9, 26, 30, 38, 64, 72, 86, 110, 126, 127, 151, 175, 185
suicide-completer/s 26, 64, 112, 117, 122, 126, 185
suicidology 3, 46–48, 126, 149, 152, 160, 162
support system 68, 158, 171

taunts 66, 72
tension/s 1, 7, 40, 47, 66, 67, 73, 76, 89, 91, 105, 118, 139
traits 9, 10, 16, 23, 27, 47, 52, 63, 75–78, 138, 139, 140, 141, 183
Traskman-Bendz 9

unconscious 7, 30, 71, 73, 89, 105, 116
unemployed 21, 175, 180
upper class 64, 183
urbanization 1, 21, 143, 145

values 3, 8, 12, 25, 30, 35, 43, 63, 75, 90, 124, 148, 150
van Orden, K.A. 67, 100, 130, 131
Varnik, Peeter 14
vicious cycle 81, 87–90
Vijayakumar, Lakshmi 14, 23, 24, 86, 90, 150
violence 14, 19, 24, 27, 31, 46, 147, 150, 167, 171, 176
vulnerability 8, 12, 16, 18, 23, 65, 81, 82, 100, 109, 123, 127, 135, 172
vulnerable group/s 21, 160

Wagner, Barry M. 12, 27
Werlang, Blanca G. 41, 45
WHO 1, 13, 14, 24, 26, 35, 81, 82, 147, 148, 152, 154, 155, 160, 173
worries 70–72, 81, 86, 104, 107, 118, 122, 135, 141, 184

Yin, R. K. 33, 48, 51
Yip, P. S. 14, 86
Young, T. 44, 111, 115, 116, 119
youth 1, 13–15, 19, 137, 154, 160, 162, 172

For Product Safety Concerns and Information please contact our EU representative GPSR@taylorandfrancis.com
Taylor & Francis Verlag GmbH, Kaufingerstraße 24, 80331 München, Germany

www.ingramcontent.com/pod-product-compliance
Lightning Source LLC
LaVergne TN
LVHW021126300926
849160LV00010B/880

9780367639006